The Moral Rhetoric of Political Economy

T0330749

This book examines the effects of the moral rhetoric of the market concept of justice on our understanding of justice. Market theory's elevation of the role of commutative justice, or justice in exchange and property, is often taken as liberalism's revolutionary change in priorities of justice in parting from the feudal world. This change has come at the expense of diminishing the role of distributive justice, or justice in what the community owes its members. This diminishment rules out discussion in the public sphere of any questions about our obligations to each other outside the market, relegating such questions instead to the purview of social decorum; so at the very historical moment in which equality of persons becomes the foundational condition for political liberty, the implications of that equality for how we should treat each other cease to be admissible as live political issues – that is, discussable as justice.

This shift in elevating commutative justice is traced through the moral rhetoric of praise and blame in the political economy of Adam Smith and Milton Friedman. Their theories of the market serve to implicitly position social and market decorum alongside an explicit commutative framework as the condition for a naturally self-regulating market. Their appeal to decorum is presented as a naturally occurring source of social stability. The book examines how these fundamental features of the economic argument represented by Smith and Friedman appear influentially in moral and political philosophy, among critics as well as supporters of the market system. The consistent problem is the persistent neglect of the genesis of individual identity's constitution in community, resulting in an overvaluation of individualism and an under-acknowledgment of the significance of belonging. Resolving this problem must necessarily focus on making relational complaints about justice part of public discussion again.

This book should be of interest to graduate students and researchers looking at communication or rhetoric in the history of economic thought, political thought as well as moral philosophy and ethics.

Paul Turpin is Assistant Professor of Communication at University of the Pacific, USA.

Routledge frontiers of political economy

The Moral Rhetoric of Political Economy

Justice and modern economic thought

Paul Turpin

LONDON AND NEW YORK

First published 2011
by Routledge
2 Park Square, Milton Park, Abingdon, Oxon OX14 4RN

Simultaneously published in the USA and Canada
by Routledge
711 Third Avenue, New York, NY 10017

Routledge is an imprint of the Taylor & Francis Group, an informa business

Typeset in Times by Wearset Ltd, Boldon, Tyne and Wear

British Library Cataloguing in Publication Data
A catalogue record for this book is available from the British Library

Library of Congress Cataloging in Publication Data
Turpin, Paul, 1949–
The moral rhetoric of political economy: justice and modern economic
thought/by Paul Turpin.
p. cm.
Includes bibliographical references and index.
1. Economics–Moral and ethical aspects. 2. Economics literature–History
and criticism. 3. Justice. 4. Distributive justice. I. Title.
HB72.T895 2011
174–dc22

2010031911

ISBN 978-0-415-74743-1 (pbk)
ISBN 978-0-415-77392-8 (hbk)
ISBN 978-0-203-83226-4 (ebk)

First issued in paperback in 2013

Contents

Acknowledgments

A project with a long genesis like this one leaves a trail of contributions that are a challenge to adequately acknowledge. Some of the assistance came in the form of specific engagement with the topic; for others, it was more general stimulation and challenge to my thinking; for still others, it was the steady support of friendship and love.

This book grew out of my doctoral research, with the core analysis of Adam Smith and Milton Friedman becoming the basis for my dissertation. I began graduate school in 1994 after a couple of decades working in construction, knowing I was interested in how stories were used to persuade, and I was fortunate enough to find Walter R. Fisher, who became my dissertation director. His direction, encouragement, and patience made it possible for me to pursue my interest in the project from its earliest beginnings to this fruition. For starting me on the path in political economy, the late John Elliott deserves a special mention. A professor of economics and of political economy at the University of Southern California, John Elliott's graduate seminar in the history of political economy was where I first encountered Adam Smith's *Wealth of Nations* and wrote my first paper on Smith's language strategies. Stephen O'Leary provided steady help as a member of my dissertation committee and sounding board. The late Stephen Toulmin deserves special thanks for stepping in to take John Elliott's place on my dissertation committee and giving me new impetus in my thinking. Randy Lake of USC Annenberg saw early drafts of these ideas and proved to be a steady interlocuter. Deirdre McCloskey of the University of Illinois has been a continuing influence, first in print, and then in our subsequent acquaintance and interaction over the years. Her intellectual generosity of spirit has been a blessing.

A special note of thanks is due to Felipe Gutterriez at UC Berkeley, whom I first met when we were twelve years old. Felipe preceded me into the field of rhetoric, and his interest and willingness to share his intellectual excitement was an important factor in my return to school. A lifetime of conversation and grappling with ideas has only become richer.

I must also acknowledge my greatest influence, my spouse, Susan. Her encouragement more than any others led me on the path to this work, and her companionship throughout the process has been invaluable, both in terms of steady support and in material terms of countless conversations and readings of drafts. Most of whatever clarity is in this book I must credit to her relentless pursuit of what I wanted to say. We discovered that spouses really *earn* their dedications! Thanks also go to my sisters, Nancy and Linda, for their support.

I was supported and stimulated by colleagues at the schools at which I taught while working on the project, in Communication Departments at the University of Colorado Boulder, the University of Nevada Las Vegas, Willamette University, Gustavus Adolphus College, and my current position at the University of the Pacific. I thank all my students, who have kept me stimulated and engaged with my research. Thanks also go to my editors at Routledge, who encouraged me and helped this project come into print.

Finally, I must acknowledge my parents, Paul W. and Laura Turpin, who passed away in 2003. The memory of their love and encouragement remains.

Introduction

Economic thought, moral persuasion, and justice

The purpose of this book is to draw attention to a significant blind spot in the development of political liberalism, understood broadly as the political philosophy of individual freedom within a framework of individual rights in the tradition claiming John Locke as one of its early articulators. I say at the outset that, while the argument I present is a critique of liberalism, I mean it as a contribution to the ongoing effort that is part of the history of liberalism's development to help the liberal project achieve its goal of promoting human freedom and flourishing. I believe there is hope for liberalism, but caution that a self-congratulatory attitude that the project of liberalism is now fully complete can ruin any such hopes.

The argument of this book is fairly simple, but counter-intuitive: the development of economic theory in the modern era has reconfigured the way we think about justice, leading us to think about justice primarily in terms of bargaining and ownership, especially of material goods, and not to think about justice in terms of relational matters. This reconfiguration happened as part of the historical development of political liberalism through the foregrounding and elevation of justice in exchange – commutative justice – in economic theory. As a consequence of this elevation of commutative justice, the idea of what the community owes the individual – distributive justice – was diminished into norms of appropriate behaviors in social and market interactions, in the process diminishing relational justice into decorum.[1]

Economic theorizing developed the animating principle of economic activity as an independent domain of social interaction, articulating the hitherto misunderstood natural dynamics of the economic operation of society. By ceasing or removing mistaken efforts to direct and control economic life, so the story went, the market would naturally find its own productive equilibrium and greatly increase its productive output – the invisible hand thesis. In order for this increase in wealth to happen, all that was necessary besides removing controls was a commutative framework of law and legal institutions, and the following of social and market norms of behavior; this process would become self-reinforcing and self-reproducing, and could therefore be called a "natural" outcome that would lead to greater wealth all around.

This promising picture of natural self-regulation is problematic, however, because it depends on the persuasiveness of the social and market norms in question, persuasive enough that people use them to guide and change behavior. This persuasiveness is what I mean by moral rhetoric – as a first approximation, the use of praise and blame that work to valorize the norms in question. While moral rhetoric is necessary to the arguments of Adam Smith and Milton Friedman, as I will show, it has produced unintended consequences that belie the promise of a naturally ethical, naturally productive self-regulating economic order.

Praise and blame comprise the character-oriented language of rhetoric, and its field of operation is the backdrop of normative appropriateness as understood by an audience. Social and market norms of behavior generate standards of behavior – including speech as behavior – that come under the general heading of decorum, or appropriateness. To know what to do or say in a given situation is to be cognizant of the situation's decorum, what it calls for. To understand a situation well means being able to understand not only the gross circumstances of time and place, but also how others view the situation and how one stands in relation to them.

So to say that the relational dimensions of distributive justice have shrunk into decorum is to say that those demands of distributive justice are now performed by participation in the decorums of social and market interaction. The problem this produces is that the decorums in question may be about appropriateness, but they are too circumscribed to handle the burden of demands of justice. To put this another way, to revive a substantial distributive justice would entail being able to call a particular decorum – that is, a set of norms and its corresponding expectations of behavior – into question as unjust.

The reliance on decorum in the modern elevation of commutative justice is inadequate to this function of distributive justice. This has led to distortions because of commutative justice's insufficiency in providing an adequate background understanding by which individuals would be able to comprehend their places in the social order relative to others. Such a background understanding is fundamental to self-perception as a social being, and is the basis – call it the condition of possibility – for making any assessment of what appropriate norms would be, and only against such a background could an appeal to injustice in relational behavior be made.

I argue that an understanding of the workings of rhetoric help us understand how language of praise and blame functions to construct a decorum – a set of norms of appropriateness – that creates a picture of how people ought to stand in relation to one another, including what their possibilities for action and communication are in given situations. The economic arguments I find in my textual analysis of Adam Smith and Milton Friedman portray the process I described above: an explicit argument for an unconstrained market within bounds of commutative justice that only works because of an implicit argument for the need to follow social and market decorum.

Smith's and Friedman's explicit argument is that freeing economic interaction from various efforts at control, especially government control, within a framework of commutative justice will be more productive of wealth than any other arrangement. The problem of controlling markets for both Smith and Friedman is that it limits competition, so making sure of competition is the key to a productive and just economy. The ubiquity of efforts to control the market, however, raises doubts about whether competition will actually occur.

These doubts are answered by Smith's and Friedman's implicit argument about the need for appropriate behavior – that is, social and market decorum; the moral rhetoric works not simply by instructing the reader in virtuous behavior, which it does to some extent, but even more by enlisting the reader's identification with moral disapproval of those who would thwart competition. Hence this moral rhetoric that competition is worthy has a political edge: it invites us not so much to judge ourselves as to judge the behavior of others. The economic system will work, then, when we, the readers, direct our disapproval against those who would thwart competition, lend our support to norms of behavior that encourage competition, and in short, become members of the discourse community Smith and Friedman invite us to join.

To say that moral rhetoric is persuasive in this way is to raise the question of how persuasion happens, how rhetoric works. Two broad and differing views of rhetoric come down to us from classical times: one, that rhetoric is about manipulating people to get what one wants of them; the other, that rhetoric is about solving problems of contingent judgment. The second of these is the correct way to think of rhetoric, in my view; in fact, these two views are of different orders. The "manipulation" perspective focuses primarily on the issue of ethics, and especially intent to deceive. The "contingent judgment" perspective is more broadly and more functionally a way of thinking about practical reason.

So to be critical of Smith's and Friedman's use of moral rhetoric does not mean that I must believe they are manipulative. The question is not whether I believe they intend to deceive their readers. Deception usually is concerned with concealing something. The important thing to discover is what they *do* want their readers to think, how they want their readers to perceive situations, judge character, and evaluate actions – in short, which attitudes and dispositions they would like their readers to share.

To share attitudes is part of the process of identifying with another, establishing or finding common ground, that is the powerful outcome of effective persuasion. Still, what does it mean to be persuaded in this sense of coming to share attitudes? The argument I advance in this book is that the best way to understand the operation of persuasion, of rhetoric, is that it operates within discourse communities – that is, among people who share overlapping sets of mutually understood ways of looking at the world. Discourse communities are purposive insofar as their discourses – speech, writing, symbolism of any sort – are *about* something that engages their members. Discourse communities are likewise always works-in-progress, and as such inherently rhetorical, as their members participate in their maintenance and revision.

Discourse communities are therefore multiple; they are communities of interests. Each of us holds membership in dozens of such discursive communities to the extent that we participate in their discourses; we can detect that by thinking of tastes we share in music, movies, reading, and so on, but also in our political inclinations, our religious worship, our family arrangements, and so on. Discourse communities can provide a sense of belonging that we need to shape our identities. We join these communities because they speak to us in some way that we value. Sometimes we can even remember the event that sparked our desire to join – the book read, the song heard.

So in thinking of persuasion as an invitation into a discourse community, Smith's and Friedman's moral arguments matter not just because they may incline a reader to agree with their economic arguments, i.e., find the explicit economic argument convincing because the implicit moral argument is appealing. Their moral arguments matter because they also work to shape the reader's attitudes, to bring them more fully into the discourse community of economics understood as a science of natural phenomena of human social behavior.

Pointing out the presence and function of the moral persuasion in economic argument in the first part of the book leads to a consideration of the consequences of a commutative–distributional paradigm in the second part. The argument for a market society grounded in commutative justice that is in turn supplemented by social and market decorum has become a tremendously powerful influence, making distributive justice outmoded and irrelevant, in effect. In the second part of the book, I look at the shortcomings of such a vision of a natural social order. The elevation of commutative justice as the primary principle of justice, I argue, has inadvertently assigned to it the function of relational coordination formerly done by distributive justice; that is, the scheme of how we are to understand our relation to each other comes through the lens of commutative justice. The modern transformation of distributive justice to mean material distribution generates three bad outcomes: (1) it separates material distribution from a relational framework; (2) it puts an undue relational burden on ordinary social decorum; and (3) it develops a market decorum that increasingly and ironically threatens commutative justice itself.

In the first bad consequence, divorcing distribution from any but market terms of relationship can lead to welfare distribution accompanied by contempt. In the second, the operation of distribution through the market subordinates ordinary social decorum into a kind of social lubricant, but the demands of the market, in being preeminent, degrade social decorum's standards of appropriateness. This is the kind of problem that we encounter when we hear someone (ourselves, perhaps) saying "it's nothing personal" or "it's just business," when saying or hearing those words means we have to swallow a reaction of *in*appropriateness ("but, but…"). Social appropriateness must bow to market precedence, which erodes social decorum's purview, grinding appropriateness down to a generalized and increasingly meaningless conventionality. Alternatively, social decorum reacts defensively, lessening the scope of its reach but jealously guarding what authority remains.

In the third bad consequence, market decorum – appropriateness in doing business – itself comes under pressure from the burden of the relational significance that the market takes on under the elevation of commutative justice. More than just the manners of buyer and seller are at stake; to be worthy of honor, one must succeed in the marketplace. As a result, not only is the satisfaction of self-interest at stake in the market, but also the satisfaction of the need for approbation that underlies sociability. The constraining influence of approbation on self-interest that marks Smith's and Friedman's arguments becomes reversed, and competition becomes transformed into gaining an advantage in agreements. Coming as it does at the historical moment when justice in exchange becomes even more purely identified with the sheer fact of agreement itself, the act of mutual consent in contract that constitutes its justice, commutative justice is made problematic by the desire for advantage, for getting the upper hand.

In addition to these problems with the asserted natural development of a productive and just commutative economic order, the discourse of the market has also heavily influenced attempts to think critically about the market order. Even critics of the condition of the market order remain caught in the distributional understanding of distributive justice and do not pay enough heed to the relational problems. In effect, even important critical perspectives continue to partake overmuch in the commutative–distributional paradigm, accepting its principles as basic elements of a market society.

The influence of the commutative–distributional paradigm in moral and political philosophy can be seen in the work of John Rawls and Jürgen Habermas. The appropriations of Kantian deontology by Rawls and Habermas neglect important relational matters. Rawls's theory of justice as fairness accepts the commutative paradigm too completely, even down to his theoretical model of the social contract. Habermas's adaptation of Kantian deontology similarly suffers from an inadequate view of relational matters, though differently from Rawls in that Habermas attempts to develop a communicative theory of rationality (unlike Rawls's bargaining agent in the original position, who engages in solitary reflection).

I assess Habermas's theory of communicative action as not communicative *enough*, that is to say, not *relational* enough, especially with respect to his theory of language and his theory of moral development. On the question of language, a critique from a rhetorical perspective shows a way to amend his language theory of universal pragmatics, which is inadequately relational in nature, and hence commutatively oriented. On the issue of moral development, Habermas's reliance on Lawrence Kohlberg's theory of moral development is hurt by Kohlberg's basic acceptance of a commutative paradigm. Carol Gilligan's critique helps clarify Kohlberg's commutative orientation and its narrow relational awareness and points toward a more rhetoric-compatible sensibility in the development of narratives in the moral imagination.

A different critique of current conditions that offers a more promising path is found in the exchange between Nancy Fraser and Axel Honneth in *Redistribution or Recognition?* Honneth's effort to adapt Hegel's theory of recognition shows promise for bringing relational questions back into prominence. Fraser's argument, on the other hand, as critical of current market society as it is, remains pretty much within the terms of the modern commutative–distributional framework. Honneth's adaptation of recognition as a crucial concept moves more decisively in the direction of relational matters of justice, but Honneth appears to accept too readily the standards of achievement in the current social order as the basis for recognition, standards that have been distorted by the commutative–distributional paradigm.

While Fraser, Honneth, and others are working toward understanding and cultivating some degree of solidarity as a way of correcting distributional problems, solidarity within a commutative–distributional paradigm is nevertheless still not promising for resolving the relational problem. Recognition may help foster solidarity, but if recognition's price is achievement in a commutative–distributional framework it will recreate the problem. Recognition as a concept needs to have another basis besides achievement. Restoring a distributive perspective that takes relational matters seriously, I argue, is a communicative problem; simply put, it is only by being able to talk about relational matters *as* justice that we can *do* justice to them. If it is to restore distributive justice to its place, recognition must encompass the acknowledgment that complaints about relational injustice have a right to be heard. That could upset a narrowly conceived solidarity.

To illustrate what such acknowledgment would look like, I turn to Stanley Cavell's work on moral perfectionism to note the central role played by the moral demand to be heard. Cavell's idea – to want the world as it is and to want it to change – brings the problem of the distortion of the commutative–distributional order into focus: the distortion prevents us from thinking of such demands to be heard as being moral at all, as being matters of justice at all. The problem of assigning norms of appropriateness entirely to social or market decorum is that in those decorums, claims cannot take on the weight of a claim about injustice. Only by restoring a willingness to listen can such a claim be heard, and willingness to listen can be developed by cultivating a rhetorical sensibility that consists of more than just deliberative expediency.

So my argument is not that we should not have markets, or that commutative justice is not important, but that markets and commutative justice are distorted, and distort us, by our acceptance of the idea that commutative justice is the only justice that matters. Similarly, issues of material distribution *are* important, but they too become distorted without a relational connection. A rhetorical awareness helps us notice how moral persuasion functions, and also helps us increase our awareness of how we live much of our lives in our discourse communities – not just communities of interests, but communities of meanings as well. Small wonder, then, that how we talk to each other matters – that speaking, being heard, and hearing matters, even to the level of justice.

A persuasive invitation to join, or help shape, or revise a discourse community continues to matter. Habermas goes too far in claiming that practical reason can no longer be of use in public judgment, having been relegated to the guidance of personal life. That ignores the ever-ongoing development of practical reason in discourse communities that occurs through the constant inventional processes of trying out revised identities and new strategies to keep pace with the changing shape of the world. Habermas is correct to say there is not a single form of practical reason with which all would agree, but to acknowledge the place of discourse communities in the communicative interaction of our lives is to admit to our membership in many smaller communities.

Keeping these discourse communities alive, which is to say lively and full of life, is important. That is where people live their lives, and where recognition enables self-development. But unwillingness to listen and failure to recognize puts a strain on discourse communities, and these failures come from the dominance of the commutative–distributional paradigm. It remains powerful and is deeply embedded in our habits of thought. Changing those habits will not be easy.

1   Moral rhetoric and political economy

Mid-eighteenth century England and France saw the emergence of the idea of the self-regulating market economy, autonomous and independent from the state. Adam Smith's *Wealth of Nations* was a decisive milestone in promulgating the concept of the self-regulating market. A central feature of Adam Smith's economic theory was the concept that markets would provide for the material subsistence of society as long as they were left open to competition instead of being controlled by the state. Smith's economic theory became the basis for the development of the current free-market gospel of a globalized economy, a development of market-based economic theory from Smith through the present I shall call liberal political economy.[1]

The advent of liberal political economy marked a revolution in economic thought, one that paralleled the political revolutions of 1776 and 1789 and the emergence of liberalism as an Enlightenment political philosophy of individual freedom.[2] The concept of a naturally self-regulating market was revolutionary because it altered the way people had previously thought about problems in the distribution of material wealth, particularly with respect to the survival of the poor. With a self-regulating market, the relief of the poor would be achieved by the natural operation of the market rather than by deliberate action of church or state. As a result, Smith's theory and its subsequent elaboration in liberal political economy led to a greatly reduced scope for public discussion of the justice of the distribution of wealth by assigning the question of subsistence in distributive justice to the natural operations of the market.[3]

There are a number of methods liberal political economy uses to persuade its audience to stop worrying about distributive justice and trust the market. As case studies, I examine Adam Smith's (1759) *Theory of Moral Sentiments* (*TMS*) in Chapter 2, his (1776) *Wealth of Nations* (*WN*) in Chapter 3, and Milton Friedman's (1962) *Capitalism and Freedom* (*CF*) in Chapter 4. A common thread that I trace in all three works is the presence of a moral rhetoric: language of praise and blame used to portray character and ascribe motivations. This moral rhetoric, I argue, consists of more than colorful examples meant to keep the reader's attention: the characterizations and implied narratives are saturated with moral judgments that are essential to the persuasive justifications for trusting the market, justifications that are fundamental to liberal political economy.

Liberal political economy relies on moral rhetoric that constructs a certain picture of decorum, or a certain set of criteria by which judgments about appropriateness or fittingness of behavior are made. The behaviors are represented in narrative form, showing characters in action, even when the narrative is only implied by an ascription of character. The moral rhetoric and narrative framework that displays a certain decorum not only indicates that a persuasive effort is at work, but also that certain standards of behavior and their concomitant expectations are portrayed as the content of that persuasion. The decorum that liberal political economy presents is the decorum of eighteenth-century British commercial society and its successors. That decorum is an essential feature, I argue, in the theoretical justifications of a self-regulating market.

Distributive justice, however, is not necessarily limited to questions of material subsistence but has historically also included issues such as social place and status. Distributive justice and decorum share in common a concern with *what is proper* with respect to members of a community. Aristotle, in his discussion of distributive justice in Book V of *Nicomachean Ethics*, refers to "distributions of honour or money or the other things that fall to be divided among those who have a share in the constitution."[4] The common concern with what is proper indicates that decorum can be thought of as a form of operationalized distributive justice – that is, what members of an actual community understand is due each other across the range of situations of their mutual encounters. With this in mind, the understanding of a decorum of a commercial society with its roots in eighteenth century Britain can be elaborated more fully: the decorum of social standing must be included with the decorum of buying, selling, and other economic interactions. The tensions, however, between a newly emerging commercial decorum and a decorum of social standing that holds to a traditional view of social order and status trouble Smith's argument and become a continuing tension in the development of liberalism from its inception.

So what is proper, in other words, depends not only on one's behavior in economic interactions, but also on the approval of one's behavior and the evaluation of its appropriateness for one's social position. The decorum of liberal political economy is not merely that of a commercial society, but of a commercial society emerging in a social world of class differences. Social class, in other words, becomes a significant category of social decorum. The naturalizing of distributive justice in its assignment to the market therefore has the effect of naturalizing social differences in class as well, making them equally difficult to discuss as a public matter.

So, in addition to doubts about whether the market is distributively just in its self-regulation (that is, whether people get what is due them as members of a community), there may also be doubts about the fairness of social positions, especially with respect to how differences in social power may affect the fairness of economic interactions. These doubts pose a problem for liberalism's central premise of individual freedom.

The core tenet at risk is that, given the right institutional arrangements of rule of law, etc., liberalism's removal of constraints leading to an increase of individual liberty ought naturally to result in a nondogmatic, just, and self-regulating order. In order to achieve such a natural and just outcome, however, the norms or decorum of a commercial, but nevertheless class-structured society are necessary to ensure that liberal economic and social systems are not at the mercy of arbitrary exercises of power. The critical role these norms play in the theories of self-regulating market and social systems means that liberal thought, at the very moment it dismisses dogma and ancient custom with one hand, reintroduces a dogmatic decorum with the other – that is, one that favors a particular social status quo. The dilemma created by those norms is that liberal political economy is covertly dogmatic. People are free to be themselves as long as they correspond to the right decorum. This is a dilemma because the universal reach of the principle of liberty forces liberalism either to invite pluralism or to demand conformity. The problem of pluralism is the friction, if not outright clash, of differences among different stations of life and the social practices they entail. The problem with demanding conformity is being two-faced about liberty.[5]

Liberal political economy demands conformity to its decorum, but the demand is subtle, not overt or explicit, inviting one to identify with liberal political economy's expectations and make oneself over into its image. This invitation is a central feature of foundational texts in liberal political economy. An understanding of the tensions within liberalism helps explain the problems that liberalism and its economic thought still face, including the extent to which matters of distributive justice are still live public issues.

Understanding the deployment of moral rhetoric in political–economic argument helps us understand how differences about economic policy also involve questions of distributive justice, and thereby comprise a substantial portion of our current political controversies. Understanding how the moral rhetoric at work in our present controversies relates to questions of justice in economic affairs is essential to understanding our contemporary situation. Understanding Adam Smith is useful to us because, as Anthony Giddens puts it, "[early modern] theories of the state retain a relevance to social or political reflection today ... exactly because they have contributed to constituting the social world we now live in."[6]

Political economy and economics

Political economy is a broader term than economics in that it situates, in social and political contexts, the analyses of economic interaction referred to as economics. The distinction between the two terms is important. Political economy encompasses the full range of the social and political situation in which economic interaction takes place, especially with respect to institutions, accepted practices, law, political debate over desirable and undesirable policies, and presumptions about human nature and social relations, including distributive justice. Economics, as a science, encompasses methods of technical analysis of economic phenomena, perhaps most vividly represented by the mathematical formulations of the effects of changes in supply and demand on prices that is one of the prime heritages of neoclassical economics and its close cousins.

Political economy and economics of a given type will share basic presumptions about economic principles, understandings of human nature, orientations toward the role of the state in the economy, and the like. The modern welfare state, for example, comprises a different political economy from the laissez-faire state, and both are quite different from the state socialism that still exists in the People's Republic of China. Welfare and laissez-faire states for the most part share economic presumptions about the dynamics of production and consumption (open markets) and the nature of economic actors (self-directing), and they disagree about the extent of the state's role in responding to market failures. State-socialism, by contrast, attempts to prevent market failures by controlling markets and strongly directing the activities of economic actors.

The large narratives of each of these forms of political economy help define what qualifies as public issues in them, and the respective audiences for those narratives are the educated citizens in the public arena. As political economies, all these systems importantly rely on their grounding narratives as legitimating functions (and, it should be noted, the very notions of "citizen" and "public" are both defined and legitimated in those narratives). Economics as a science, on the other hand, is a technical form of analysis, and its audience is twofold: (a) economists, as scholars of the science; and (b) the public and its policymaking representatives, as recipients of technical advice.

This project concerns political economy, not economics per se, but I must stress that even a strongly laissez-faire economics that sets itself apart from political oversight, such as Milton Friedman represents, nevertheless has a political economy in mind – that is, a social and political situation comprised of a certain set of beliefs and values, including claims about justice – that it views as necessary for the autonomy and hence successful operation of the economic system. In the specific case of liberal political economy, given its presumptions about the natural self-regulation of the market, economic advice is argued in the name of efficiency and freedom of action. Critics of liberal political economy, less convinced of the market's ability to be fair, respond with proposals to ameliorate what they perceive as problems with distributive justice.

From the mid-eighteenth century to the latter half of the nineteenth century, "political economy" was the term used to refer to the study of economic phenomena. The shift to the appellation "economics" came about in the late nineteenth century with the development of neoclassical economics, a move that emphasized even more strongly than the earlier classical political economists the autonomy and self-regulating dynamics of the market, separate and independent from political oversight. My appellation of "liberal political economy" is intended to note the common thread of economic autonomy and independence from political oversight that remains a common theme despite the changes in the shift from the political economy of Smith's day to the economics of today.

My critique of liberal political economy examines the connection between the social functions of decorum and the political pressures of distributive justice.

Smith's and Friedman's moral rhetoric works not only to construct the identities of economic actors but also to form their moral judgments and political dispositions as well. Moral judgment in liberal political economy transposes into a legitimation of the diminution of distributive justice; moral rhetoric is thus more than merely sociological in nature, but political as well because of the relation of power and justice to the political constitution of any community.

Lineaments of the rhetorical approach

The opportunity of a rhetorical approach is accompanied by a problem of categorizing this book. Though it discusses economic ideas, it is not a book on economics as that word is normally used. I discuss figures and ideas from the history of economics, but neither is the book, strictly speaking, a history of economic thought. I talk about justice and ethics, but the book is not an exercise in moral philosophy, nor an exercise in modern social-psychology.[7] I use rhetorical methods, but this book is neither a history of rhetoric nor quite a work of rhetorical theory (although there is some of the latter at work). I discuss historical influences, but for hermeneutic rather than antiquarian purposes. I am primarily motivated by a desire to understand how we think *now*, but I recognize the influence of ideas across time. I am attempting to illuminate the place where liberalism's understandings of economics, ethics and justice, and politics as public life rub up against each other, shaping and being shaped by each other through moral persuasion. Call that nexus a political life of the mind.

My approach is best described as an effort at criticism, a critical reading of justice and economic thought. Mary Mothersill's account of criticism offers a good definition:

> In criticism ... success or failure hinges on getting something across, except that what has to be transmitted is neither a message, a bit of information, nor a skill, but a mode of perception or understanding. Criticism is also like psychotherapy in that it tries to establish, not by fiat or by persuasion, but by *exposition*, the difference between appropriate and inappropriate feeling response.
>
> (1975: 30, original emphasis)

Mothersill articulates this definition in the course of a discussion of Stanley Cavell's writing on the philosophy of art (Cavell will figure later in this book), and one of her general conditions for criticism is its object "being aesthetically interesting" (ibid.). The question naturally arises about how a reflection on justice and economic thought can be considered aesthetically interesting. The answer to this question requires an expanded account of what I mean by rhetoric, and what I mean more specifically by moral rhetoric.

Defining rhetoric is particularly fraught since its commonplace meaning is trickery or empty talk, an idea at least as old as Plato's critiques of the sophists.[8] This pejorative sense of rhetoric stems from taking rhetoric strictly as an instrumental art of fooling or manipulating audiences to serve the rhetor's inter-ests. A slightly less pejorative version of this attitude survives from the more recent early modern version that restricts rhetoric to the use of figurative language and other such "flowers" of rhetoric.[9] In both of these pejorative versions of rhet-oric, the aesthetic and the cognitive are diametrically opposed to each other; rhet-oric is the enemy or at least obfuscator of reason and therefore to be unmasked.

Such views are inadequate representations of rhetoric understood as the art of practical reasoning by audiences facing contingent situations, given its first and still valuable articulation in Aristotle's (1954) *Rhetoric*. In Aristotle's rhetorical theory, the cognitive and the aesthetic work together in an ethical framework, reinforcing each other. Thomas Farrell's (1993) account of Aristotelian princi-ples captures the ethical dimension of rhetoric by noting how, "alone among the arts, it presents a public audience with the possibility of becoming, for a time, an accountable moral agent" (9). What makes rhetoric ethical is its audience-oriented, reason-giving dynamic; rhetoric as persuasion is the proferring of a *possibility for human action* in the face of a need to act. The aesthetic dimension of rhetoric, as I shall develop later at more length, is more than just flowery lan-guage or even an attention-getting device; it also is essential to the process of cognitive invention through the operation of metaphor, the discover of like-but-unlike resemblances that make new insights available – an idea present in rhe-torical theory since the Greeks and articulated by Vico in the late Renaissance.[10]

Farrell aptly describes Aristotelian rhetoric as consisting of a *dunamis* (capacity) and *technai* (artistic proofs). Aristotle's modes of persuasion, the artis-tic appeals, are fairly well known: reasoning about probabilities within the frame-works of audience beliefs (*logos*); the frame of mind or emotional attitude toward a subject (*pathos*); and the presentation of trustworthy character in the person of the persuader (*ethos*). Less well known but even more important is the dynamic capacity of being able to observe the persuasive possibilities in a given situation; this is the definition Aristotle gives as the essential art of rhetoric. The signifi-cance of this definition is that the capacity for rhetorical judgment is the capacity to size up situations and their attendant audiences with a sensitivity to which deployments of logos, pathos, and ethos are likeliest to be persuasive. This sensi-tivity requires the rhetor's putting herself imaginatively in the audience's place, one which I shall argue is essential to the moral imagination. Similarly so for the "reflective imagination" that critics demand of rhetoric in the name of being a responsible art (Farrell 1993: 66): the "practical" in practical reason encompasses the imaginative ability to entertain alternatives to things-as-they-are. This imagi-native ability points to the basis for Farrell's argument that figuration is at root a matter of reasoning as well as of aesthetics. Similarly, the ability to size up situ-ations means to understand the audiences that matter in and to those situations. This is the foundation of the ethical dimension of rhetoric – accountability to an audience that is the hallmark of what Farrell calls a rhetorical culture.

Closely connected to this awareness of audiences as situated – that is, as living in specific historical and cultural circumstances with their unique problems – is the governing principle of appropriateness. The register of appropriateness is fundamental to the possibility of sizing up situations correctly. I use the rhetorical term *decorum* to stand for this fundamental need to address appropriateness as a continuous demand of rhetoric. Far from being merely conventionality, or the dead hand of the past, decorum is the live, sometimes minute-by-minute demand to be alert to an actual audience and situation. Rhetorical decorum shares with Aristotle's ethical theory the idea that actual situations can be so variable in their particulars that they cannot be determined in advance by formula; in Aristotle's conception of virtue, one must navigate between excess and deficiency to find the mean of virtuous behavior – hence, the value of prudence as a keystone virtue in aiding that navigation.[11] In similar fashion, decorum can be understood as the capacity to assess situations with appropriateness as a key criterion.

This is not to deny that decorum can become sedimented and ossified into a weapon of domination; it is rather to note that claims to decorum of this sort are moves to claim power, the power to define or declaim or otherwise enforce a particular notion of appropriateness. To the degree that the powerless are constrained from answering back in disagreement, what happens is not persuasion but coercion. In this case, decorum tends to become a frozen code that is used as a policing mechanism; to speak of mere conventionality is to speak of a mild form of this deadening of appropriateness as a live issue. The history of social conflict is certainly replete with instances of codes of appropriateness used to mark off and defend territory, but it is important to keep in mind the ever-present shifting challenge that change brings to all notions of appropriateness. Decorum, in other words, is continually a pressure on the rhetorical situations we face.

I look to extend Farrell's project in two ways. First, I consider Farrell's argument about public deliberation to focus rhetoric too strongly in the ambit of deliberative rhetoric. This is not to say that public deliberation is not highly important, but rather to make more room for consideration of rhetoric's valuation processes (about which more shortly). A deliberative focus for rhetoric restricts, in my view, rhetoric's broader architectonic scope as a theory of language and symbolic interaction.[12]

A second extension of Farrell's approach is to focus attention on the discursive underpinnings of active public deliberation. One of the shortcomings of a strongly deliberative view of rhetoric is the tendency to keep attention focused at the level of current policy debate and its search for opportunities for action. As necessary as policy debate is, it can take for granted the network of assumptions and valuations that pervade the discourse that underpins any given policy position. Discourse here refers to the writings and prior policy arguments that undergird the live interchange of active policy debate, including the presumptions and assumptions of the discourse community engaged with the policy debate. The purpose of this book is to search out these presumptions and assumptions in an examination of how our attitudes about justice are influenced by our attitudes toward economics.

Attention to the valuational processes of rhetoric and the discursive underpinnings of active deliberation point up the problem of how we are to understand audiences in the first place. There is no simple answer to this. On one hand, there is a theoretical–analytical approach that generalizes features of audiences; this is clearly the case where Aristotle and his many adapters, including myself, claim that audiences are persuaded by reasoning based on beliefs they hold to be true, by emotional attitudes they care about, and by relational trust. On the other hand, how any of those beliefs, etc. actually take shape and mean something to a particular audience, historically and culturally situated in a particular moment, remains to be specified. Any such specification by its nature is an interpretation, and because it takes place against a background of possible competing interpretations, it takes the special shape of criticism, as I noted earlier.

An additional problem in thinking about audiences is the ethical problem. What of objections that "sizing up" means to treat an audience as an opportunity for manipulation? For Aristotle, this factor was straightforwardly a question of moral purpose on the rhetor's part, and as such no different from other arts in terms of moral risk. The primary hedge against this risk is the capacity of the audience to be aware of manipulation; for Aristotle, such awareness depends on the audience having something important at stake in the persuasive situation.[13] Having something important at stake keeps an audience alert to the arguments and appeals.

Farrell takes the question of moral risk a step further in his emphasis on reflexiveness as a norm of rhetorical culture. If the basis of ethics is attention to the demands of audience, then an ongoing test of the moral quality of that attention is reflection on the rhetorical production at play in the public space. Hence criticism, as the reflexive counterpart to rhetorical production, is what helps to keep rhetorical culture honest.

A third issue is the presumption of a single, unitary audience. Farrell, for example, writes at times as though there were a single public culture or rhetorical culture. His resistance to postmodern objections seems at least partly to stem from his disagreement with the postmodern demurral that some people do not trust the dominant public culture, do not feel that it speaks to them or for them, and want nothing to do with it.[14] Farrell seems to feel such people should become part of the public culture because we need them to be part of it in order for it to really be the public's culture. This opens Farrell to a charge of idealism, with the unfortunate implications of liberal bullying that attend on idealism in the public sphere these days. Farrell's purpose would be served as well, I believe, by acknowledging the fragmentation of public culture – without having to cede fragmentation as inevitable or having to consider differences as fragmentation – and focusing his argument on the discourse communities that comprise the fragments of public culture.[15]

Understanding audiences as discourse communities is a way to think concretely about what audiences think and care about. I include here both communities of face-to-face interaction as well as those that exist through writing or other symbolic communication. Discourse communities acknowledge both the similarities and sympathies we may share as well as real differences we may have; we experience those phenomena because we share some discourse communities but not others. The condition of modernity is experienced as fragmented because of these differences, and attempts to overcome the fragmentation are themselves constituted in discourse communities. We become members by participating, by learning and practicing, and one of the important lessons we learn is how to speak and act appropriately – we learn our community's decorum.

The concept of membership in a discourse community helps to keep in mind the embeddedness of individual identity within social structures. One of anthropologist Claude Levi-Strauss's most significant insights in his structuralist approach to anthropology called into question the classical tradition since Aristotle of identifying the biological family as the "germ" of society. Levi-Strauss recognized that families can only form within the context of a social order that structures the possibilities for new familial arrangements between men and women who were formerly unrelated.[16] In this view, a social structure must pre-exist families in order for new families to come into being.

Levi-Strauss's insight about the contextual ground that social structure provides, illustrates the function I am claiming for decorum as an architectonic principle in the perception of social place. The claim that decorum is distinct from prudence (i.e., is not merely tactical) means that judgments about the possibilities and proprieties for words and deeds, like rhetoric writ large, are matters of reasonableness, emotional valence, and relational import. Because decorum references the relational ground through which people identify themselves and their place in terms of appropriateness, it should not be a surprise to see decorum linked to distributive justice. My argument about distributive justice's naturalization into decorum is that the move functions to privatize it, removing it from legitimate public discussion as justice. For Smith and Friedman, this naturalization is not a problem. To see how Smith's and Friedman's works on political economy invite us to join their discourse communities, I turn to a closer account of how rhetoric works.

Strategic and constitutive rhetoric

A key function of discourse communities is to provide a framework for the constitution of identity. This constitution happens in parallel with how strategic and constitutive rhetoric work together. The ordinary way of understanding rhetoric is that it is strategic in nature: intentional persuasion towards a goal. Strategic rhetoric attempts to persuade its audience with arguments for explicit deliberative judgments. Smith and Friedman wish to persuade us, their readers, of the problems they see with their respective historical periods and of the rightness of their solutions, so they craft arguments and offer evidence that they intend to be persuasive. The propositional logic of their economic thinking occupies the foreground of this kind of argumentation.

In similar fashion, the ordinary way of thinking about rhetorical style and aesthetics is that they are merely supplementary embellishments to an argument's strategic logic that are meant to keep the reader's interest and attention. Style, however, involves more than just attention-attracting qualities, or to put it slightly differently, style and aesthetics are able to draw attention because they connect the audience with a way of being. Style in its fullest sense is constitutive of identity.[17] To speak of constitutive rhetoric is to acknowledge that identification with a way of being and acting is as powerfully persuasive as the pull of logic. Thus the constitution of the corresponding features of identity and character (being and acting) are the ultimate point of style, whether in enacting the identity of the rhetor, as one would speak of a rhetor's "style," or more broadly in the direct elaboration of a portrait of character by a rhetor.

Unlike strategic rhetoric, constitutive rhetoric may or may not be foregrounded, but what counts with constitutive rhetoric is its artfulness, the way it constructs a unique identity. This is most true where artfulness concerns the representation of human character in action, which is what narratives do. Because the persuasive pull of identification is so strong, narrative through its portrayal of character is a strongly effective mode of representing expectations of behavior – what I have been calling decorum.[18]

The connection between character (being and acting) and decorum (expectations) means that constitutive rhetoric necessarily invokes a social framework with which an audience can identify itself – that is, a framework by which members of an audience understand themselves in relation to other members as well as in relation to the rhetor. Identity, in other words, exists within a social network, and its actions take place within that network. The judgments that underlie what I am calling constitutive rhetoric, comprised as they are of the classical elements of pathos and ethos, communicate to the audience the attitude to take towards the subject under discussion (pathos – e.g., this situation deserves our sympathy) *and* to take toward their fellows (ethos – e.g., people of good character naturally feel sympathy at times like this). By implication, those judgments also communicate the attitudes one's fellows will take toward oneself.

Constitutive rhetoric models how values form character, how in turn character forms identity, and how identity itself is constructed out of a milieu of social recognition and its sets of expectations – decorum. Constitutive rhetoric, therefore, participates in the recursive relationship between the individual and the social that frames and contextualizes one's actions, contributing to how one learns to act appropriately by being persuaded to value a certain view of oneself and one's fellows.

So the explicit arguments of strategic rhetoric pursue their persuasive goal by means of the types of reasoning and evidence offered, while the constitutive rhetoric encompasses the identities and associated values that are constructed/portrayed for the reader to identify with, and by implication, sympathize with and wish to emulate, thereby contextualizing and framing the moves of strategic argument.

Constitutive rhetoric: decorum and narrative, character and moral judgment

My argument about the persuasiveness of liberal political economy in Smith's and Friedman's writings can thus be interpreted as framing the question in terms of the implications of how they each construct identity for legitimating their policy arguments. So far, my analysis has maintained that decorum stands at the juncture of political economy and rhetoric, pointing in one direction toward the values and practices that legitimate the relations between individuals and institutions, and pointing in the other direction toward the persuasive modeling of social practices that occurs in narratives. To follow more closely the way in which the reader can be drawn to identify with an identity, I turn now to consider how narratives function persuasively.

Understanding rhetoric's constitutive nature facilitates the investigation of decorum as it is expressed (or implied) in narratives. Narratives are embodied and/or emplotted in character, and character in turn implicates identity. That is, character implies a disposition to act in certain kinds of ways. In short, structures of decorum appear in traces of character, and evaluations of decorum come in the judgments – moral judgments of approval or disapproval – made about particular actions and even about certain kinds of dispositions. In a narrative, in other words, one not only judges a character's actions, one also judges the character's *character*. These judgments are the brushstrokes of decorum.

Identification with character occurs textually through the engagement of a reader's sympathies, both through the direct portrayal of action and through the signs of the author's attitude toward the portrayed character. Wayne Booth (1983), in describing the rhetoric of fiction, used the telling/showing distinction in his opening chapter to describe the way rhetorical features had previously been distinguished from aesthetic features in a text. Telling, or direct authorial commentary to the reader, was rhetorical, while dramatic portrayal of characters and actions was aesthetic. Booth demonstrated that dramatic portrayals also contained authorial commentary, points of view, and shadings of attitudes toward characters that had moral import, such that it was impossible to separate the aesthetic from the rhetorical.

Booth emphasized the strategic imperatives that texts reveal about their authors' attitudes, not in the sense of wondering, for example, what Jane Austen wanted the reader to think or feel, but in the sense of what the reader can infer about Austen's attitudes toward her characters in reading a text like *Emma*.[19] To do this, Booth discriminates among different senses of the author: the flesh-and-blood author (the real person); the implied author (our impression of the author from the text); and the narrating voice of the story.[20]

Of these three, the implied author is the most significant for my argument. The implied author is a persona, a crafted representation of an authorial self that gives the impression of a coherent set of values and attitudes that contribute to the overall ambience of a text. The implied author, in other words, is who the reader thinks the author is, based on the text. Where the implied author is the persona of the author of a text – the impression of the author's character – the implied reader is the persona of the audience who would agree with and identify with the implied author's judgments and attitudes. Just as Booth read Austen for her attitudes toward her characters, I intend to read Smith and Friedman for their attitudes in the characterization they portray and valorize.

Classical roots of moral rhetoric: praise, blame, and character

Constitutive rhetoric, as I have been calling it, has its roots in Aristotle's conception of rhetoric, especially in the genre of epideictic rhetoric and the mode of persuasion known as ethos. Praiseworthiness has its roots in Aristotle's genre of epideictic rhetoric, where the subject of the genre is honor and dishonor, and the means of the genre are praise and blame. The subject of the praiseworthy combines two intertwined elements: (1) definitions of virtue, especially as regards question of character, and (2) conceptions of the audiences who share those definitions. Virtue, in this model, never stands alone as an absolute standard, but rather is always situated in the esteem of some particular audience whose recognition and approbation is necessary or desirable (even if that audience is an ideal or imaginary one).

The praiseworthy is also a link between values and action, and is an adjunct to issues of expediency in deliberation. This is another way of conceiving what I have called the relation between strategic and constitutive rhetoric. This is apparent in Aristotle's (1954) *Rhetoric* in the chapter on epideictic rhetoric (Bk. 1, ch. 9):

> To praise a man is in one respect to urge a course of action.... Consequently, whenever you want to praise any one, think what you would urge people to do; and when you want to urge the doing of anything, think what you would praise a man for having done.
>
> (1367b, 1.36f.)

From this perspective, epideictic rhetoric links to deliberative rhetoric as a preliminary moment, rather than being merely a form of entertainment as traditional neo-Aristotelian criticism would have it.[21]

The praiseworthy also has a natural affinity for proofs of ethos; that is to say, epideictic works best when its primary mode of proof is an ethical, as distinct from emotional or rational appeal. In Book I,9 of the *Rhetoric*, immediately following his discussion of the forms of government, Aristotle writes,

> We have now to consider Virtue and Vice, the Noble and the Base, since these are the objects of praise and blame. In doing so, we shall at the same time be finding out how to make our hearers take the required view of our own characters – our second method of persuasion [i.e., ethos].[22]

Ethos, as a mode of rhetorical proof, encompasses several apparently different ideas which may not initially seem congruent with each other: it is often called an appeal to authority (and one can find this usage even extending into academic writing with some idea, condition, or event 'authorizing' another). At other times, ethos seems connected to particular personalities, when it is *personal* character that is emphasized (as Aristotle does in 1356a, 1.5).

What these two ideas have in common are trustworthiness, credibility, and reliability. Aristotle writes about the issue of character in Book II as prologue to his catalog of the emotions:

There are three things which inspire confidence in the orator's own character – the three, namely, that induce us to believe a thing apart from any
proof of it: good sense, good moral character, and goodwill ... any one
who is thought to have all three of these good qualities will inspire trust in
his audience. The way to make ourselves be thought to be sensible and
morally good must be gathered from the analysis of goodness already given
[in Bk. I, ch. 9]: *the way to establish your own goodness is the same as the
way to establish that of others.* Good will and friendliness of disposition
will form part of our discussion of the emotions [in Bk II, ch. 4 – emphasis
added] ... (1378a 5–6, 15–19) ... We may describe friendly feelings
toward anyone as wishing for him what you believe to be good things, not
for your own sake but for his, and being inclined, so far as you can, to
bring these things about.

(1380b 34 through 1381a 1)

Clearly, establishing one's ethos is part and parcel of epideictic, and the seam-
less aspect of such a unity of purpose is the compelling – i.e., persuasive – aspect
of an epideictic discourse: it heightens the effect of naturalness.[23] Moreover, in
the formulation of the three elements of ethos, one can see all three modes of
persuasion embodied in the speaker, further heightening the natural rightness of
the epideictic discourse: good sense, good moral character, and goodwill stand
in for logos, ethos, and pathos, all embodied in the speaker.

In keeping with the close relation between epideictic and ethos, it is important
to keep in mind that deployments of epideictic which blame rather than praise
also employ a mode of polemic that is an attack on the ethos of one's opponent –
i.e., polemic aims to undermine at least one of the three elements of ethos and
thus undermine the opponent's credibility. This construction of polemic is very
much in line with Walter Fisher's idea that the "rhetoric of subversion occurs in
situations in which a communicator attempts to weaken or destroy an ideology
... Subversive rhetoric is an anti-ethos rhetoric..."[24] Smith's explicit polemics
are very much of this kind, but there is also more subtle moral rhetoric at work
in Smith's writing.

Moral rhetoric: A first look at invoking decorum

To read for constitutive rhetoric, then, is to bring an awareness of how the language of praise and blame is used to evaluate characters, and how that evaluation says something about the social order which those characters inhabit, and
ultimately, I argue, about the moral order of the political and economic interactions with each other. I will conclude this chapter with a sample reading before
turning to a consideration of Adam Smith's arguments.

A great many commentators have ascribed moral qualities to political
economy, but few have acknowledged how fundamentally moral its underlying
narratives are. George Stigler is a representative example. A 1982 Nobel Laure-
ate in Economics and a leading figure in economics in the latter part of the

twentieth century, Stigler (1982) wrote about moral language in "The Economist as Preacher." In defining what he meant by preaching, Stigler wrote,

> When Adam Smith speaks of the debasement of the currency [in *Wealth of Nations*] ... he says,
>
>> By means of those [debasing] operations the princes and sovereign states which performed them were enabled, in appearance, to pay their debts and to fulfill their engagements with a smaller quantity of silver than would otherwise have been requisite. It was indeed in appearance only; for their creditors were really defrauded of a part of what was due to them.[25]
>
> I consider this to be preaching since "fraud" is not merely a descriptive word. On this mild and I hope reasonable definition of a moral judgment, I have just quoted the only clear example of preaching in the first hundred pages of the *Wealth of Nations*.[26]

While acknowledging that Smith has a number of other places in which he engages in polemics farther on in *WN*, Stigler goes on to imply that that the rest of Smith's first hundred pages is scientific in nature rather than being moral preaching. Stigler's estimation of Smith's moral language is fairly typical among interpreters of Smith's work[27]; they note Smith's explicit polemics and consider his exhortations and condemnations to be the morally rhetorical part of his argument.

While accusing someone of fraud is certainly an expression of moral judgment and accusing a sovereign of fraud is certainly polemical, there are other forms of moral judgment equally as disapproving if not so explicitly an indictment of immoral behavior. By way of an opening example, let us consider a broader appreciation of what is implicitly possible in moral rhetoric in two other parts of Smith's initial chapters. Two passages within the first twenty pages of *WN* serve to illustrate an implicit moral rhetoric. The first is an oft-quoted one:

> ...and yet it may be true, perhaps, that the accommodation of an European prince does not always so much exceed that of an industrious and frugal peasant, as the accommodation of the latter exceeds that of many an African king, the absolute master of the lives and liberties of ten thousand naked savages.[28]

This passage concludes Chapter 1 after a page-long description of all the specialized labor that goes into the production of a simple laborer's woolen coat. The moral of the story in the contrast of the woolen coat with the state of the "naked savages" that ends the sentence is that the division of labor provides wealth, and the moral of the story structures the moral rhetoric, which in turn seeks to form the moral judgment of the reader as the reader identifies with the story.

The passage performs, however, yet another rhetorical function that builds on the comparisons and contrasts even more subtly. The contrasts of clothed/naked, rich/poor, and royal/common also illuminate how Smith characterizes workers earlier in the chapter. In the passage above, the moral qualifier in Smith's comparison is that the peasant is "industrious and frugal" (16). The European prince and the African king are named by their rank, while both the peasant and the "savage" subjects are denoted by qualifiers – industrious and frugal versus naked – that have a moral coloration both in terms of self-reliance versus dependency and in terms of temperate versus intemperate character.

The discussions that preceded the passage are worth considering at length. Earlier in Chapter 1, Smith discusses the three circumstances that make the division of labor advantageous. The first, dexterity, is identified with the speed acquired through specialization, using such expressions as "utmost diligence" (11) and "when they exerted themselves" (12). By contrast, the second circumstance, which involves the saving of time, is illustrated by a negative example – by the time wasted by the agricultural laborer who moves from task to task instead of specializing in a single one. The description Smith uses here is that the laborer "saunters a little in turning his hand from one sort of employment to another," leading to the following judgment:

> The habit of sauntering and of indolent careless application, which is naturally, or rather necessarily acquired by every country workman ... renders him almost always slothful and lazy, and incapable of any vigorous application even on the most pressing occasions.
>
> (12)

Here one can see an implicit structuring of moral categories of workers' qualities in the form of the relation between motivations and actions. The concept of laziness as an obstacle to productivity is introduced, which Smith initially characterizes as structural rather than willful. The phrase "naturally, or rather necessarily" in this passage functions to place the origin of the laziness in the nature of the work itself, but the final effect by the end of the passage is that the *laborer* is "almost always slothful and lazy." The initial impetus of the metanoia (a "change of mind or heart; a correction"),[29] which is to place the blame for laziness on the work's nature, rather than on the worker's nature, is compromised by the end of the passage.

So Chapter 1 sets a foil in place – the indolent and careless farmhand – for the arrival of the figure of the industrious and frugal peasant four pages later at the end of the chapter. A structure of implicit moral judgment is taking place alongside the explicit judgments of Smith's polemics like the "fraud" that Stigler noted. A moral economy is beginning to take shape inside the financial economy, and it is discernible through the language of the praise and blame in judgments of character.

Smith uses vivid language, but these narratives are more than "merely" figurative speech. Smith is appealing to the audience's common knowledge, its beliefs and values. What these excerpts from *WN* and Stigler's commentary have in common is that they are all implied moral narratives: in each case, a representation of character is made about the qualities or motives of an implied action. The reader can supply, in her or his imagination, the scenes in which these characters exist, and can create some picture of the activities in which they engage. In short, readers take fragments, in the form of characters or actions, and make inferences that fill out narrative structures, making the implicit come alive.[30] When one does this narrative filling-out as a reader, one also finds oneself making moral judgments where the language of praise or blame, approval or disapproval, is attached to portrayals of the motivations and actions of characters.

The judgments readers are invited to make are the judgments of the implied audience – that is, the audience implied by the text. As readers identify with the implied audience, they come to identify with the sense of appropriateness to situation, or decorum, that discriminates the indolent farmhand from the industrious peasant. This kind of identification is quiet in its operation. It occurs through many small expressions of moral judgment, tributaries of praise and blame in descriptions of character and motive that together feed a strong moral current. As I shall demonstrate, this rhetoric of praise and blame is an integral aspect of Smith's and Friedman's efforts to initiate the reader into the decorum of liberal political economy, and ultimately shaping how we think about justice.

The core of my argument in the following two chapters is that Adam Smith's two published works were necessarily and closely connected with each other through the social theory implied by Smith's separation of commutative and distributive justice, a social theory that grounded support for competition in a natural moral approval. In the next chapter I examine Smith's first book, *The Theory of Moral Sentiments* (*TMS*), which comprises Smith's argument about the development of social order through the operation of moral judgment and the faculty of sympathy. It was in Smith's discussion of justice and the social order that he separated commutative and distributive justice, a move he made based on the basis of the relative strength of moral judgments that he observed in the commercial society emerging from the remains of feudalism. Based on what he saw as universal sympathy for enforcing precepts of protecting life and property, Smith assigned commutative justice to the operation of government and law. He then removed distributive justice from the political realm on the grounds that our sympathies for its enforcement were relatively weak and not widely shared, and assigned it instead to persuasion in personal relationships.

Thus, by taking the values and moral judgments of his commercial society and naming them natural features of human nature, Smith merged a realist analysis of the historical evolution of society with a normative prescription, abstracting the values of the predominant social groups around him into a version of natural law – that is, justice derived from natural moral sentiments. In his separation of commutative and distributive justice, however, Smith hedged, recognizing that a minimum of distributive justice in the form of a minimum of propriety was necessary for the stability of a social order; he therefore brought a modicum of distributive justice back into his concept of what was necessary for a just social order. That aspect of distributive justice functions as a social decorum – a set of expectations about conduct that govern behavior. Smith's treatment of moral judgment, justice, and the social order constituted a social theory – that is, a comprehensive explanation of the dynamics by which the social order maintains its stability and reproduces itself. In short, *TMS* was not merely Smith's theory of the individual psychology of moral judgment, but also a theory of society as well – and one based on a separation of commutative and distributive justice.

2 Sympathy and justice in *Theory of Moral Sentiments*

For generations of scholars *the* problem of interpreting the connections between Smith's various writings was, of course, that of reconciling the sympathetic ethic of the *Theory of Moral Sentiments* with the selfish ethic of the *Wealth of Nations*. Few scholars now believe that this is how the problem should be posed, though there is still scope for a discussion of how Smith's complex interpersonal approach to morals and social ethics should be reconciled with the more impersonal and anonymous world depicted in the *Wealth of Nations*; and whether, and in what respects, it is legitimate to use the ethical work as a court of appeal for resolving difficulties in the economic work.[1]

Donald Winch

The nature of the relationship between Adam Smith's *Theory of Moral Sentiments* (*TMS*) and *Wealth of Nations* (*WN*) has absorbed scholarly interest virtually from *WN*'s first publication in 1776. There appeared to be a disjunction between a "sympathetic ethic" (*TMS*) and an economics of selfishness (*WN*). By the mid-nineteenth century, critics of the German Historical School had named the issue Das Adam Smith Problem (hereafter, DAS Problem).[2] In my reading of *TMS* and *WN*, I argue that, although most critiques of DAS Problem are misreadings of Smith, there nevertheless is a genuine Adam Smith Problem. The problem derives from Smith's separation of distributive justice from commutative justice, and the consequences of that separation for Smith's theory of society. How the separation happens is the subject of this chapter, and its significance for understanding *WN* is the subject of the next chapter.

Winch's comment on the relationship between *TMS* and *WN* represents a view now common: that, though *WN* does not discuss the concept of sympathy so central to *TMS*, both works share concepts of prudential self-interest and the role of government in protecting property.[3] In my view, however, the two works are not merely compatible but essential for each other, because the broad work that they accomplish together is to complete the process of reconfiguring how justice was conceived, a process begun by secular natural law theorists like Hugo Grotius in the preceding century.[4] Smith completed the movement of the secular natural law theorists' attempts to separate distributive justice from commutative justice. Smith accomplished this in *TMS* by removing distributive justice from the province of government – and thus from politics and public deliberation as well – by assigning its functions to two interconnected natural processes: (1) the natural sources of moral judgment in human psychology; and (2) the functions of social control that emerged from interactions among people who not only have wants of their own but also desire the approval of others.

By the mid-eighteenth century, when Adam Smith took up his teaching and writing, a long process of gradually shifting the duties of distributive justice from the church to civil authority had been heavily influenced by the arguments of the secular natural law theorists that only commutative justice really counted as justice. The two pressing questions were (1) the problem of a moral social order, or how morality and social stability could be maintained in the face of the increasing pressures of the pursuit of self-interest in an expanding market economy, and (2) how the sovereign – the state – should manage its affairs, including its duty of managing distributive justice. Adam Smith answered those questions in *TMS* with a theory of moral psychology that led to a natural, self-regulating civil society, which greatly furthered the separation of commutative from distributive justice and removed the latter from the duties of the sovereign. Smith completed this process, as I shall argue in the next chapter on *WN*, by assigning the practical duties of distributive justice (material provisioning) to a naturally self-regulating market.[5] This did not, however, fully account for distributive justice.

The central theme of *TMS* is Smith's view of the natural psychological dynamics of sympathy in moral judgment. More accurately, *TMS* is a social-psychology, in that the individual psychological process of sympathy and judgment is always situated in social context; this means not merely that more than one person is involved, but that judgment occurs within a framework of specific time-and-place norms of appropriateness – within, in other words, an actual social context. For Smith, the desire for approval leads one, through a natural ability (i.e., sympathy), to imagine how people might judge oneself and hence to control one's behavior. Thus, moral judgment is always socially situated.

The necessarily social nature of moral judgment led Smith to a theory of how moral judgments interact in a way that enables society to persist. In arguing that some moral judgments – specifically those concerning protection of person, reputation, and property – were more important than others because of their greater claim on sympathy, Smith participated in the reconfiguration of how justice should be understood. Commutative justice became, for Smith, the only real justice. Commutative justice is concerned with rendering to everyone what belongs to her, and so comes to include fairness in exchange, property, and so on.[6] For Smith, commutative justice was, therefore, the province of government and law, while matters of distributive justice – what one was due as a member of a community – was relegated to persuasion and the social controls of approval and disapproval. Smith's relegation of distributive justice to civil society was only possible because Smith's theory of moral judgment cast civil society as a natural system whose central gyroscope was its set of norms of appropriateness – in rhetorical terms, its system of decorum.

This chapter traces out the significance of Smith's moral theory for his theory of justice and hence of society in *TMS*. The background for Smith's work can be traced across key conceptions of distributive justice, first from Aristotle's discussion of justice, then in the Christian church across the Medieval period, and finally in the emergence of a secular natural law movement in the seventeenth century that were Smith's immediate predecessors. Against this background, I then turn to *TMS*, examining its placement in the secular natural law controversies, its exposition of the dynamics of sympathy in moral judgment, and the consequences of such dynamics for a theory of justice and society.

The historical development of distributive justice

Aristotle's discussion of justice in *Nicomachean Ethics* is generally taken to be the early source for most of Western thinking on distributive justice.[7] In his discussion of the distributive aspect of justice, Aristotle describes it as a "kind [of justice] that is ... manifested in distributions of honour or money or the other things that fall to be divided among those who have a share in the constitution." A few lines later, Aristotle, acknowledging that different political arrangements may exist, says more specifically that the definition of who may share and what may be divided will differ among democrats, oligarchs, and aristocrats.[8]

The more immediate background against which liberal political economy developed was the long rise and subsequent decline of the influence of Christianity in Europe and the emerging course of economic development and trade. The condition of the poor, a central concern of the church for doctrinal reasons, occupied a great deal of church thought on economic matters. Chief among these were the injunctions against usury, the concept of a "just price," and the duty of charity to the poor.[9]

Church thought was not only ecclesiastical, however, but was also bound up in a society of feudal relationships. The feudal view of social relations, with every rank having its proper station in a hierarchy of life, was inevitably a factor in the church's assessments of economic justice. The main focus of the three central economic concerns of the church – usury, just price, and charity – was on the condition of the poor, and especially on the condition of those *in extremis* through destitution or disaster. The church sought security, in other words, by controlling markets directly through establishing interest rates, controlling prices, and acting as a clearinghouse for charitable giving. This was achieved partly by moral influence, but also by influence with the civil authorities and most typically by functioning as a court of appeals, often with the power to impose civil penalties, on complaints about interest rates and prices.[10] Tithes were a primary source of funds for charity, and they were administered then, as now, with a religious message.

As Europe developed economically and began to trade more extensively, however, the church's attempt to control prices and interest rates became more and more problematic. The injunction against usury was intended to prevent unscrupulous gouging of the poor when a disaster had rendered them helpless.[11]

That same injunction was a hindrance to merchants for whom a line of credit was the most sensible way of doing business across long distances and for whom paying interest was an ordinary cost of doing business.[12] Controlling prices similarly became unwieldly when markets were not simple matters of local produce on local stalls.

Political as well as economic changes influenced the evolving nature of distributive problems. In Aristotle's ethics, "constitution" referred to the form of political organization and its relation to justice. With the rise of the modern nation-state, distributive justice came to be considered one of the duties of the sovereign, though the content of the justice varied according to the form of government, as Aristotle had indicated. In Western Europe the influence of Christianity and the principles of charity for the poor gradually came to include the principle that the sovereign should not stand by and watch the poor starve without trying to ameliorate their situation.[13] A promise of subsistence, in other words, became part of the concern of the sovereign, whether the reality of subsistence was achieved or not.

So the church was not alone in attempting to do something about the poor. While the church's doctrinal inspiration for being concerned with poverty had its source in scripture, the civil authorities were well aware of potentials for civil unrest. Seeing to the poor was as much about controlling populations as it was about compassion. The Elizabethan Poor Laws remanded the poor to the care of their parishes while simultaneously forbidding them to leave their parishes (a policy Smith was later to criticize vehemently in *WN*).[14] As the church's influence over economic decisions gradually waned, it was taken up more and more by the civil authorities, so that eventually the satisfaction of distributive justice was viewed as a duty of the sovereign (nicely summed up in the phrase "Elizabethan Poor Laws").[15]

As the civil authorities gained more power over economic matters relative to the church, the rationales for their doing so began to vie with traditional church teachings. The seventeenth-century revival of a secular natural law theory grounded in Roman civil law rather than Christian doctrine was a significant move in preparing the way for the economic theorists of the eighteenth century. Roman civil law centered around legal questions having to do with the ownership of property, the relation of the citizen to the state, and the role of the state in administering justice through courts.[16]

The development of a secular natural law theory and its contest with religious teaching took place, however, in the midst of a debate over the sources of human moral behavior. Secular natural law meant that the church's moral authority and the sanctions of divine commands were no longer adequate warrants for moral strictures. Nature, and human nature in particular, became the locus of the search for moral warrants, and a significant division emerged among natural law proponents over whether reason or feeling was the primary source of moral judgment.[17] Thomas Hobbes, with his theory of Leviathan (the state) as a bargain struck by rational agents for their mutual security, was a key figure on the rationalist side, along with Hugo Grotius and others.[18] Opposed to the rationalists, a line of thinkers progressing from Francis Hutcheson, through David Hume, to Adam Smith argued that moral judgments were primarily initiated by sentiments.

The differences between the rationalist and sentimentalist camps on economic issues are illustrated by Bernard Mandeville's (1732) *The Fable of the Bees* and Adam Smith's critique of it in *TMS* (VII.ii.4.6).[19] Mandeville's fable argued that vice would produce virtue: that the rich and indolent, in pursuit of vice, would spend money that would in turn enable others to live. Mandeville's argument captures the sense of unintended consequences that Smith was later to elaborate in *WN*, and Mandeville is certainly describing an economy of open market exchange. The problem was that Mandeville's picture was scandalous; it upset the notion that economic interaction would be moral. The unadulterated and rational pursuit of self-interest looked like the beginning of the end for a moral order.

Smith, however, argued that Mandeville was incorrect, not because of the unintended dynamics of market exchanges, but because his understanding of human motivation, and therefore of morality, was faulty. Smith argued that human nature is motivated by more than merely naked self-interest; it is also motivated by a desire for sociability that springs from the emotions, not from a process of rational calculation. In his critique of Mandeville, Smith offered a positive factor in human nature for the moral conduct of economic affairs: the desire for approval yields sociability.

Even with Smith's rejoinder to Mandeville, though, an important shift in thinking about the morality of economic behavior had already occurred that distinguished the secular natural law proponents generally from earlier Christian thought, including Thomistic natural law. The pursuit of self-interest was suspect from a Christian perspective in part because of the danger of harming the poor; this was the problem of distributive justice that the church had tried to manage by its injunctions against usury and its effort to control prices. Natural law proponents of open markets, of whom Smith was the most recognizably successful, claimed to solve that problem with the theory of a naturally self-regulating market. There was a second danger, however, that the church was concerned with, which was the damage that the pursuit of self-interest might pose to the soul of the pursuer: the problem of Mammon that tempts one to seek happiness in material possessions. As Robert Heilbroner (1985) noted, this part of the religious objection to the pursuit of self-interest in economic behavior was ignored and overridden by the rising tide of individualism.[20]

By Smith's time in the mid-eighteenth century, the religious and political strategies for dealing with the poor were under attack for a variety of reasons. The feudal system's treatment of non-economic distributive justice (everyone in their social ranks) had contributed to economic distributive justice by virtue of the reciprocal duties among the social classes. The erosion of those reciprocal duties in the rising tide of liberal individualism lent fresh urgency to the issue of distributive justice.

Adam Smith and the natural law tradition; empiricism vs. rationalism in natural law

Smith's elaboration of the secular natural law tradition, in keeping with the interest Smith shared with Hutcheson and Hume in the sentiments, had one fundamental difference from earlier theorists like Grotius and Mandeville: Smith sought to put natural law tradition on an empirical rather than a rationalist or egoistic footing. Whereas Grotius and other predecessors attempted to articulate general laws that would serve as guiding first principles, Smith sought to ground natural law in human experience – specifically, the sentiments that prompted moral judgment.[21]

Smith's theory is simultaneously a moral psychology and a social theory, or more specifically, a social theory that grows out of a psychology of moral judgment. That is, Smith makes claims about psychological dynamics and propensities in forming moral judgments, but his claims are not about pure subjectivity, but rather rely on the context of what happens psychologically in the course of interactions with others. Smith postulates principles of justice on the basis of the natural operation of the sentiments rather than as *a priori* propositions; the natural operation of the sentiments accounts for how society manages to persist. Together, these principles of psychological dynamics and their social consequences (including justice) constitute Smith's basic social theory. His principles of social cohesion are the locus of his argument about the nature of justice, and it is here that Smith's distinction between distributive and commutative justice first takes shape. In order to see how he arrives at this social-psychology of moral judgment, I now turn to an assessment of the ways Smith describes the fundamental dynamics of sympathy and the sentiments.

Sympathy and the psychology of moral judgment

Sympathy

The central dynamic of sympathy is the ability to recognize and identify with another's feelings. To be sympathetic in Smith's sense of the word is to imagine what one's own reaction would be in another's situation; sympathy is not empathy. One does not feel the other person's feeling, but rather imagines what one would feel in the same circumstances. This is a necessarily attenuated fellow-feeling in that an observer cannot enter as fully into a feeling as the person affected does. As Smith describes it, the more intense the expression of emotion, the more attenuated the potential for sympathy; one is, for example, more able to sympathize with controlled than with hysterical grief.

The reason for the attenuation is an early indication of a rhetorical dynamic at work in Smith's theory: attention to audience. According to his argument, one's own experience of the difficulty of sympathizing with others' strong emotions leads one to moderate one's own expression of emotion so as to gain the sympathy of others (*TMS* I.ii.3.1). That is, others are seen as an audience of observers. The natural desire for others' approval is the engine that drives the self-command that Smith so admires, but, as he later argues in contradistinction to Hume, the desire for approval does not simply translate into a desire for praise, but into the desire to see oneself as praiseworthy. What begins as a process of observation and reaction becomes an internalized judgment and, ultimately, the development of conscience.

The concept of sympathy is translated into a visual metaphor for Smith; one identifies with those whom one can see, and who can see oneself in turn. This visual horizon serves as the source for Smith's everyday examples of face-to-face interactions, like the example of the "butcher and brewer," that occur later in *WN*. The visual metaphor also gets figured, both literally and metaphorically, into the imagination itself. The "mind's eye" not only performs the act of imaginatively "seeing" the examples Smith offers – that is, through reading his examples – it also becomes personified in the figure of the impartial spectator.

The impartial spectator

Sympathy itself is described as operating through the metaphor of the impartial spectator, the "man within the breast" (*TMS* III.2.32). The visual metaphor extends beyond simply observing the actions of others to encompass a horizon of the visible through which the structures of social relations are known. This is the horizon of the visible time-and-place content of social relations, including such things as customs, status, and the like – in short, decorum.

For Smith, however, moral judgment is not constrained to be little more than the voice of convention. The development of conscience that marks full moral development, while growing out of a social milieu, provides a resource of independent judgment with which not only to withstand the force of popular opinion but also to judge the worth of conventional wisdom.[22] Perhaps counter-intuitively, conscience for Smith relies heavily on an operation of sympathy capable of exceeding the limits of convention, so that one has the opportunity to sympathize outside the limits of conventionally scripted judgments. The ability to exceed convention is one of the significant reasons for Smith's insistence that the desire for praiseworthiness, rather than for praise itself, as Hume had suggested, is the motivating principle in the desire for approval.

Propriety and merit

The ability to identify and sympathize with another's passions and behavior leads to making judgments of propriety and merit for Smith:

> In the suitableness or unsuitableness, in the proportion or disproportion which the affection seems to bear to the cause or object which excites it, consists the propriety or impropriety, the decency or ungracefulness of the consequent action.

In the beneficial or hurtful nature of the effects which the affection aims at, or tends to produce, consists the merit or demerit of the action, the qualities by which it is entitled to reward, or is deserving of punishment.

(*TMS* I.i.3.6–7)

Even in judgments of merit, for Smith, propriety is what is assessed: the propriety of an affected person's gratitude or resentment at an agent's actions. Such judgments of demerit are always tempered by judgment of the agent's propriety, though. Thus, for Smith, one cannot sympathize with strong resentment against an agent whose behavior (which includes an assessment of motive) one finds to be praiseworthy, in the same way that one can sympathize with resentment against an agent whose intentions one finds blamable. Judgments about the propriety of the agent temper judgments of merit.

The standard of judgment to which Smith appeals is the reader's own sympathetic feelings. Throughout the first book of *TMS*, Smith constructs numerous examples of different kinds of behavior, mostly hypothetical – of grief, of good fortune, of friendship – to illustrate the different degrees of sympathy that are possible for different kinds of passions. The standards of propriety rely, in other words, on an intuitive commonality: the ability to know propriety and impropriety when one sees it. This is the function of moral judgment that Griswold (1991) refers to as Smith's appeal to the "self-understanding of ordinary moral actors" (219). The plural is significant: to say that ordinary moral actors share a self-understanding is, in effect, to declare the presence of decorum. The appeal to self-understanding for Smith becomes de facto the appeal to the decorum of the dominant social order of his time, yet as decorum it is primarily performative – that is, it finds expression in example and story rather than in propositional claims.

Moral judgment, justice, and the nature of society

Smith's theory of justice grows out of a natural sympathy with proper resentment against harm, with the standard of what is "proper" being identified as an appeal to self-understanding, but with the imputation that the standard of propriety will conform to a dominant decorum. So even though an agent's motives may more readily garner sympathy, proper resentment against injury will carry greater weight; the preponderant weight of sympathies in resentment of injury then gives legitimacy to the use of force in serving justice. The way that Smith discriminates between the ready sympathy involved in judgments of an agent's propriety and the indirect but weightier sympathy of judgments of demerit is by comparing the virtues of beneficence and justice:

Actions of a beneficial tendency, which proceed from proper motives, seem alone to require reward; because such alone are the approved objects of gratitude, or excite the sympathetic gratitude of the spectator.

Actions of a hurtful tendency, which proceed from improper motives, seem alone to deserve punishment; because such alone are the approved objects of resentment, or excite the sympathetic resentment of the spectator.

(*TMS* II.ii.1.1–2)

When someone sympathizes with another's resentment at an injury, she does not merely judge the offense itself as harmful (though that is necessary), she also gauges the propriety of the offended person's reaction – his resentment – as an appropriate response to the harm.[23] The key to sympathy is the ability to enter into another's feelings, not just to assess their behavior by an external criterion; this is in line with Smith's effort to empirically ground moral judgment and avoid the dogmatism of rationalist approaches like Grotius's.[24]

Smith's reference to the approved objects of gratitude or resentment, respectively, is a reference to the tacitly accepted dominant decorum of his time, whether positively about gratitude or negatively about resentment. By framing the question as beneficence vs. harm, Smith's argument that sympathy with resentment against the injustice of harm will always be stronger than sympathy with gratitude for beneficence leads to the conclusion that real justice can only concern injustice as harm. He argues that the need for defense, which justice provides, is more fundamentally important than disappointments that might arise when beneficence fails (*TMS* II.ii.1.4). Smith's distinction between beneficence and harm continues the process begun in the previous century of separating distributive justice (which Smith takes as beneficence) from commutative justice (which is concerned with preventing harm to what is one's own, and especially life, liberty, and property). Haakonssen (1981) notes the different functions of distributive and commutative justice, distributive having to do with the promotion of goods and commutative having to do with the prevention of harm.[25] Smith's treatment of distributive justice completed its transformation from something that is right to do because someone is due it, to something that is nice to do because it would be approved as proper.

Beneficence, in other words, is admirable when it occurs, but merely disappointing – and not an injustice – when it fails; forcing it cannot be justified. Justice, however, "may be extorted by force," since "the violation of justice is injury" (*TMS* II.ii.1.3); that is, one sympathizes with the propriety of using force because one sympathizes with the propriety of resenting injury.[26] As evidence, Smith, in an appeal to the reader's self-understanding, points to the greater felt obligation to support the principles of justice than toward the practice of other virtues like "friendship, charity, or generosity" (*TMS* II.ii.1.5). Force, in other words, may be used to make people observe the rules of justice, but cannot be so used to require propriety:

in these cases, though every body blames the conduct, nobody imagines that those who might have reason, perhaps, to expect more kindness, have any right to extort it by force. The sufferer can only complain, and the spectator can intermeddle no other way than by advice and persuasion.

(*TMS* II.ii.1.7)

Impropriety in itself, while blamable and even conceivably generating under-standable hatred, is not an injury in Smith's view.[27]

The issue of what constitutes injury and therefore what can be forced is at the heart of the question of justice for Smith. He writes,

> Among equals each individual is naturally, and *antecedent to the institution of civil government*, regarded as having a right both to defend himself from injuries, and to exact a certain degree of punishment for those which have been done to him.
>
> (*TMS* II.ii.1.7, emphasis added)

This statement is a clear natural rights argument:[28] natural sympathies approve resentment against injuries, and the approval of this resentment becomes the basis for the institution of civil government and its administration of justice – that is, the propriety of resentment against injury, affirmed by the sympathetic approval of the impartial spectator for it, becomes the ruling principle for Smith in what is legitimately public about justice.

At this point, however, Smith immediately qualifies the distinction between resentment against injury (demerit) as the realm of justice and resentment against offense (impropriety) as not, by continuing:

> A superior may, indeed, sometimes, with universal approbation, oblige those under his jurisdiction to behave, in this respect, with a certain degree of propri-ety to one another…. The civil magistrate is entrusted with the power not only of preserving the public peace by restraining injustice, but of promoting the prosperity of the commonwealth, by establishing good discipline, and by dis-couraging every sort of vice and impropriety; he may prescribe rules, therefore, which not only prohibit mutual injuries among fellow-citizens, but command mutual good offices to a certain degree…. Of all the duties of the law-giver, however, this, perhaps, is that which it requires the greatest delicacy and reserve to execute with propriety and judgment. To neglect it altogether exposes the commonwealth to many gross disorders and shocking enormities, and to push it too far is destructive of all liberty, security, and justice.
>
> (*TMS* II.ii.1.8)

What Smith does in this passage is to exclude distributive justice from "real justice" (par. 7), and then reimport it under the same aegis of sympathetic legiti-macy for the resentment against injury that warrants the enforcement of commu-tative justice. The "certain degree of propriety" in the passage above is a necessary minimum of distributive justice that must accompany commutative justice. The relationship between the two is articulated in the line, "not only pro-hibit mutual injuries among fellow-citizens [commutative justice], but command mutual good offices to a certain degree [the minimum of distributive justice]."[29]

By approaching justice through a distinction between beneficence and harm, Smith separated distributive justice from commutative justice. In relegating beneficence, in effect, to private life, Smith defined away distributive justice as a public matter – yet immediately thereafter, brought it back in to a "certain degree." This recuperation of a "certain degree of propriety" in Smith's conception of real justice, I claim, is the reimportation of a basic decorum of the dominant social order – that is, some part of the sets of the "approved objects of gratitude" and the "approved objects of resentment." Smith leaves the content of the minimum of decorum ambiguous, but the implication is that the dominant social order's sensitivities will be the test of what constitutes a disruption. Nondominant views are invisible.

So, beginning from a natural human disposition, Smith arrives at a theory of justice – a natural jurisprudence. His theory of justice is essentially commutative in nature, though with a minimum of propriety that is also necessary. The nature of that minimum is undefined (at this point) except that it is necessary to prevent "many gross disorders and shocking enormities" (ibid.).

Smith proceeds from his theory of natural jurisprudence directly to its consequences for understanding society. In doing so, Smith implies a social theory – that is, a theory of how society persists and reproduces itself. In outlining his theory of the natural development of moral judgment, Smith is ultimately making an argument for the natural self-regulation of the social order. Smith makes a direct connection between justice and social stability where he writes:

> It is thus that man, who can subsist only in society, was fitted by nature to that situation for which he was made. All the members of human society stand in need of each others [sic] assistance, and are likewise exposed to mutual injuries. Where the necessary assistance is reciprocally offered from love, from gratitude, from friendship, and esteem, the society flourishes and is happy. All the different members of it are bound together by the agreeable bands of love and affection, and are, as it were, drawn to one common center of mutual good offices.
>
> But though the necessary assistance should not be afforded from such generous and disinterested motives, though among the different members of the society there should be no mutual love and affection, the society, though less happy and agreeable, will not necessarily be dissolved. Society may subsist among different men, as among different merchants, from a sense of its utility, without any mutual love or affection; and though no man in it should owe any obligation, or be bound in gratitude to any other, it may still be upheld by a mercenary exchange of good offices according to an agreed valuation.
>
> Society, however, cannot subsist among those who are at all times ready to hurt and injure one another.... Beneficence, therefore, is less essential to the existence of society than justice. Society may subsist, though not in the most comfortable state, without beneficence; but the prevalence of injustice must utterly destroy it.
>
> (*TMS* II.ii.3.1–3)

Smith outlines three types of societies here, and they correspond to: (1) a society in which distributive as well as commutative justice is widely held in common; (2) a commercial society in which distributive justice may be deficient but which observes commutative justice; and (3) a disintegrating society where neither type of justice is observed. While the first type of society may be preferable, the second type is viable for Smith.

With this connection of justice to a theory of social order, Smith implies the content of the minimum of propriety that is needed to accompany commutative justice: "society may subsist among different men, as among different merchants." The minimum decorum that must accompany commutative justice is, let me call it, the decorum of a commercial society, one such as Smith saw in Holland and emerging in Great Britain. With this move, two potential sets of decorum are at hand to justify the social order – the decorum of the dominant social order of civil society and the decorum of commercial enterprise.

Summary of Smith's argument in *TMS*

Smith's answer in *TMS* to the problem of egoism posed by figures like Mandeville – that self-interest would dominate all – was that self-interest would be balanced by a desire for the approval of others. In developing his social-psychology of moral judgment based on the response to being observed and judged by others, Smith's balancing dynamic appears to function for a society that shares a metaphorical horizon of visibility – that is, a sense of caring about the approval or disapproval of others who are aware of one's behavior.

Smith also notes, however, that sympathy is not wholly reliable, and it especially attenuates with distance (again, metaphorically as well as literally). How does this not undo his solution to egoism? Smith's solution has two parts: (1) his conception of natural jurisprudence, which separates distributive justice from commutative justice, and (2) his theory of society, in which commutative justice (with a minimum of distributive justice) can enable society to persist, as in a society of merchants. So the answer to the conflict between sympathy and self-interest is twofold: (1) for cases where one feels the weight of others' judgment, sympathy leads to self-command and balances self-interest; (2) for cases where distance attenuates fellow-feeling, a sympathy for certain minimum requirements of distributive justice accompanies and legitimates the enforcement of (commutative) justice and thereby constrains self-interest. The legitimation of law, in other words, takes up where the limit of sympathy as a form of social control leaves off.

Reconsidering Das Adam Smith Problem

While the full Adam Smith Problem is about the relationship between *TMS* and *WN* and must wait until I have examined Smith's economic argument in *WN*, there are already several objections to the traditional framing of the problem as one of virtue in *TMS* vs. self-interest in *WN* that my analysis of *TMS* raises. *TMS* is not merely about virtue; its argument about a natural ground for moral judgment is also a theory of both justice and society. *TMS* is not simply a treatise on human behavior and moral judgment; it is also an explanation of how society manages to regulate itself. It is, as T. D. Campbell suggested, a "science of society."[30]

Recognizing *TMS* as a science of society leaves a new problem, namely the ambiguity about what the standards for the minimum degree of propriety in justice will be – or perhaps more to the point, *whose* standards they will be. Smith's tacit ground of judgment appears to be that of the dominant social order. Ideally, this would describe Smith's best-case type of society, where a harmonious social order provides for distributive justice and the law for commutative justice, and a social decorum would fit neatly with law. But less than ideal societies are also possible and even likely. A commercial society will develop its own standards of decorum. If a commercial society can persist primarily with commutative justice, the minimum of propriety itself may come to be defined in commutative terms. Self-interest itself may increasingly take on the dress of propriety; how self-interest is defined in doing business may itself become what is proper.

Even more likely, there could be a mixture of a traditional social order and an emerging commercial society, much as what Smith was observing around him. There, a contestation of proprieties might vie for preeminence, a contest for dominance between a traditional social order intent on maintaining its dominance and an emerging commercial order. Such a conflict may well "resolve" (that is, avoid resolving) by the unacknowledged development of a double standard: one may shift between a traditional or commercial standard as justice in the interest of maintaining one's place.

The question of what one is due as a member of a community, of one's social place as a public matter, is no longer a problem for Smith. It is defined either in terms of the natural operation of the system of sympathy, moral judgment, and justice, or in terms of private life. What remains of distributive justice are the economic issues – material provisioning and the survival of the poor. Those are the subjects Smith takes up in *WN*, to which I now turn.

3 Sympathy and moral horizons in *Wealth of Nations*[1]

Justice and natural systems

In the previous chapter I argued that in *TMS* Smith is engaged in the project of detailing which aspects of justice need to be consciously articulated and enforced by human effort and which can safely be left to the operation of autonomous natural systems.[2] In *TMS* he argued that the natural desire for approval and the psychological operation of sympathy create a positive motive for cooperative behavior. Therefore, *TMS* can be viewed as establishing a social–psychological basis for the natural emergence and self-regulation of civil society. In the process of making his argument in *TMS*, Smith distinguished "real justice" from beneficence, a move I described as separating commutative justice from distributive justice, assigning the first to law and the second to individual acts of benevolence. I also pointed out that Smith made a reservation in his theory of justice by making a place, though vaguely defined, for a certain minimum of propriety. The ultimate effect in *TMS* was to make a distinction among three separate realms: (1) civil society, organized and maintained around the social–psychological dynamics of sympathy and moral judgment; (2) an adequate social stability organized around observance of law (and of a certain minimum of propriety that remains ambiguous); and (3) the practice of virtue, the highest of which is benevolence, in private life. My argument about these separate realms is that distributive justice, understood as what one is due as a member of a community, pervades each of these realms, albeit possibly in different and conflicting forms.

This chapter demonstrates that *WN* continues Smith's project, begun in *TMS*, of identifying autonomous, self-regulating social systems. In *WN*, Smith argues that the principle of prudential self-interest, under the right conditions of competitive markets – and right conditions include the right decorum – can do the best possible job of providing for the material provisioning of society. In doing so, Smith satisfies distributive justice's essential duty of providing for material subsistence that was alluded to but left undeveloped in *TMS*. Smith accomplishes this task in *WN* by describing the operation of an economic system in which markets simultaneously (a) generate the greatest possible abundance of wealth and (b) provide for adequate distribution to serve the community as a whole.

That is to say, *WN* makes the argument that a market economy can provide distributive justice in terms of material goods.[3]

WN is specifically designed to show how commutative justice sets the conditions in which a market economy can self-regulate and satisfy the need for subsistence. In this respect, *WN* can be viewed as a form of deliberative rhetoric: a set of policy proposals that argue for eliminating rules and practices that interfere with the operation of the market by restricting competition, and for structuring governmental duties to promote and sustain the market. This is the aspect of *WN* where one can discuss with some confidence Smith's purposeful, strategic rhetoric.

In addition to the strategic policy argument that Smith makes, however, there is also an implicit appeal to propriety in *WN* that is much the same as the certain minimum of propriety in *TMS* required for the effective operation of "real justice." The minimum of propriety is as essential for Smith's thinking in *WN* as it was for *TMS*. In *WN*, propriety is presented through the scenarios, examples, and attribution of character and motive that guide the reader's evaluations. This presentation of propriety differs from *TMS*'s discussion of it in that *WN* performs rather than explains propriety, constructing a sense of decorum through its portrayals. This performance is largely constitutive rather than strategic in nature and functions through identification. From this perspective, *WN* can be viewed as a performance of epideictic rhetoric, what Fisher (1970) calls an argument of "affirmation" (131).

The performance of a sense of propriety in *WN* contributes to its function as a narrative of identity in the modern – which is to say, commercial – world. One might say that in *WN* Smith's economic theory provides the plot (dynamics of market operations) while the moral evaluation of the portrayals of character provides the drama (judgment of the appropriateness of character and interaction in the market). The reader is invited to join with Smith in his viewpoint, to confirm and adopt his sense of propriety.

More specifically, to draw attention to the performative nature of Smith's writing is to draw attention to the relationship between the implied author and implied reader in the text. The narrative – and therefore character-oriented – expression of desirable and undesirable behavior draws the narrative reader to identify with the implied reader that is created by the structure of inferences set up by the language of praise and blame in the text. Reading *WN* rhetorically accounts for questions about the absence of sympathy from *WN* that have been raised since its original publication. The impartial spectator and her sympathies and judgments reside *in the reader*, or more precisely in the implied reader of the text, and Smith's invocation of sympathy invites the reader to occupy the position of impartial spectator.

The early questions about sympathy and the impartial spectator were part of what became known as Das Adam Smith Problem (DAS Problem), which centered around issues of consistency between the *TMS* and *WN*. A common articulation of DAS Problem was that *TMS* was about virtue and benevolence, while *WN* was about self-interest. The commentary on Smith that has focused on virtue as the key element in *TMS* and *WN*, however, is a misreading. Instead, Smith's central concern in both works is how the operation of sympathy provides a self-regulating dynamic to social systems. From this reading of DAS Problem, Smith's treatment of self-interest in *WN* becomes the central issue, one concerned with how self-interest will not disrupt the sociability necessary for a stable social order. This is the identical social question in *TMS*. The stability of social order, however, is problematic. The economic symptom of the problem is that Smith develops optimistic and pessimistic scenarios that are respectively centered around issues of competition vs. "combination" in economic affairs. The optimistic and pessimistic scenarios, in turn, define the rhetorical situation Smith faces – that is, the situation which his persuasion must address. The expression of his optimistic and pessimistic scenarios intertwine deliberative and epideictic rhetoric, in both rhetorical concepts and examples. Smith uses explicit polemics to criticize current practices as well as implicit uses of characterization and narrative scenarios to illustrate desirable forms of behavior.

Such a process of identification, I argue, demonstrates not only how propriety is to be understood in Smith's characterizations and scenarios, but also how the reader comes to identify with Smith's construction of the implied reader as an impartial spectator. Smith's use of propriety, and the sense of decorum which it necessarily implies, are indispensable to his conception of an optimistic scenario of natural liberty – or, in other words, indispensable to his theory of economic self-regulation. The sympathy of the reader for the judgments of Smith's implied reader creates a favorable orientation towards competition, legitimating both formal and informal institutions, one of which is Smith's standards of propriety.

My analysis not only works to address the ambiguities of DAS Problem by reorienting it from a focus on virtue to a focus on power and social theory, but also is applicable to liberal political economy more generally. As I argued in Chapter 2, the question of propriety links to considerations of distributive justice. The status of distributive justice hinges on the resolution of power differences. Smith's reliance on propriety to certify the fair operation of the economy ultimately leaves open both the question of what one is due as a member of a community and how that very question is to be settled.

In the end, processes of social change lead to redefinitions of propriety, and political disputes inevitably arise with respect to those redefinitions. The history of the past two centuries is testimony to the continuing pressures for some to claim distributive justice as a public cause and for others to deny its public nature. Distributive justice remains alive as a controversial and ongoing public subject, despite attempts to naturalize it away, and an inescapable part of the controversy is whether distributive justice is a legitimate subject of public discussion in the first place. Liberal political economy's answer is that it is not, and in Smith and Friedman, the move to rule out public discussion of distributive justice is made through reliance on appeals to social decorum.

Das Adam Smith Problem as a misreading

Most commentaries on Smith neglect the fundamental place propriety holds in Smith's theory of sympathy and moral judgment in *TMS*, concentrating instead on its treatment of virtue.[4] Failure to recognize the operation and significance of a sense of propriety in *WN* leads to problematic interpretations of Smith's work, both across his published works and within each text. To demonstrate this, I will briefly review the history of interpretations of Smith under the rubric of Das Adam Smith Problem (DAS Problem), as the doubts about the relationship between *TMS* and *WN* came to be known.

Doubts about Smith's purposes came early on with criticisms from Lord Kames and Thomas Reid[5] that Smith's system was not moral at all, but was rather just a restatement of a philosophy of selfishness not unlike Mandeville's (1732) *Fable of the Bees*. DAS Problem was articulated as an apparent disjunction between a treatise on morality that set benevolence as the highest virtue (*TMS*), contrasted with a treatise on economic activity that set forth self-interest as the operative human feature (*WN*). This disjunction was the basis for arguing that *TMS* and *WN* were incompatible or at least inconsistent with each other, with the implication that either Smith changed his mind or his overall project was incoherent. An early defense from Smith's admirers was that the differences could be laid to the different subject matter treated in each work: morality in *TMS* and economics in *WN*. From this view, both works are moral; they are just on different topics.

An early mistake was taking benevolence as equivalent to sympathy. This is a basic misreading of Smith that equates a virtue with a psychological dynamic. Raphael and Macfie (1984) felt justified in dismissing the whole notion of Das Adam Smith Problem once they pointed out the misreading. That mistake and its correction, however, have not prevented most of the discussion of the relation between *TMS* and *WN* from remaining focused on the same set of issues: most of the commentary on DAS Problem has been about the nature of virtue across the two works. I consider this tendency to partake of the initial misreading of *TMS* itself as being primarily concerned with virtue and benevolence. This reading kept the focus on the role of virtue in Smith's theory (and therefore on private life), instead of more properly focusing on sympathy, including the psychosocial basis for moral judgment and social cooperation.

The most important questions to investigate in Smith are (a) how he defines or accounts for justice and (b) where the dynamics of sympathy and the impartial spectator are in *WN*. Smith, having consigned the practice of virtue to private life in *TMS*, is intent on working out the implications of justice for the self-regulating systems of society and economy. Complaints about a lack of virtue[6] – or reduced virtue,[7] or even arguments about the presence of virtue[8] – in *WN* miss the main point: for Smith, "real justice" in law plus the self-regulation of society through sympathy can produce a stable civil society (*TMS*), and the self-regulation of economic relations through a competitive framework for pursuing self-interest will provide all the natural dynamics, all the material distributive justice necessary for a secure society (*WN*).[9] The competitive framework is itself ultimately grounded in sympathy (at least, in the optimistic scenario). Thus the natural social and economic dynamics needed to provide a secure place for the living of private life and its attendant practice of virtue are at hand, *as long as* the decorum/proprieties that will sustain sympathy and therefore competition are observed.

The real Adam Smith Problem is not whether people individually practice virtue (benevolence being the highest form of virtue), but whether sympathy for competition can actually be sustained in a highly individualistic social order. Competition is foundational to Smith's economic thinking.[10] The maintenance of economic competition requires a moral attitude toward self-regulation – that is, the ability to permit competition rather than thwart it when self-interest is at stake – so that cultivating impartial spectators is as essential for sustaining the economic order as it is for the social order. The impartial spectator is the only one capable of holding the necessary proprieties. In this respect, compared with benevolence, self-command is the more important virtue across the two works, which is appropriate given its place in supporting justice.

This does not mean that Smith expects economic stability simply from the self-command of all economic actors; his expectations for human excellence are more realistic than that, and he largely expects a middling sort of virtue, preeminently a prudential self-interest (as against either disinterested benevolence or unconstrained self-interest). As in *TMS*, the primary social function of the impartial spectator occurs when one's own interests are not directly at stake: the judgments of the impartial spectator primarily serve a *legitimating* function. In economic interaction, what the spectator legitimates is the institutional framework that sustains a competitive field. Part of that institutional framework is legal, part is concerned with accepted practices, and part with the norms and expectations of behavior that underlie what I have been calling decorum.

The problem of sustaining sympathy with competition, however, is not merely an issue that is economic in nature. Despite the wrong focus of much of DAS Problem, it nevertheless registered the symptoms of a genuine consistency problem that begins in *TMS* and runs through *WN*. The consistency problem is not about virtue, nor is it simply in the movement from *TMS* to *WN*; rather, it is within each of them. The inconsistency has to do with the regulation of self-interest and power, at the level of social relations in *TMS* and at the level of economic relations in *WN*. The commentators who worry about power in Smith's theories are closer to identifying the problem than those who worry about virtue.[11]

The inconsistency in Smith's view of the regulation of power exists at two levels: first, in his theory of economic interaction; and second, in his address to the reader. Both of them are managed by invoking propriety. Invoking propriety at the level of theory works along two dimensions: first, observing propriety in one's own actions could forestall self-interested abuses of power and lead to a self-regulating dynamic if everyone did so; but second, even in the event that personal self-regulation did not occur or was minimal, sympathy with the institutions that control power by promoting competition would legitimate and sustain those institutions. Invoking propriety at the level of addressing the reader – that is, rhetorically – works in that the reader can easily find the appeal to such a solution in keeping with the notions of decorum advanced in the narrative structures of both books. As Smith argues for the theoretical necessity of legitimating competition, in other words, he simultaneously invites the reader to approve and legitimate the institutions necessary to sustain it.

Smith's rhetorical situation in *Wealth of Nations*

Optimism vs. pessimism

John Kenneth Galbraith (1983) argues in *The Anatomy of Power* that the social conditioning of belief via persuasion is the predominant mode of power in the modern era:

> While condign and compensatory power [i.e., punishment and reward] are visible and objective, conditioned power, in contrast, is subjective; neither those exercising it nor those subject to it need always be aware that it is being exerted. The acceptance of authority, the submission of the will to others, becomes the higher preference of those submitting. This preference can be deliberately cultivated – by persuasion or education. This is explicit conditioning. Or it can be dictated by the culture itself; the submission is considered to be normal, proper, or traditionally correct. This is implicit conditioning. No sharp line divides one from the other; explicit conditioning shades by degrees into implicit.
>
> (Galbraith 1983: 24)

While Galbraith does not mention rhetoric, except in its usual pejorative meaning of empty talk, his distinction between explicit and implicit conditioning is a reasonable if general approximation of what I have called the distinction between strategic and constitutive rhetoric.

Galbraith identifies *WN* as a pivotal persuasive influence in the shift from Mercantilist to market capitalism (ibid., 111). He claims that Smith accomplished two main things with *WN*: he attacked and undermined the rationales for the existing Mercantilist system, and he promoted the idea of the self-correcting market – the famous "invisible hand" – which by its nature would turn the pursuit of self-interest to socially productive and desirable ends. Accomplishing these two ends framed Smith's rhetorical situation and took the form of pessimistic and optimistic scenarios about the power of self-interest (Mercantilism and Smith's extended division of labor, respectively). Navigating between the pessimistic and optimistic scenarios is Smith's rhetorical challenge in *WN*.[12]

Smith's optimism about the state of natural liberty in *WN* is in tension with his pessimism about combination. Each tendency places certain rhetorical demands on Smith's argument. The picture of a morally regulated civil society developed in *TMS* supports the optimistic argument, but it is not sufficient in *WN* for Smith to paint a happy picture of how conditions could be better to have any influence in changing policy. He also has to attack and criticize policies and orientations that he believes are wrong, though still entrenched and powerful, like those of the Mercantilists. Smith has a reasonable skepticism about the extent of natural human goodness, noting in *TMS* that beneficence is strongest, through sympathy, with those to whom one is nearest, and weakest with those from whom one is most distant. Yet, since one of the major differences between *TMS* and *WN* is that economic relations, more so than everyday social relations, are indirect and hence invisible, Smith fears there is a natural tendency for people to combine to seek a position of advantage for their own interests, the Mercantilists being a case in point.[13] This is the problem of the pessimistic scenario; seeking advantage does away with the competition necessary for the market to be self-regulating.

In support of the optimistic scenario, Smith provides primarily the decorum of the social world conceived as a horizon of visibility, as developed in *TMS*. *TMS* features scenarios of middling virtuous behavior, such as prudential self-interest, that serve as commonplaces in *WN*. Appeals to the reader's self-understanding, like the passages on the thrifty and frugal peasant and the indolent farmhand I explored in Chapter 1, are examples. The appeal to everyday experience, within a horizon of mutual judgments and expectations, demonstrates to the reader a morally regulated social order. The consequent peaceful operation of civil society becomes the basis for a flowering of economic interaction in a system of natural liberty, once external constraints like bad law and counterproductive policies are removed. This is Smith's optimistic argument.

There is, nevertheless, a tension between Smith's confidence in the "system of natural liberty" and his polemics against combination. The system of natural liberty is presented as an arrangement of free interactions among individuals who respect each other's positions – i.e., that tolerate competition. The system of natural liberty is morally attractive; it is a story of free interactions that by their nature lead to productive, if unintended, outcomes. Combination, on the other hand, seeks to evade competition by gaining a power advantage. Where Smith talks about the system of natural liberty, the obstacle he describes is government interference, but elsewhere he talks about the evils of combination in business practices. Smith condemns the tendency to combination but does not address its effects on the system of natural liberty, leaving uncertainty about how the system of natural liberty would not be disrupted by it. One might say that Smith's polemics work almost too well, with his skepticism about combination undermining his optimism about the successful spontaneity of natural liberty.

Navigating between his optimism and pessimism is Smith's rhetorical challenge in *WN*. The narratives about moral relations within a horizon of identification developed in *TMS* work to support his optimistic argument, while his explicit polemics against his opponents tend to express his pessimistic view. The behavior that calls forth Smith's polemics, however – the pursuit of self-interest within a context of indirect or distant social connection – is just as natural as the operation of sympathy at closer quarters. Because of this, Smith is never able to account explicitly for how the tendency toward combination will not thwart the development of natural liberty. Instead, Smith's resolution of the tension between his optimistic and pessimistic scenarios is *implicit*, in his elaboration of the propriety of competition as worthy of approval by the impartial spectator, and by extension, worthy of the sympathetic approval of the reader. In terms of the rhetorical argument I have been making about the role of decorum in Smith's argument, his constitutive rhetoric is indispensable in generating the necessary identification and sympathy.

Arrangement and argument in WN

Galbraith's (1983) description of Smith's achievements in *WN* as being his attack on Mercantilism and his promotion of the self-regulating market provides a good point of departure for approaching Smith's text. The problem that any scholar of Smith's work faces is the tremendous range of Smith's analysis; *Wealth of Nations* is a two-volume work comprising over a thousand pages. My analysis of *WN* will necessarily be illustrative rather than exhaustive, but the main theses of the book are well expressed in the arrangement of the book's opening and closing sections.

Smith handles the rhetorical task of negotiating between optimistic and pessimistic scenarios in the main by opening *WN* with his optimistic argument – the promotion of the self-regulating market – and only later turning to his pessimistic argument in the attack on the Mercantilists.[14] The opening chapters of *WN*, which I will examine shortly, confirm this: most of them make use of the commonplaces of everyday virtuous behavior. Smith establishes a basic narrative background of how the dynamics of sympathy drive economic behavior, giving substance to his portrayal of an optimistic picture.

The end of the book, by contrast, is an extended analysis of the bad effects of the national debt on England's economic health, debt that Smith lays at the doorstep of Mercantilists and others who have combined to restrict trade and serve their own interests. Smith assigns the evils of combination, including Britain's debt, to his opponents and closes *WN* with an analysis of the gloomy prospects in store should his advice be ignored.

In making the argument that Smith's use of constitutive rhetoric (the portrayal of character and decorum) works to reinforce and support his strategic rhetoric (promoting the self-regulating market and attacking Mercantilism), I will focus primarily on *WN*'s opening chapters, where Smith has the challenge of engaging the reader's sympathy for Smith's vision of the market. Before turning to the opening chapters, however, it would be useful to review Smith's critiques of Mercantilism, to have the problem he aims to solve freshly in mind.

Smith's objections to Mercantilism fall into four closely interrelated areas, all of which involve state actions of some kind or other that claim to be motivated by benevolent intentions. The first two areas fall under the rubric of protectionism, dividing roughly between domestic limitations on economic activity and limitations on foreign trade. The second two areas fall under national policy, and they involve both colonial policies and the national debt. In all four cases, the state is the enforcer of restrictions on economic activity, whether in restricting the movements of workers within the country in laws of settlement (*WN* i 493), restricting the corn trade (*WN* ii 29), or in burdening the nation with debt from colonial wars (*WN* ii 486).

But Smith's target is not the state itself as much as it is the influence on the state of the Mercantilists: Smith's policy goal is a reconsideration of the state's best actions with regard to "a plentiful revenue or subsistence for the people ... [and] to supply the state or commonwealth with a revenue sufficient for the public services" (*WN* i 449). In that respect, the state – i.e., those who are in a position to influence its actions – is a significant part of Smith's audience. The Mercantilists are the targets for condemnation, and Smith regularly makes them targets of polemical strategic rhetoric. Monopolizing merchants are castigated for their "mean rapacity" (*WN* i 519) and are accounted responsible for destroying the virtue of parsimony in society at large with their profligacy from all their excessive profits (*WN* ii 128).

The problem of self-interest stems from the potential conflict of interests between different parties. For Smith, this potential conflict is mediated by the desire to trade and exchange. The context for the playing-out of the tension between conflicting desires to self-maximize on the part of different actors is the situation of "natural liberty"; that is, the political situation of a peaceful social order, which is maintained by an effective state, both in defending the country from foreign predation as well as by maintaining the internal social order. Smith was well aware of the need for the state, of course. As he outlines it,

> According to the system of natural liberty, the sovereign has only three duties to attend to; three duties of great importance, indeed, but plain and intelligible to common understandings: first, the duty of protecting the society from the violence and invasion of other independent societies; secondly, the duty of protecting, as far as possible, every member of the society from the injustice or oppression of every other member of it, or the duty of establishing an exact administration of justice; and, thirdly, the duty of erecting and maintaining certain public works and certain public institutions, which it can never be for the interest of any individual, or small number of individuals, to erect and maintain; because the profit could never repay the expence [sic] to any individual or small number of individuals, though it may frequently do much more than repay it to a great society.
>
> (*WN* ii 208)

Smith's description of the ideal state – i.e., one which removes itself from economic control – comes in the last section of *WN*. Considering that his broad argument is that economic relations are self-regulating, having the relations of self-interested economic actors function properly because there is a police officer on every streetcorner would weaken rather than strengthen his case. The state is a backstop, a literal court of appeals that stands behind some other regulative means that enables the negotiation of different interests. Sympathy with competition, enabled by acceptance of Smith's standards of propriety as established in *TMS* and performed in *WN*, constitutes that regulative means, and it functions to legitimate Smith's recommendations about how competition may be sustained.[15]

The optimistic and pessimistic aspects of *WN* are often represented as signs of Smith's realism. I claim, however, that the optimistic/pessimistic divide is conceptually critical to Smith's argument, and that the tension it produces is managed rhetorically by the constitutive performance of propriety in *WN* – in Smith's attributions of moral judgment and portrayals of character. I say "performance" to answer the important question about the relation between *TMS* and *WN* with respect to the operation of sympathy and the judgments of the impartial spectator.[16]

As I suggested earlier in this chapter, my answer is that sympathy and the impartial spectator are *performed* in *WN*, and are thus in the implied reader, whose judgment the actual reader is invited to share. This acknowledgment of the role of the reader points up the unavoidably practical element in discussing propriety: in order to talk about decorum, one must necessarily participate in its construction, and one does this in the reading of *WN* by identifying with the characters and the stories – or perhaps more precisely, in one's identification with the implied author, whose attitudes toward the characters and stories help reveal the propriety at stake in each of them. Attention to reflection on the act of encountering Smith's text with an awareness of the function of decorum provides a new perspective on the inconsistencies in Smith's texts. At the end, the logic of systematic thought is not adequate on its own to provide a solution; instead, Smith's readers are able to join him in a performance of propriety and decorum in which their own sympathies are appealed to, in which they assume the position of the impartial spectator.

So Smith's rhetorical situation in *WN* is roughly as follows: his economic analysis, including its aspect of self-regulating social order, serves as the warrant for his policy recommendations. His task is to confirm his policy recommendations while attacking current Mercantilist policy. This task marks *WN* as a form of deliberative rhetoric: arguments about expediency and effectiveness. The process of confirming the desirability of Smith's ideas emphasizes fair outcomes – that is, it presumes a stable civil society (which derives from *TMS*), while his attack emphasizes abuses of power that are anti-competitive. Since both cooperation (through sympathy) and the potential for abuses of power are fundamental aspects of human nature, and since sympathy limits the range of natural self-command (i.e., the range of sympathy is limited by the potential for identification), the question of how one knows that the optimistic scenario of cooperation can prevail over the abuse of power becomes unavoidable.

So the rhetorical structure of Smith's argument is ultimately a dialectic, but one of persuasion rather than of purely rational argument. The dialectic between self-interest and the pursuit of power needs intervention, the reader's participation in it to tip the scales in favor of a cooperative outcome. So the dialectic is the interplay of deliberative and epideictic rhetoric: economic analysis and policy argument viewed through the lens of desirable human behavior.

The implicit rhetoric of the praiseworthy in *WN*

Constitutive rhetoric, as I argued in Chapter 1, can be thought of in terms of Aristotle's treatment of epideictic rhetoric, whose central concern is praiseworthiness, and its affinity for the persuasiveness of ethos, or character. The rhetoric of the praiseworthy is concerned with motives and with moral character, but it is not just mobilized in explicit epideictic discourse – for example, in outright polemical accusation or name-calling – but also indirectly in portrayals of good or bad behavior. These latter instances can be much more subtle than explicit encomia or diatribes, and are usually embedded in narrative structures.

Fisher's (1987) narrative paradigm is of use in examining narrative forms; his distinction between narrative coherence and narrative fidelity provides two different angles of appreciation on narratively embodied portrayals of character and moral value. Coherence, on the one hand, is a test of consistency and sense-making; it involves the self-cohesion and continuity of a story and its elements. Fidelity, in contrast, involves the weighing of narrative elements such as portrayals of character and expressions of moral value against the rest of a reader's experience; it asks whether a proposed value is supported by other values one holds dear. The distinction between coherence and fidelity in Fisher's paradigm provides intratextual/intertextual comparatives as a basis for assessing a narrative text, and it is especially well suited for the subtleties of implicit arguments about moral questions.

For Smith, the first step in undermining benevolence as a rationale for Mercantilist policy is simultaneous with the first step of its replacement by the motive of a more effective prudential self-interest (Smith's "self-love"), which is the basis for the division of labor and a "consequence of a certain propensity in human nature … to truck, barter, and exchange one thing for another" (*WN* i 17). But Smith does not open his treatise directly with the principle of self-interest; instead, he opens (Chapter 1) with a narrative recounting of the enormous productive capacity of the division of labor – the pin factory – and only afterwards (Chapter 2) traces back to the motives which underlie it.

Smith sets up the implicit moral argument of his work in the first three chapters of Vol. 1: "Of the Division of Labour" (one); "Of the Principle Which Gives Occasion to the Division of Labour" (two); and "That the Division of Labour Is Limited by the Extent of the Market" (three). The chapters are short – ten, eight, and five pages respectively – and their subjects seem fairly straightforward: Chapter 1 describes the great productive power generated by the division of labor, beginning with the example of the pin factory; Chapter 2 contains the famous line about the "propensity in human nature … to truck, barter, and exchange one thing for another" (*WN* i 17); and Chapter 3 establishes the limits of trade as the key factor for maximum productivity. As brief as they are, however, these chapters establish the basic decorum that will continue throughout the book.

The first thing to note about these chapters is that they model his explicit social–economic thesis. Smith's thesis is (1) that wealth can be defined as the great productive capacity of the division of labor; (2) that there is a quality of human nature, self-interest, that promotes the division of labor by manifesting itself in the desire for trade; and (3) that the limit of trade, as the potential limit of the productive capacity of the division of labor, is definable as the conditions, both material and political, which facilitate social intercourse, especially by making transportation and travel easy.

These three points can also be described in a general way as the method by which Smith combines the principle of convincing through familiarity with his didactic prose: (1) the identification of a fairly simple example through which a principle of operation can be illustrated, which is then extended to a more complex situation; (2) the justification for the operation as a natural feature of human nature; and (3) the summing up of descriptions of physical or material conditions into a developmental – i.e., law-governed – historical and political narrative.[17]

Smith's opening lines establish his argument about the division of labor and simultaneously work to construct his ethos as a scientist. His assertion about the productiveness of the division of labor is accompanied by the caution that ordinary observation is not adequate to the task of understanding. He therefore simplifies for the reader a complex process, to "be more easily understood" (*WN* i 7). What he actually produces, though, is a doubled simplification – first, from the general business of society to that of some manufactures, and then from some manufactures to "a very trifling manufacture" (the pin factory) that can be "placed at once under the view of the spectator" (*WN* i 8).

"Spectator" is a significant term in late eighteenth-century natural science, and for Smith himself as well since it figured prominently in his theory of sociability in *TMS*. Smith, however, both nods to the scientific nature of observation and exceeds it in opening his discussion of the pin factory. While he alludes directly to a "spectator" (*WN* i 8), he does so by talking about the limits of a spectator's ability to see the connections among diverse workers in a division of labor. The spectator, in other words, is limited in comparison with Smith; Smith is able to "see" things which are not visible, simply by the grasp of his understanding. The example of the pin factory, therefore, is an example tailored by Smith to fit the limited capacity of the spectator/(reader). The example of the pin factory also functions as a kind of inverse argument *a fortiori*; i.e., if even this simple instance of the division of labor is complex, how much more so must the genuinely complex industries be. Here is where Smith establishes his ethos as a scientist: he can explain the invisible relations between visible phenomena in a way that is not directly observable or apparent.[18]

Smith illustrates the extent and productivity of the division of labor in several different ways in the first chapter, combining extended examples and brief ones. The pin factory is the first extended example, and it is followed by the example of the benefits (in terms of productivity) of specialization with the nail-making example, which comes in under the first of the three different circumstances which Smith defines as benefits of the division of labor – the improvement of dexterity (*WN* i 11). Brief examples are interspersed, as is a brief mention of

> How many different trades are employed in each branch of the linen and woollen [sic] manufactures, from the growers of the flax and the wool, to the bleachers and smoothers of the linen, or the dyers and dressers of the cloth!
>
> (WN i 9).

The third extended example forms the closing paragraph of the chapter, and is the most complex; it begins, "Observe the accommodation of the common artificer or day-labourer in a civilized or thriving country...." (*WN* i 15), and proceeds to trace out the division of labor *and* the role of trade (which is in effect a preview, since "trade" will not be developed until Chapters 2 and 3). The first point of departure is,

> The woollen [sic] coat, for example, which covers the day-labourer, as coarse and rough as it may appear, is the produce of the joint labour of a great multitude of workmen. The shepherd, the sorter of the wool, the wool-comber or carder, the dyer, the scribbler, the spinner, the weaver, the fuller, the dresser, with many others, must all join their arts to complete even this homely production.
>
> (*WN* i 15)

This listing is a condensed version of the division of labor given in the example of the pin factory; the condensation is important, for the list on its face might be no more than a *sorites*[19] – a heap of workmen. What redeems it is the implied narrative of necessary sequence represented in the listing. At the same time, it partakes of some of the rhetorical force of a *sorites*: not only this worker, but that, and then the next, and so forth and so on; the evidence piles up, so to speak.

Smith then shifts to the subject of trade in the next line, and begins alternating between trade and the division of labor:

> How many merchants and carriers, besides, must have been employed in transporting the materials from some of those workmen to others who often live in a very distant part of the country! how much commerce and navigation in particular, how many ship-builders, sailors, sail-makers, rope-makers, must have been employed in order to bring the different drugs made use of by the dyer, which often come from the remotest corner of the world!
>
> (*WN* i 15)

This extended example, which proceeds to move from product to product for a page and three-quarters at the end of Chapter 1, traces out an extensive network of the division of labor, and culminates in an assertion and a comparison. The assertion is that, in examining these issues according to Smith's guidelines, we shall be sensible that without the assistance and co-operation of many thousands, the very meanest person in a civilized country could not be provided, even according to what we very falsely imagine, the easy and simple manner in which he is commonly accommodated.

(*WN* i 16)

The comparison seeks to demonstrate the superiority of modern European methods to primitive methods:

and yet it may be true, perhaps, that the accommodation of an European prince does not always so much exceed that of an industrious and frugal peasant, as the accommodation of the latter exceeds that of many an African king, the absolute master of the lives and liberties of ten thousand naked savages.

(*WN* i 16)

Several different things are happening in this final one-quarter of a page in the first chapter. Part of this section was the example I used in Chapter 1 of Smith's moral rhetoric; let me now look again at this section in more detail. In the assertion, Smith's authorial ethos is reasserted; the "we" is Smith being generous to his audience. The "we" who falsely imagines how simple it is to accommodate "the very meanest person" certainly does not include Smith himself, who knows very well that the matter is much more complicated. The comparison serves several different purposes. First, it continues the method of comparing one country's level of development to another's (a comparison which Smith initiates in Chapter 1, which I have not yet mentioned, and which is developed at much greater length in Chapter 3). Second, there is a specific moral (as in "moral of the story") for the entire extended example which begins with the woolen coat, and it is the contrast of the state of the "naked savages" which closes the paragraph. Civilized/uncivilized is concretized in this comparison as clothed/naked, which would undoubtedly appeal to Smith's readers as a kind of rhetorical proof, and in particular a moral one in the sense of standards of right and wrong, but also a moral as in the moral of a story – a practical lesson about wealth vs. poverty. The third purpose served by the comparison at the end of Chapter 1 is connected with the moral tone implied by the contrast of clothed/naked, but is even more subtly moral, and is a way into recognizing the constitutive moral argument, anchored to decorum, that Smith makes: it concerns the characterization of workers earlier in Chapter 1.

In the final comparison itself, the moral qualifier that hedges Smith's comparison is that the peasant is "industrious and frugal" (*WN* i 16). It is worth noticing that both the European prince and the African king are only noted by their social rank, and not by any other quality, while both the peasant and the "savage" subjects are denoted by qualifiers – industrious and frugal versus naked. Part of this is hyperbole; Muller (1993) traces the origin of the civilized/savage metaphor to Locke's Second Treatise (1952), where Locke describes America as a place where "A King of a large and fruitful territory there feeds, lodges, and is clad worse than a day Labourer in England."[20] Muller further notices that Smith extends Locke's metaphor in an early draft of *Wealth of Nations* where he writes, "a European prince does not so much exceed that of an industrious and frugal peasant, as the accommodation of this last exceeds that of the chief of a savage nation in North America" (1993: 66).

Something else is going on as well, though, with the characterization of the peasant as industrious and frugal. These qualifiers mark the moral subtext of Smith's argument, and some review of that subtext in Chapter 1 is now in order. Smith sets up another set of contrasting terms when he discusses the three circumstances that make the division of labor advantageous, but the contrast is indirect rather than explicit. As I noted in my opening example in Chapter 1, in the discussion of the first circumstance, dexterity (discussed above with reference to nail-making), Smith identifies it with the speed acquired through specialization, using such expressions as "utmost diligence" (*WN* i 11) and "when they exerted themselves" (*WN* i 12). By contrast, the second circumstance, which involves the saving of time, is illustrated by a negative example – i.e., by the time wasted by the agricultural laborer who moves from task to task instead of specializing in a single one. The expression Smith uses here is "saunters a little in turning his hand from one sort of employment to another" (*WN* i 12) and this leads to the following judgment:

> The habit of sauntering and of indolent careless application, which is naturally, or rather necessarily acquired by every country workman ... renders him almost always slothful and lazy, and incapable of any vigorous application even on the most pressing occasions.
>
> (*WN* i 12)

An implicit structuring of moral categories of workers' qualities is emerging in this passage in the form of the relation between motivations and actions. The concept of laziness as an obstacle to productivity is introduced, which Smith initially characterizes as structural rather than willful. The phrase "naturally, or rather necessarily" in this passage functions as a metanoia – a self-correction – to place the origin of the laziness in the nature of the work itself, but the final effect by the end of the passage is that the agricultural laborer is "almost always slothful and lazy." The initial impetus of the metanoia, which is to place the blame for laziness on the work's nature, rather than on the worker's nature, is compromised by the end of the passage.

So by the end of the chapter, a foil has already been set in place for the figure of the industrious and frugal peasant: the indolent and careless farmhand. A moral economy begins to take shape within the economy of material production from the start, and it is discernible through the language of praiseworthy character and the appeals of decorum.

Throughout the rest of the book, the contrasts of thrift/profligacy are interwoven with those of independence/dependency and freedom/tyranny. The explicit polemics that Smith engages in against the Mercantilists and the Church are counterpoised by the naturalness and everyday quality of his "heroic" figures: the industrious worker, the honestly self-interested retailer. Consider one of *WN*'s most famous lines, from Chapter 2; in discussing the proclivity to trade, Smith writes,

> It is not from the benevolence of the butcher, the brewer, or the baker that we expect our dinner, but from their regard to their own interest. We address ourselves, not to their humanity but to their self-love, and never talk to them of our own necessities but of their advantages. Nobody but a beggar chuses [sic] to depend chiefly upon the benevolence of his fellow-citizens.
>
> (*WN* i 18)

Certainly, this passage is a clear statement of the central place of self-interest in *WN*, but what passes unremarked in the usual treatments of DAS Problem is how this passage invokes *propriety*. In rhetorical terms, the confirmation of Smith's reasoning lies in the reader's everyday experience of propriety.

In similar fashion, the evils of the Mercantilist system and religious rule are both personal and political; they not only degrade the people who are forced into dependency, but they also harm the nation. The harm itself is twofold; the loss of liberty weakens the state, and the monopolizing of advantage robs the state of its potential wealth – i.e., it keeps wealth from *rising* – and keeps it centralized in the hands of a small group. The harm also triggers a distrust of institutional benevolence.

The everyday qualities of Smith's heroes are the evidence for the reader's tests of fidelity: is it proper to appeal to the butcher's self-interest when I want to buy dinner? The reader's sympathetic approbation of reasonable self-interest advances Smith's case. The villains in Smith's story are not nearly so matter of fact; they are deceptive and have ulterior motives, and most especially have a desire for power over others. The ethos of the Church and of the Mercantilists is fatally compromised by the discovery that their true motives are holding power for themselves and keeping others dependent on them.[21] These elements fuel the antipathy Smith is able to generate with his polemics.

The explicit rhetoric of the praiseworthy

While the genuine problem that the Mercantilists pose for society is not simply their greed per se but their power and the bad example they set, they are nevertheless part of an established social order that Smith must undermine if he is to undermine their legitimacy. Smith's polemics against the greed of the Mercantilists play against Smith's earlier move in *TMS* to displace benevolence as a reliable motive for social policy. Smith reframes the problem of Mercantilism by calling the entire system of patronage into question, and he does it by eliminating benevolence from a reliable role in economic matters. Benevolence as a motive for social policy is the lynchpin of a system of patronage: with it, a distributively just Christian social order, such as the Middle Ages dreamed about, is possible;[22] without it, power becomes tyrannical. Smith's appeal to our positive understanding of the "butcher, the brewer, or the baker" (*WN* i 18) helps to later undo benevolence as a motive with his castigation of the Mercantilists and the Church, setting the stage for his subsequent attack on a system of patronage which has been stripped of its justification. The translation of distributive justice into beneficence in *TMS* takes shape in *WN* as benevolence being an unworthy motive for state policy.

Much of the explicit rhetoric of the praiseworthy in *WN* actually takes place in the negative – i.e., in polemics and attacks on policies that Smith is arguing against. After arguing for a repeal of the settlement laws, for example, that prevented workers from leaving their town or agricultural district to find employment elsewhere, Smith writes,

> To expect, indeed, that the freedom of trade should ever be entirely restored in Great Britain, is as absurd as to expect that an Oceana or Utopia should ever be established in it. Not only the prejudices of the public, but what is more unconquerable, the private interests of many individuals, irresistibly oppose it. Were the officers of the army to oppose with the same zeal and unanimity any reduction in the number of forces, with which master manufacturers set themselves against every law that is likely to increase the number of their rivals in the home market; were the former to animate their soldiers, in the same manner as the latter enflame their workmen, to attack with violence and outrage the proposers of any such regulation; to attempt to reduce the army would be as dangerous as it has now become to attempt to diminish in any respect the monopoly which our manufacturers have obtained against us.
>
> (*WN* i 493)

and Smith goes on for the same length again before he finishes this passage with language just as strong. As noted earlier, "monopolizing merchants" are castigated for their "mean rapacity" (*WN* i 519) and are accounted responsible for destroying the virtue of parsimony in society at large with their profligacy from all their excessive profits (*WN* ii 128).

The Roman Catholic Church comes in for a blistering attack as well. While most of the religious civil war was finished by Smith's time, the Jacobite uprising of 1745 occurred during his time as a young man at Oxford, and there was continual suspicion of Catholic motives. Smith writes,

> ...the constitution of the church of Rome may be considered as the most formidable combination that was formed against the authority and security of civil government, as well as against the liberty, reason, and happiness of mankind, which can flourish only where civil government is able to protect them.
>
> (*WN* ii 325)

Nor is education exempt from his criticisms; Smith also blasts policies that give professors a living that makes them independent of their students' needs. He writes of Oxford, where he went, "the greater part of the public professors [there] have, for these many years, given up altogether the pretence of teaching" (*WN* ii 284). Smith's polemical criticisms are a blend of exposing bad faith, wrong-headedness, and corrupt self-interest. They are all indictments of moral character in one way or another, and questions of moral character have been at the center of rhetoric's concern with the place of character in persuasion and its relation to the expectations about proper behavior in decorum.

The consequences of bad faith and bad policy

While the opening chapters of *WN* can be taken as establishing the pursuit of self-interest as a basis for free market relations, the closing chapter can be taken as an illustration of the worst consequences of a controlled market in which government serves the interests of the Mercantilists. The last chapter of *WN* is on Public Debts, and it comes as the close of Book 5, "Of the Revenue of the Sovereign or Commonwealth." This chapter makes an analysis of the national debt and ends with the somewhat startling recommendation that Great Britain should cut loose the American colonies.[23]

Smith's views on America are particularly interesting for seeing the obverse of the American justification for rebellion against England. A central American complaint was that of being taxed without representation, which violated a central precept of British citizenship; the complaint was that Americans, as British subjects, were not being treated as fairly as Britons, by not being given seats in Parliament. Smith's view was that the American colonies were a *drain* on Britain's treasury – that they were not, in other words, paying their fair share and were thus being subsidized. Smith's recommendation was to grant the Americans parliamentary representation and to then *increase* their taxes – or, failing that, to cut them loose and grant their independence. Smith was not unsympathetic to the American cause, but he was much more sympathetic to Britain's problem with its national debt.

The British debt and colonial policies were intertwined with each other, although the link was not direct. The main complaint that Smith had about the debt is that it concealed the real costs of wars by spreading the payment for them out over many years – in fact eventually over several generations.[24] The real cost of the debt is that it diverts the money raised by taxation to pay the interest on money obtained from lenders. The lenders themselves not only make money out of this situation, at the expense of the rest of the country's taxes, but also continue to make money ad infinitum since the principal is never paid down.

The problem is compounded by the extent to which, in Smith's analysis, the borrowed money is used to finance colonial expansion – both in terms of subsidizing colonial operations and in terms of waging wars of conquest or wars in defense of colonized areas. It is important to remember that Britain's colonial policy was protectionist and monopolistic at the time – exactly the things that

Smith was arguing *against* in Mercantilist policy. In effect, the colonial monopolies were enriching themselves with government assistance, and the government, in order to give that assistance, was enriching the shareholders of the Bank of England by taxing the rest of the country to pay the interest on the growing debt. That taxation, to return to Smith's thesis – because it did not extend and expand the limit of trade – failed to stimulate the division of labor as much as it might otherwise, and thus acted as a drag on economic growth.

Smith sets up two contrasting policies: one (his) which promotes trade and growth which benefits the whole society, and the other (the Mercantilist or Physiocratic) which serves the interests of some at the expense of others. Mercantilist policies benefit the few, especially colonial monopolists and the Bank of England, at the expense of the great part of the rest of the country who pays those taxes. The economic harm is twofold: the money given to inappropriate taxation is not only lost for use as productive capital, it is also wasted because it only pays on the interest of the debt and does nothing to secure a more productive future. The dismal consequences of these policies are condensed by Smith into the final sentence of *WN*:

> If any of the provinces of the British Empire cannot be made to contribute towards the support of the whole empire, it is surely time that Great Britain should free herself from the expence [sic] of defending those provinces in time of war, and of supporting any part of their civil or military establishments in time of peace, and endeavor to accommodate her future views and designs to the real mediocrity of her circumstances.
>
> (*WN* ii 486)

Propriety, theoretical necessity, and persuasive performance

The foregoing examples of strategic and constitutive rhetoric indicate the ways in which Smith attempts to construct a favorable attitude toward his economic theory and his policy recommendations. Smith's economic system in *WN*, far from being a social landscape empty of moral virtue, is one highly dependent on it. The role of sympathy that Smith develops in *TMS* is also necessary in *WN*; it is this sympathy *in the reader* that makes his appeal to the example of the butcher and brewer so rhetorically effective. This is the moral key to Smith's system: the division of labor and a wide extent of trade will develop and regulate itself as long as sympathy for competition motivates policy. That sympathy most effectively takes the form of propriety. It is only when selfish forces thwart competition and seek a monopoly or similar advantage that the system of free and open trade does not promote the general welfare. At those times the invisible hand is thwarted, and serves only private interests. Smith's deployment of propriety is, therefore, rhetorical in the deepest sense: it is a persuasive appeal, but the success of the appeal is essential to the theoretical success of the economic system *qua* system. Propriety itself – and the sympathy it seeks to engage – is necessary not only to theoretically explain the economy but also practically for its just operation.

Returning to my larger argument about the social theory implicit in Smith's work in *TMS* and *WN*, propriety is a key concept because of its function as the element of distributive justice that cannot be apportioned either to the market itself or to the private practice of virtue. Propriety, and the sense of decorum that gauges its standards, functions as the means by which individuals locate themselves in their communities and are able to generate their individual identities through their interactions with others. From this perspective, Smith's work in *TMS* and *WN* functions as a primer, an instruction manual that is both an introduction and an initiation into a discourse community whose standards bring the community itself into being.

The dilemma of Smith's work, however, remains the tension between the desire for approval that underlies human sociability on the one hand, and the unregulated power of the pursuit of self-interest on the other. Propriety is essential to managing that tension, but in practice, propriety is a contested concept and subject to change and resistance. Smith's version of propriety is that of a commercial society, a "society of strangers" as Richard Teichgraeber has put it.[25] Propriety as a way of defining or delimiting a community, however, has other possibilities, other claims on the nature of community and membership in it.

My overarching argument is that the role propriety plays in Smith's social theory points to the central tension in liberalism itself: the promise of freedom on one hand, with a demand to accept a given propriety on the other. That tension existed at the inception of the United States, in the acceptance of a definition of community whose propriety included a place for slavery. While Smith was an adamant foe of slavery, the limited nature of his view of a proper social order can be clearly seen in examples like his treatment of the topic of women's education; assigning women entirely to the domestic sphere, Smith argued in effect that literary or higher education generally was wasted on them (*WN* ii 302).

The prospect of a changing propriety is important because of its essential connection to distributive justice. Recall that the natural law theorists' efforts to define "real justice" as commutative justice was also an effort to define distributive justice as virtue, thus rendering it private and removing it from public discussion. Smith's treatment of justice contributes without question to what became the liberal distinction between the public and the private.

Conclusion: *TMS* and *WN* as social theory

I have argued that Adam Smith's two published works are necessarily and closely connected with each other through the social theory implied by Smith's separation of commutative and distributive justice. The first book, *TMS*, comprises Smith's argument about the development of social order based on the psychology of moral judgment and the faculty of sympathy; it is here, in his discussion of justice and the social order, that Smith separates commutative and distributive justice, assigning the first to the operation of government and law and removing the second from the political realm, assigning it instead to persuasion in personal relationships.

In Chapter 2 I argued that Smith, in hedging about a minimum of propriety being necessary for the stability of a social order, brought a modicum of distributive justice back into his concept of what was necessary for a just social order. That aspect of distributive justice, I claimed, functions as a social decorum – a set of expectations about conduct that govern behavior. I further argued that Smith's treatment of moral judgment, justice, and the social order constituted a social theory – that is, a comprehensive explanation of the dynamics by which the social order maintains its stability and reproduces itself. In short, I argued that *TMS* was not merely Smith's theory of the individual psychology of moral judgment, but also a theory of society as well – and one based on a separation of commutative and distributive justice.

In Chapter 3, I have argued that *WN*, far from being in opposition to or disconnected from *TMS*, as suggested by the controversy of Das Adam Smith Problem, was in fact a further extension of Smith's social theory, not only consistent with *TMS* but in fact dependent on its theory of justice and social order. I argued that *WN* completed the work begun in *TMS* of Smith demonstrating how attention to distributive justice was no longer necessary because its functions would be handled by natural social systems. *TMS* described the workings of a natural and self-sustaining social order that satisfied the demands of distributive justice regarding one's place in society, and *WN* described the workings of a natural and self-sustaining – that is, self-regulating – market that satisfied distributive justice's demands for material subsistence. Because these two great systems of society and economy were driven by features of human nature, Smith thought, they would deal with distributive justice without the need for deliberate control.

I have claimed, however, that Smith's conclusions about self-regulation in both his economic and social theory were problematic. The self-regulation of the economy was dependent on competition to achieve the fairness and full production that would implicitly serve distributive justice's material demands for subsistence. Yet competition, though supported by the sentiment of approving fairness, was threatened by an equally natural sentiment of self-interest. The conundrum in Smith's theory is why competition would prevail over self-interest. The function of decorum in the social order from *TMS*, I argued, was how Smith tipped the scales toward competition in *WN* by his portrayal of that decorum in the constitutive rhetoric of characterization and authorial approval. Absent such a decorum, the self-regulating nature of Smith's economy is open to question.

A similar problem plagues Smith's picture of a self-sustaining social order. The dilemma is that Smith's view of the necessary minimum of decorum winds up favoring the advantaged classes since they are the ones with the wealth and property that commutative justice is largely concerned with. With distributive justice relegated to private life, those without advantages have little recourse for talking about their situations in terms of justice; complaints about social justice lose legitimacy and can be written off as personal grumbling and sour grapes. Motives for adherence to the necessary decorum become strained. The ability of a weakened condition of decorum to sustain approval for its own social order, much less for competition, becomes open to doubt.

In short, Smith's attempt to complement Newton's science of the physical universe with a science of society has not succeeded, in large part because solving persisting problems of distributive justice that disrupt the social order and the economic world by assigning them to natural dynamics has not succeeded. Problems in distributive justice find expression in political discourse when they are not successfully handled otherwise, despite the argument that they should not be political matters.

Smith's treatment of justice is not merely a curiosity of Enlightenment thought. Smith's concept of the pursuit of self-interest in a self-regulating market was a powerful addition to the liberal vocabulary of individualism. His ideas remain influential insofar as his treatment of justice – i.e., separating commutative and distributive justice – has become a basic principle of classical liberalism. I now turn to an examination of Milton Friedman's *Capitalism and Freedom (CF)* to demonstrate that Friedman, like Smith, holds fast to this classical liberal conceptualization of justice, and with similar problematic results. In *CF*, I examine how Friedman's treatment of individualism and the principle of liberty relies on the same kinds of appeals to character and decorum as Smith's, and does so for the same purposes of confirming commutative justice as the only public justice.

4 The subordination of distributive justice in Milton Friedman's *Capitalism and Freedom*

Roughly two centuries separate Adam Smith and Milton Friedman. The connection I wish to draw between their ideas is not a direct line of causation so much as to point out shared and ongoing foundational assumptions about justice, assumptions that I claim characterize liberal political economy. The thesis I have been arguing is the apparent disappearance of distributive justice from public view with the advent of liberal political economy in the late eighteenth century. I say apparent because, as I argued about his economic theory in *Wealth of Nations* (*WN*), Smith's powerful concept of a naturally self-regulating market relied on a theory of social order that took a prevailing distributive order of society as natural and acceptable, while simultaneously excluding discussion of distributive justice from the public realm of politics. This exclusion constitutes the "disappearance" of distributive justice, but the acceptance of a prevailing social order gives mute testimony to the presence of a distributive order that resists questioning – a distributive order that defines the two central demands of distributive justice (one's place in society and one's subsistence) in terms of a commercial society.

Smith's exclusion of distributive justice from discussions of "real justice" (i.e., commutative justice) in *Theory of Moral Sentiments* (*TMS*) exerted a powerful influence in the intensive focus on individual freedom that developed with classical liberalism out of the eighteenth century into the nineteenth, and it continues to influence thinking today. Smith's exclusion of distributive justice relegated it to private concerns, with the effect that *both* commutative and distributive justice came to concern the individual: commutative justice, as it had been before, being concerned with those aspects of the individual worthy of public attention like protection of life and property, and, in its new configuration, distributive justice concerned with those aspects of the individual *not* worthy of public attention – one's position as an individual in relation to other individuals instead of one's worth as a member of society. This is not to say that social standing as a measure of worth ceased to exist; rather, social standing was declared to be a function of individual measure, while still being practiced as sharing the status of a group. Social connections, in other words, remained important in actual (private) life but became obscured in public discourse in favor of an increasing emphasis on individualism and on societal decorum – a decorum that shifted between that of a dominant social order and that of a commercial society.

So from Smith's time, a dynamic of accepting a dominant social order while excluding public discussion of distributive justice during the growth of a commercial society becomes a mark of liberal individualism. The exclusion of distributive justice worked by a process of naturalizing it, assigning its demands to the natural systems of society and economy, a process which was communicated by the use of appeals to character and characterization to establish a compelling picture of a proper decorum. This same dynamic is at work in Milton Friedman's *Capitalism and Freedom (CF)*.[1]

While some of the specifics of Friedman's arguments differ from Smith's, the two share a common orientation in their strategic arguments: (1) to "real" justice defined commutatively; (2) to the divisions of public and private life that follow from the exclusion of distributive justice; (3) to the autonomous and natural self-regulation of both the social order and the market; and (4) to the central importance of competition in the market for that self-regulation. Their portrayals of a commercial decorum of proper behavior and marked approvals and disapprovals of character are how the prevailing social order's distribution is accepted and confirmed as just.

The exclusion of distributive justice in Smith's *TMS* became taken for granted in Smith's account in *WN* of how a free market would operate. By Friedman's time, two centuries after the publication of *TMS*, the exclusion is barely remembered; distributive justice has become entirely subordinated to commutative justice, becoming a blind spot in liberalism's theory of individual freedom.

Friedman's Whig history

While *CF*. is a much shorter book than *WN* at only 202 pages, it presents its own challenge to a rhetorical reading. Where Smith's work presents the challenge of an overwhelming amount of detail, Friedman's exhibits the opposite problem of a spare treatise without a great deal of detail. Friedman's claims very often take the form of assertions with little in the way of analysis or evidence to support them – or more precisely, they take the form of claims, the support for which is itself a series of assertions that culminate in an appeal to a value, most often and most prominently, an appeal to the value of liberty. At the heart of the problem with reading Friedman rhetorically is his commitment to a Whig interpretation of history.

As described by historian Herbert Butterfield (1931), Whig history views events in terms of broad marches of progress, and the Whig historian "very quickly busies himself with dividing the world into the friends and enemies of progress" (5). Historical figures are abstracted from their times and inhabit a nearly melodramatic scene (34). Friends of progress, however defined, are heroes; enemies are villains.

At first view, a Whig interpretation of history looks like an ideal candidate for rhetorical analysis. To its critics, Whig history may appear to be *entirely* rhetorical, and insofar as it is polemical by nature, rhetoric naturally comes to mind. The temptation, however, is to stop with this reflection and fall into the everyday (and inadequate) understanding of rhetoric as strong language that masks a lack of content or sense. As I have argued throughout this book, the myriad ways in which identity is constructed and claimed contribute to the formation of character in the texts under discussion, and the constructions of character, in turn, invoke appeals to decorum that reveal important beliefs about the natures of the individual and of society and articulates values having to do with the relation between them. So to identify Friedman as engaged in writing a type of Whig history is only the point of departure, not the final destination of the analysis. The question remains: how does Friedman constitute character and decorum in *CF*, and how do those constitutions work together with his admittedly polemical strategic argument to reveal attitudes toward justice?

The strongly polemical tone of Friedman's Whig-historical orientation results in a more direct authorial commentary with Friedman than with Smith. Wayne Booth's (1983) telling/showing distinction helps to clarify what this means. Booth's contribution, as I noted in Chapter 1, was to demonstrate that "showing" (dramatic portrayal of a character) could be just as rhetorical as "telling" (direct commentary by an author), thereby unsettling the dictum that telling was rhetorical while showing was artistic. Thus, as I argued about Smith's *WN*, moral persuasion was at stake in Smith's miniature narratives, hypothetical scenarios, and sketches of character. While *CF* is not devoid of narratives, it nevertheless has a higher proportion of direct commentary than *WN*. Because of the greater extent of direct commentary, Friedman's implied author appears to be as close to him as the live author. Friedman constructs character strongly through the representation of his own character, and addresses the reader in terms that invite familiar agreement.[2]

This process is apparent where Friedman identifies himself with the tradition of classical liberalism at the beginning of *CF*. He lays specific emphasis on the Latin root of "liber" – free – that underlies the terms liberalism and liberty. Individual freedom is Friedman's central social principle:

> As liberals, we take freedom of the individual, or perhaps the family, as our ultimate goal in judging social interrelations among people … in a society freedom has nothing to say about what an individual does with his freedom; it is not an all-embracing ethic. Indeed, a major aim of the liberal is to leave the ethical problem for the individual to wrestle with. The "really" important ethical problems are those that face an individual in a free society – what he should do with his freedom. Thus there are two sets of values that a liberal will emphasize – the values that are relevant to relations among people, which is the context in which he assigns first priority to freedom; and the values that are relevant to the individual in the exercise of his freedom, which is the realm of individual ethics and philosophy.

(CF 12)

This treatment of individual freedom fits what has become a standard model of the difference between public and private life. Friedman's generality, "values that are relevant to relations among people," is translated in political terms; that is, they are the values that have the most widespread appeal and agreement. This is consistent with Smith's criteria for commutative justice – that they have a universal appeal – and with his relegation of distributive justice to individual ethics in private life.

The essence of character then, in Friedman's view, is the adherence to first principles, which in public affairs ought to be the principle of liberty. This is, of course, a public virtue, or more precisely, a virtue with respect to public affairs, and indeed, in Friedman's view the only really necessary public virtue. All other virtues, according to his definition, are either private or philosophical questions. So Friedman's view of the primary duties of government are similarly consistent with those developed in classical liberalism, including by Smith, that fit with a commutative understanding of justice as the only real justice appropriate for government and hence for political life. Commutative justice is expressed in the protection of life and property, so chief government duties include national defense and domestic peacekeeping, along with the tasks of defining property rights and enforcing contracts. Friedman also adds the duty of "foster[ing] competitive markets" (*CF* 2) to support his argument about the primacy of economic freedom. Competition, as Friedman defines it negatively, is about the absence of collusion, whether collusion among private parties or, much worse, for Friedman, government sanction that creates a collusive arrangement protected by law.[3]

Friedman's primary focus, however, is less on politics per se than on economic matters; his "major theme [is] the role of competitive capitalism ... as a system of economic freedom and a necessary condition of political freedom" (*CF* 4). Competition is essential to Friedman's system because his definition of economic liberty encompasses the freedom of consumers and producers to find alternative suppliers or buyers (*CF* 14). Restricting competition would restrict such alternatives, and thus would restrict freedom. By implication, increasing choices would increase freedom.

Friedman, however, reproduces the same dilemma as Smith with respect to the central importance of competition in liberal capitalist economic theory: the dilemma that competition, while essential for the operation of the market, is only made possible from outside the market by a social order that values competition and disapproves of non-competition. For both Friedman and Smith, in order for the market to be self-regulating, it must be competitive, but the tendency of individual behavior in the market to avoid or control competition generates a problem of coherence. If people have a natural preference for non-competition in their economic affairs, which for both Smith and Friedman appears to be the case, how can competition be required by government without violating that preference, and therefore contravening their liberty? Thus, Friedman's argument for economic liberty appears to yield the same coherence problem as Smith's.

Friedman's answer is framed in terms of character; in effect, people with the right attitude do not have a preference for non-competition; they are able to practice "self-denial" (*CF* 18). This is a much more direct appeal to virtue than Smith makes, but it shares the quality of Smith's use of moral argument in that its main force is aimed less at improving the reader's own virtue in making sacrifices than at enlisting the reader's resentment at those who try to avoid or control competition. Friedman's moral argument, in other words, works as a legitimating appeal rather than as an appeal to personal virtue – as being concerned with attitudes one should take toward others rather than toward oneself.

Thus, in Friedman's framework, individual preference for non-competition is not as much of a problem as government sanctions that give particular narrow interests an unfair advantage. Accordingly, for Friedman liberty is served by preventing collusion and getting rid of government sanctions; there is no need to look further for other advantaged interests, since Friedman minimizes potential bad effects from non-governmental power. This answer to the problem of competition, however, creates a problem in the fidelity of his argument. In American history, government regulation, whatever its outcomes, often developed in the first place to mitigate an advantage one group had over another – in other words, to address imbalances of power in society that create non-competitive situations.

Neither Smith nor Friedman acknowledges the problem of coherence and fidelity raised by the dilemma of competition. According to their explicit arguments, competition would naturally emerge once government sanctions that restrict it were removed. In Smith, this view culminated in his "system of natural liberty" (*WN* ii 208); for Friedman, freedom is the first principle of social relations – that is, an end in itself. The reader, however, is left with the indelible impression that the natural desire to avoid competition, whether out of greed or from a desire for security, is as natural and widespread as any other feature of human nature; hence the reader can legitimately wonder how the inclination to avoid or control competition can be compensated for, and be turned instead into an attitude of approval of competition.

The importance of the toleration of competition, moreover, is not achieved simply by a direct appeal to the reader's personal virtue – that is, to encourage the reader to be willing to tolerate competition herself – but rather by cultivating an attitude, through the implied reader, in harmony with a decorum that judges the willingness of *others* to tolerate competition with themselves. Ultimately, I argue, this strategy relies on portraying, again through the implied reader, a decorum of justified resentment of those who will not tolerate competition. This model is as apt for Friedman as it was for Smith. Their strategic reasons for cultivating a negative judgment are the same: they both argue to build support for reversals in government policy, so they have to establish the existing policies as problems needing resolution. There is an additional function, however, that resentment performs constitutively: it appeals to social condemnation as a form of control, not only inviting the implied reader to join in the implied author's judgments, but also pressing her to choose sides – to either condemn or be condemned.

Friedman's rhetorical situation

Friedman's rhetorical situation is to change what twentieth-century American political and economic history means to most of his audience – primarily the American public. Friedman faces the obstacle of a widespread historical belief of his audience that the Great Depression of the 1930s was a failure of free market economics and that the government's actions in response (the New Deal) helped restore the country's vitality. Friedman's rhetorical task when *CF* was written in the 1950s and 1960s was to convince his audience that free-market policies are morally and productively superior to those favoring government intervention in the economy that came into vogue as a result of the Depression, among them Keynesian economics and the New Deal, which in his view are wrongheaded and contrary to principles of freedom. Friedman faces the problem, in other words, of changing his audience's minds about their understandings of these broad historical events.

Friedman uses two strategies of appealing to common ground, one positive and one negative. The positive common ground that Friedman uses is the value of freedom, which has wide currency among American audiences. For Friedman, the two major sources of audience resistance are a historical distrust of the market that generates approval for government regulation, and (in his view) conceptual misunderstandings of economic principles, exemplified by their support for the Federal Reserve System and Keynesian economics, that led to misinterpretation of economic problems and their solutions.

The negative common ground that Friedman uses to frame his argument is the distrust and fear of totalitarianism, which is identified primarily with communism but which is also exemplified by Hitler's Nazi Germany. Friedman draws a clear line with the first paragraph of the first chapter, arguing that considering "democratic socialism" to be possible is a "delusion" (*CF* 7–8). Friedman's argument establishes a stark contrast: on one side, his view of freedom; on the other, an inevitable slide from government intervention in the economy, to the welfare state, to democratic socialism, to "totalitarian socialism" (*CF* 7) and the oppression represented by the Soviet Union.

To counter the interpretation of the Depression as a failure of capitalism, Friedman relies strongly on appeals to values of individualism and freedom that are the heritage of Smith's reconfiguration of justice. Friedman's combination of appeal to the ethic of individual freedom together with fear of totalitarianism comprise the common ground he seeks to create, from which point he expands his conceptual argument from economic freedom to political freedom (Chapter 1), to the limited functions government should perform (Chapter 2), and thence to his critique of the Federal Reserve System, Keynesian economics, and the New Deal (Chapters 3 through 5). So Friedman's primary historical message – that the Great Depression, contrary to what the reader might think, was not capitalism's fault but rather the fault of an interventionist government acting on incorrect economic theory – comes only after he has taken the opportunity to engage the audience through their positive attitudes toward individual freedom and their negative attitudes toward totalitarianism.

Understanding Friedman's rhetorical situation helps clarify his strategic rhetoric – what he hopes to persuade his audience to believe and the arguments and reasons he uses to persuade them. Just as Smith's argument was that Mercantilist policies limited the extent of trade and, therefore, stunted the wealth of the nation, Friedman's argument is that government involvement in the economy is inefficient and unfair, leading to distorted decisions about investment, limiting competition, and infringing on freedom. Friedman's goal is to generate support for policy changes that would, in his estimation, remove government from wrongheaded entanglements in the economy.

Whig history and Manichean argument

With the goal of changing the prevailing attitude that the Great Depression was capitalism's fault, Friedman's strategic argument relies strongly on establishing first principles as governing ideals, and he puts these relatively abstract arguments together with his constitutive rhetoric of character. Friedman reproduces the antithetical oppositions of Whig history in his conceptual frameworks, creating a quasi-Manichean picture of a world composed of light and darkness, of the virtue of liberty and the vice of collectivism, and of heroes and villains. A combination of argument from definition and disjunctive (either/or) reasoning that plays off highly polarized dualistic oppositions characterizes Friedman's conceptual reasoning both in his grand themes and in his case studies. Friedman typically identifies a key concept, defines the concept as an ideal, and repeats and refines the definition throughout his case studies. His logic then moves to generating disjunctive choices around the concept, such as: friends vs. enemies of capitalism; liberty vs. tyranny; individualism vs. collectivism; or diversity (of the market) vs. conformity (of government).

Friedman's pattern of argument from definition and pejorative juxtaposition also occurs in his broad historical themes and is evident in his construction of the rhetorical situation. Friedman views history almost exclusively in the light of his view of liberty, which leads to his use of history primarily to highlight or introduce a concept. Friedman himself notes that "Historical evidence by itself can never be convincing" (*CF* 11) as he shifts from the historical overview with which he opens Chapter 1 to a discussion of freedom as a concept. Friedman's historical interpretation in this section is framed to illustrate movements that were either individualist or collectivist. Anything in-between only counted as a moment in the movement toward or away from individual freedom or collectivist tyranny.

Friedman's conceptual emphasis affects his selection of historical, social, and political examples; they are chosen with an eye toward illustrating his abstract principles (or their opposites), but his examples often are partial and distorted. His historical examples often feel taken out of context, for instance, with attention to illustrating his principles but not to their own historical periods or their own internal logics. His social and political examples share the same selectiveness. This creates serious fidelity problems even for only moderately well-informed readers insofar as Friedman's examples seem strained or one-sided.

Example 1 – liberalism and its enemies

Friedman clearly states that capitalism's moral value derives from being the manifestation of liberty in the use of property.[4] Liberty is the moral ground of capitalism, and the first principle of Friedman's argument. In his description of the organization of the book (*CF* 4), he notes that the first two chapters set out the abstract principles of economic and political freedom that he subsequently applies to a series of cases. Friedman's definition of liberty, quoted earlier, is a recurring touchstone in his argument, and his logic moves by conceptualizing a polar opposite to liberty that becomes the other branch of a disjunctive choice.

The method of framing polar oppositions that Friedman uses repeatedly throughout the book also exhibits his moral judgment: they are pejorative juxtapositions. For example, in the first few pages of the Introduction, Friedman defends his use of the term liberalism instead of conservatism to characterize his views; he approvingly quotes Joseph Schumpeter's remark that " 'the enemies of the system of private enterprise have thought it wise to appropriate its label'."[5] Two paragraphs later, Friedman writes, "[Liberalism in the twentieth century] came to be associated with a readiness to rely primarily on the state rather than on private voluntary arrangements to achieve objectives regarded as desirable" (*CF* 5). The polarized dualisms in these oppositions are strongly inflected with morally weighted language, as indicated by "enemies," and typify the recurring thematic of disjunctive, either or logic. Either, following Schumpeter, one is a friend of capitalism or an enemy; either one relies primarily on private arrangements and is a friend of capitalism, or primarily on the state and is an enemy of capitalism. There is no in-between. Allowing no in-between and no shades of gray, Friedman's polarizing approach also conflates shades of difference together, either explicitly as Friedman does in describing communism, socialism, and the welfare state as all being "guises" of collectivism (*CF* 34), or implicitly in the "primarily state" vs. "primarily private" opposition that Friedman sets up.

The net strategic effect of Friedman's disjunctive approach is to put the reader in a position where she must choose sides – or doesn't have to, since the implication is that she agrees. This air of a disjunctive choice that is not really a choice at all indicates the constitutive rhetoric that underlies Friedman's argument here. No one of good character would be a proponent of collectivism and an enemy of capitalism.

Example 2 – disjunctive weaknesses

A disjunctive framework has the weakness of being vulnerable to alternatives that fit neither side of the either or choice. Friedman's 1982 Preface to the twentieth anniversary edition of *CF* has an apparently unnoticed irony where he mentions the televised series based on his *Free to Choose* (1980) (*CF* vii). There Friedman argues that it would be wrong to attribute the success of *Free to Choose* to its popularization by television, claiming instead that there had been a shift in the climate of opinion between 1962 and 1980. While Friedman is accurate that there had certainly been political shifts, the irony lies with Friedman's leaving unmentioned that the Public Broadcasting Service (PBS), that carried the television series, is a welfare-state institution. Friedman fails to note that PBS, as a publicly funded media venue, does not fit his disjunctive model. This is a symptom of the more general absence in Friedman's analysis of the place and role of institutions as mediating frameworks.

This particular example stands in sharp contrast to the disjunctive picture Friedman paints at the end of the first chapter (*CF* 16–20) of the extremes of a free market in public communication in capitalism vs. a state-controlled media in the collectivist totalitarian model. In that model, the only communication venues possible in Friedman's scenario are either pure free-market or pure state-controlled. The success of his own show was accomplished through a public communication medium that was neither because it was both – a mixture of market and government elements. Even more to the point, Friedman's show was *not* shown on purely commercial television, which his own theorizing suggested should have been the case.

Example 3 – weakness of Whig history in analysis

Friedman's translation of Whig history into ideal concepts partakes of Whig history's tendency to ignore difficult facts or events. The partial readings of history are a weak support that raise questions of fidelity. One of Friedman's partial readings of historical examples occurs in the first chapter, where he argues for economic freedom as a necessary condition for political freedom. In speaking favorably about the relation between economic freedom and political freedom, Friedman is willing to elide differences among a market economy, a free market, and capitalism, as he invokes classical Greece and Rome and the experiences of Europe and the United States in the nineteenth and twentieth centuries, totalitarian states (Nazism and communism) excepted (*CF* 10). In his account of the relationship between economic and political freedom, Friedman writes that Jeremy Bentham's arguments for political reform led an initial support for market-friendly laissez-faire policies in England. After that initial support, however,

> The triumph of Benthamite liberalism in nineteenth-century England was followed by a reaction toward increasing intervention by the government in economic affairs. This tendency to collectivism was greatly accelerated, both in England and elsewhere, by the two World Wars. Welfare rather than freedom became the dominant note in democratic countries.
>
> (*CF* 10)

With this description, Friedman sums up nearly one hundred years of the heart of the modern era with no analysis at all about why or how welfare replaced freedom as a dominant concern. The strategic point of this comment, for

Friedman, is that political freedom does not necessarily advance economic freedom, and hence cannot be trusted. He gives no analysis of the conflicts and problems which comprise the history of those decades, no hint as to how freedom and welfare might have come into conflict. Friedman's use of history in this section works solely to advance the assertion *that* the cause of freedom had been harmed by the rising emphasis on welfare.

Example 4 – assertion without analysis

Friedman makes the claim that the Interstate Commerce Commission (I.C.C.), while legitimately created to forestall bad effects of technical monopoly when railroads were the dominant mode of transport, should have been discontinued once trucking and airlines offered alternative forms of transportation (*CF* 29). In this example of argument by assertion, Friedman implicitly claims that railroads, trucking, and air transportation constitute adequate competition. He makes no analysis of the possible role of business practices in restraint of trade, no comparisons between industries to make the case that the different modes of transportation offer genuine alternatives to each other – which is his own standard for free exchange (*CF* 14–15) – and offers no argument for why the Commission's function does not come under the heading of "rules of the game" (*CF* 25). For Friedman, the example stands simply as evidence that government intervention never shrinks but only grows. This creates a coherence problem – i.e., is the problem as bad as he says it is? – that relies on his general warrant that government regulation is always bad.

Individuals, the social order, and justice

In addition to the problems of coherence and/or fidelity that Friedman's argumentation raises, there are also presumptions about the relations that should obtain between the individual and society, especially with regard to justice. I will examine three of Friedman's cases: market vs. government; the relation of citizen to government; and the relation of individual to individual.

Market vs. government

The conclusion of *CF*'s first chapter provides an example of how Friedman's blind spot about distributive justice and his reliance on abstract concepts influence his portrayals of individuals and social groups, especially in his contrast of market and government with respect to justice. In discussing the effects of McCarthyism on government employees targeted by McCarthy who lost their jobs, Friedman concludes the first chapter with comments about their fates that are worth quoting at length:

> It is of interest to note that a disproportionately large fraction of the people involved apparently went into the most competitive sectors of the economy

– small business, trade, farming – where the market approaches most closely the ideal free market. No one who buys bread knows whether the wheat from which it was made was grown by a Communist or a Republican, by a constitutionalist or a Fascist, or, for that matter, by a Negro or a white. This illustrates how an impersonal market separates economic activities from political views and protects men from being discriminated against in their economic activities for reasons that are irrelevant to their productivity – whether these reasons are associated with their views or their color.

As this example suggests, the groups in our society that have the most at stake in the preservation and strengthening of competitive capitalism are those minority groups which can most easily become the object of the *distrust and enmity of the majority* – the Negroes, the Jews, the foreign-born, to mention only the most obvious. Yet, *paradoxically enough*, the enemies of the free market – the Socialists and Communists – have been recruited in disproportionate measure from these groups. Instead of recognizing that the existence of the market has protected them from the attitudes of their fellow countrymen, they mistakenly attribute the residual discrimination to the market.

(*CF* 21, emphasis added)

First, the conceptual generalization: "No one who buys bread knows" stands for Friedman as the mark of the impersonality of the market. The economic relation it expresses might be better expressed by saying that the supermarket shopper buying bread does not know who grew the wheat for it, but to use an example like this to define a market relationship is a gross oversimplification that glosses over the relationships that do, in fact, obtain in nearly every market, and most especially those close to Friedman's "ideal free market." The shopper does not know the wheat farmer, but he may well know the grocer, the grocer the distributor, the distributor the baker, and the baker the miller, and so on and on until we arrive at the farmer. This sort of network of relationships is exactly what the complexity of the division of labor is about, and those relationships may have factors other than simply considerations of price. The actuality of the market may not reflect the principle Friedman attributes to it, and it may very well reflect the social order in which it operates. Friedman's fidelity suffers here where he does not take the time to assess markets as they are within their social contexts.

If that social order maintains itself through unjust exclusions, it will have problems of distributive justice (in that one's "place" is either denied or made subordinate), but those problems would be invisible *qua* justice to Friedman and would be interpreted merely as expressions of personal preferences. This follows from Friedman's earlier distinction between public virtue (liberty as first principle) and private virtue. Hence Friedman's assessment of a paradox; his view does not account for the attraction of socialism or similar political philosophies as other than a mistake, failing to note that the main force driving the rising importance of welfare and equality from the mid-nineteenth to the mid-twentieth century, one that motivated a host of political reforms as well as inspiring socialism and communism, was perceived injustices of exclusion.

Friedman's reference to the existing social order ("the attitudes of their fellow countrymen") in the final paragraph has strategic significance as the avowed reason why minorities should favor an impersonal market system – because they can "most easily become the object of the distrust and enmity of the majority," a problem which is attributed in the closing sentence to "residual discrimination" (*CF* 21). Friedman's constitutive rhetoric in this passage is in the performative mode; it is part of the establishment of Friedman's ethos – the representation of his attitude toward the subjects he discusses. While we have seen quite explicit language at work, as with his adoption of Schumpeter's use of the term "enemies," there are also implicit, more subtle forms of attitude. The attitude expressed in the first chapter's concluding paragraph is contained in the words "those minority groups which can most easily become the object of the distrust and enmity of the majority" (*CF* 21). In his strategic argument, these words indicate that Friedman is facing facts here; he is being a realist, and recommending his view as one.

While Friedman's very realism outwardly implies neither approval nor disapproval of such majority, his neutrality functions as a tacit acceptance of the social order implied by such a majority. His neutrality is evident by there being no shadow of a suggestion that minorities subject to distrust and enmity have any cause to think that such an attitude toward them is an injustice.

Compare this orientation with his discussion two pages later of the role of government:

> The use of political channels, while inevitable, tends to strain the social cohesion necessary for a stable society. The strain is least if agreement for joint action need be reached only on a limited range of issues on which people in any event have common views. Every extension of the range of issues for which explicit agreement is sought strains further the delicate threads that hold society together. If it goes so far as to touch an issue on which men feel deeply yet differently, it may well disrupt the society.
>
> (*CF* 23)

The criterion here is issues that are felt "deeply but differently," and the purpose to be served is to not strain the social fabric. Yet, clearly, deep feelings on the part of the majority count in a way that those of the minority do not, and the dissatisfaction of the majority places a strain on the social fabric which the dissatisfaction of the minority *should* not. The proper course of action, by implication, is that things as they are should not be disturbed. This tacit approval of the existing decorum of the social order transforms it from a realist position (nothing can be done) to a normative one (nothing should be done).

Citizen and government

Friedman opens his Introduction with President Kennedy's inaugural address phrase, "ask not what your country can do for you – ask what you can do for your country." Friedman's quotation of Kennedy is the beginning of a rhetorical attack. Friedman's disapproval is clear: "Neither half of the statement expresses a relation between the citizen and his government that is worthy of the ideals of free men in a free society" (*CF* 1). Friedman interprets Kennedy's statement as narrowing the choices of citizenship to either paternalism ("do for you") or to a master–servant relationship ("do for your country"). His strategic intent is clearly to disturb the regard in which Kennedy's address is held.

Friedman's attitude in his critique of Kennedy's famous line is discernible in his interpretation of it. Kennedy himself exploited an ambiguity in the word "country," so that his line could be interpreted as: ask not what your government can do for you, but ask what you can do for your community. With this reading, Kennedy's line is seen as a call for public service. Friedman's interpretation exploits the ambiguity in a different way, with "government" being the implicit meaning of "country" in both instances. The effect of Friedman's interpretation is to block the conventional invocation of community and replace it with a picture of admirable individualism, and simultaneously block the image of government as a collective expression of citizens ("us") and replace it with a picture of government as tyrant ("them").

This view of government is not surprising in the context of a Whig-historical view such as Friedman espouses. Kennedy was representative of the same political orientation as Franklin Roosevelt, one that Friedman viewed, at best, as being on a slippery slope to socialism and communism. The root of the problem, as Friedman defines it, is "that the great threat to freedom is the concentration of power" (*CF* 2), and government, and especially centralized government, is the primary danger.

Friedman's tendency to Manichean disjunctions leads him to some odd characterizations of government. One of the oddest is in Chapter 6, "The Role of Government in Education." Friedman's main argument in this section is in favor of replacing the public school system with a voucher system. He distinguishes between the rationale for funding education through public funds, with which he agrees, and the rationale for administering schools through a public agency, with which he disagrees. In making this distinction, Friedman writes, "the actual administration of educational institutions by the government, the 'nationalization,' as it were, of the bulk of the 'education industry' is much more difficult to justify.... The desirability of such nationalization has seldom been faced explicitly" (*CF* 89). Two pages later, in arguing for vouchers, Friedman writes that "denationalizing schooling would widen the range of choice available to parents" (*CF* 91). After his initial use of quotation marks and the modifying phrase "as it were," Friedman simply uses the term "nationalization" throughout the rest of the chapter.

The fidelity problem here is that schooling (K-12 is at issue here) has never been nationalized in the U.S., unlike many other countries. To the contrary, school districts have traditionally been the most local of local governances. The contrast between these remarks about education and Friedman's earlier remarks about the dangers of centralization and the preferability of small, local governance is striking.

The ambivalence in Friedman's treatment of politics and government finally appears in his Preface to the fortieth anniversary edition in 2002. The contrast between his original text and his reflections four decades later is telling. First, his original text:

> Historical evidence speaks with a single voice on the relation between political freedom and a free market. I know of no example in time or place of a society that has been marked by a large measure of political freedom, and that has not also used something comparable to a free market to organize the bulk of economic activity.
>
> (*CF* 9)

Next, from the 2002 Preface:

> If there is one major change I would make, it would be to replace the dichotomy of economic freedom and political freedom with the trichotomy of economic freedom, civil freedom, and political freedom. After I finished the book, Hong Kong, before it was returned to China, persuaded me that while economic freedom is a necessary condition for civil and political freedom, political freedom, desirable though it may be, is not a necessary condition for economic freedom and civil freedom. Along these lines, the one major defect in the book seems to me an inadequate treatment of the role of political freedom, which under some circumstances promotes economics and civic freedom, and under others, inhibits economic and civic freedom.
>
> (Friedman 2002: x)

The contrast between these two passages is clear. The reason for contrasting them is not to suggest that Friedman may not change his mind in retrospect, but rather to note that his change of mind focuses specifically on distinguishing between civil and political freedom. His alliance of economic and civil freedom, especially with the example of Hong Kong, suggests that he is most concerned with a certain rule of law, one that is primarily oriented toward commutative justice.

Individual to individual justice.

Friedman uses the figure of Robinson Crusoe in several places in the book as an exemplar of individualism. The most striking example with respect to questions of justice is in Chapter 10, "The Distribution of Income." Friedman sets up a hypothetical example, in which there are "four Robinson Crusoes, independently marooned on four islands in the same neighborhood." One island is well endowed, the others marginal. "One day, they discover the existence of one another." As Friedman poses the question, the rich one could be generous, but would the other three be justified in compelling him to share the wealth?

> Many a reader will be tempted to say yes. But before yielding to this temptation, consider precisely the same situation in a different guise. Suppose you and three friends are walking along the street and you happen to spy

and retrieve a $20 bill on the pavement. It would be generous of you, of course, if you were to divide it equally with them, or at least blow them to a drink. But suppose you do not? Would the other three be justified in joining forces and compelling you to share the $20 equally with them? I suspect most readers would be tempted to say no.

...Can we be judges in our own case, deciding on our own when we are entitled to use force to extract what we regard as our due from others?

(*CF* 165)

This extended passage is an exact rhetorical parallel to Adam Smith's line about appealing to the self-love of the butcher, the brewer, and the baker when we want our dinner. What I pointed out about Smith's passage is equally true here: the force of the comparison relies on the reader's sense of the decorum of the situation. The decorum itself is taken entirely for granted.

The question that naturally arises is whether the comparison is, in fact, an exact one, as Friedman claims. My point in underscoring the role of decorum in assessing the persuasiveness of the analogy is that here, Friedman simultaneously disavows decorum and relies completely upon it. This passage is an enactment of what Smith performed in *TMS* when he ruled out distributive justice with one hand and brought some of it back with the other. Friedman's use of "Robinson Crusoe" functions to universalize (that is, to make abstract) while simultaneously personifying individuality. The move to universalize the desert island scenario is a move to eliminate issues of decorum from the equation of the analogy. Yet, at the same time, the direct appeal to the reader ("you") and her friends tacitly relies upon an evaluation of the decorum of the situation as clearly as Smith's analogy of shopping for one's dinner.

Finally, Friedman's last line in this passage, "[are we] entitled to use force to extract what we regard as our due," leads him into the process of alluding to concepts of distributive justice only to subordinate them – just as Smith does – to commutative justice. I now turn to Friedman's explicit discussion of distributive justice.

The subordination of distributive justice

Friedman's discussion of distributive justice happens in Chapter 10, "The Distribution of Income," in the section titled "The Instrumental Role of Distribution According to Product." While he uses the term "distributive," however, his discussion of justice is actually about commutative justice, not distributive justice. This constitutes Friedman's complete subordination of the idea of distributive justice to that of commutative justice.

Where Friedman writes "distribution according to product," the distribution to which he refers is the distribution of payment. Here is the paragraph in which he uses the term distributive justice:

Though the essential function of payment in accordance with product in a market society is to enable resources to be allocated efficiently without

compulsion, it is unlikely to be tolerated unless it is also regarded as yield-
ing distributive justice. No society can be stable unless there is a basic core
of value judgments that are unthinkingly accepted by the great bulk of its
members. Some key institutions must be accepted as "absolutes," not simply
as instrumental. I believe that payment in accordance with product has been,
and, in large measure, still is, one of these accepted value judgments or
institutions.

(CF 167)

Following this paragraph, Friedman goes on to say that even Marxism, though
critical of capitalism, relies on the notion that payment should fully recompense
the producer.[6]

Payment, however, falls under the heading of commutative justice. Consider
again Aristotle's (1987) distinction between distributive and commutative
justice, where he discusses the role of money in being a measure that enables
people to do justice in exchange (Bk. V, ch. 6–8). Exchange is about the reciprocity in value that commutative justice is concerned with. Friedman has interpreted distributive justice as commutative justice, just as, in the desert island
scenario, he framed the issue in terms of what could legitimately be forced.
Commutative justice is real justice, in Friedman as in Smith; distributive justice
has no public place.

These examples of portraying character promote Friedman's attempt to create
the decorum of a society of individualists, whose only ground of community is
the sharing of a first principle of freedom as Friedman defines it. The vision of
such a foundation for the social order is the grounds for invoking resentment at
portrayals of favoritism and special interests in his later chapters (labor unions,
physicians, and teachers, among others) and is the fertile ground for his argument about competition. Yet at the same time, Friedman acknowledges and
tacitly accepts an existing social order that is governed by the preferences of its
members rather than by his first principle of freedom. The dissonance between
these two social orders, the ideal and the actual, is what finally emerges as a
problem of fidelity in Friedman's argument.

Conclusion: Individualism in a naturalized social order

I have argued in this chapter that, despite developments in the technical understanding of economics and two centuries' distance in time, Friedman's *CF*
expresses the same kind of moral argument about political economy with respect
to justice that Smith does in *TMS* and *WN*. That moral argument focuses on commutative justice – an emphasis on law heavily concerned with property and
exchange – as the only real justice, and dispenses with discussion of distributive
justice by naturalizing it into the social order and into private life.

The rhetorical form of that moral argument is the construction of character
and an associated societal decorum that carries the valence of approval and disapproval. Friedman's reliance on a Whig perspective of history serves the

purpose of instantly framing the broad issues of political economy that he addresses in terms of friends and enemies, heroes and villains. Friedman accentuates that basic frame with his own authorial commentary, as with his "counting noses" comment,[7] and with his distillation of the themes of Whig history into a set of ideals. The highest of these is the principle that liberty is the first principle of political relations among people, with other ethical issues being either personal/private or philosophical in nature. The principle of liberty, identified with liberty in economic relations, or the free market, then becomes a form of confirming appeal, or rhetorical proof, in his arguments. Adherence to this view of liberty becomes itself the mark of good character, the touchstone of value by which the implied reader is to assess Friedman's judgments.

With this view of character, Friedman's strategic goal is to change public perceptions of government in general and the New Deal in particular. Friedman's argument follows the pattern of heroes and villains set out in Whig history, adapted into disjunctive conceptual argument (rather than history per se) such as his opposition of free market vs. complete government regulation. The black-and-white character of his argument and his authorial tone of approval and disapproval work in concert together.

The issue of one's place in society, as I have framed the question of distributive justice, is submerged in Friedman's arguments into the realms of private life and a tacitly accepted and natural social order. Real justice is commutative in nature, as with Smith.

Finally, the same conundrum about competition in Smith appears in Friedman's argument. After reading case upon case in *CF* of efforts made by companies, labor unions, teachers, physicians, bankers, etc., etc., to avoid or control competition, the question remains: if people are so determinedly disposed to avoid competition, what can be done to keep the economy competitive and therefore just? Friedman's answer – implied in his definition of who should have freedom, "only for people who are willing to practice self-denial" (*CF* 18) – is, like Smith's, to cultivate resentment against those who would thwart competition as well as to instruct the characters of the readers. The cultivation of resentment, again like Smith's, is above all a political appeal – that is, an appeal to legitimate the writer's political recommendations.

Yet the problem of the exercise of power by a dominant social order that is taken as given (because natural) still persists. The vision of a social order supportive of competition stands in place of an actual social order that may not support competition – in Friedman's terms, that is not willing to practice self-denial.[8] The attractiveness of the vision of a social order that supports competition is its liberty and implicit equality, and it is this vision that provides the moral persuasiveness of Friedman's argument. The shortcoming of the argument is the cognizance that the implicit equality not only may *not* exist, but also may be actively opposed by the social order whose interests are best served by a persisting inequality. This is the issue of distributive justice, and it is one that liberal political economy has left without a voice.

5   The materialization of distributive justice

> Principles of distributive justice are normative principles designed to guide the allocation of the benefits and burdens of economic activity.
>
> *Stanford Encyclopedia of Philosophy*, entry on Distributive Justice[1]

In reading Adam Smith's and Milton Friedman's texts for the role moral persuasion plays in them, I followed the play of praise and blame in the characterizations that explicitly or implicitly seek moral legitimation through generating sympathies for competition as a way of confirming the market as a self-regulating and independent (from politics) dynamic social system. These characterizations influence our view of the market economy through a narrative invocation of decorum – expectations of appropriate behavior; this invocation of decorum serves the function of moral judgment, which is to say justification, that is necessary to political legitimation insofar as this moral judgment delineates the relation between the economic and political domains as respectively private and public.

Three consequences followed from this. The first was that distributive justice became entirely instead of only partially about material distribution. This is what I mean by saying distributive justice became *materialized*.[2] The second consequence was the naturalization of distributive justice's criteria of appropriateness into social decorum, which provided an imprimatur of authority to the dominant social order's decorum. The third consequence was the elevation of the decorum of the marketplace itself into contention with social decorum. Each of these consequences in turn contributed to the distortion. The question of justice in material distribution disappeared into the distribution of the marketplace itself, either wholly, in classical liberalism's natural rights view of property and the efficacy of market exchange, or mostly, in what became modern liberalism's view of correcting for market failures of various degrees. Social decorum became a matter of personal preference, private taste, and interpersonal dynamics, and so outside the domain of justice entirely. Market decorum took on the nonmaterial functional tasks of relational social coordination served by distributive justice – the functions of enabling individuals to identify themselves in terms of self-understanding and in terms of relation to others. Achievement in the marketplace became the measure of merit, and the source of honor and esteem.

In theory, especially from Adam Smith's vantage point, everything could proceed from that point forward. In seeking to satisfy their self-interests, social actors would be constrained by the requirements of appropriate behavior found in social and market decorum. Smith's task was overcoming the strongly hierarchical remnants of feudal economic arrangements and opening up a freedom of movement in trade. Doing away with the residual feudal view of distributive justice – birth, social rank, and so on – was clearly necessary.[3] Opening up opportunities for new achievement looked to be a brave new world. But from the beginning there were problems. Social and market decorums were often in conflict, and dominant social orders clung tenaciously to their privileges and ranks as long as they could. The social orders also worried, with reason, that the market would be corrosive of bonds of tradition, not least because of the dislocation of populations. The process of urbanization in the nineteenth century meant that living in cities was truly a matter of being in the company of strangers. The economic and cultural shocks and problems of poverty, both rural and urban, kept reoccurring even as economic and technological progress accelerated. These problems kept pressure on material distributional issues and on the relational elements embedded in social and market decorums.

Let me restate the claim of distortion here, to clarify the import of the consequences. The problem with distributive and commutative justice changing places, as it were, is that the broader function of social ordering once performed by distributive justice became instead taken over by the narrower sense of commutative justice.[4] This is a problem and a distortion because commutative justice's range is too narrow. By this, I mean to draw attention to commutative justice's central focus on the transactional nature of economic interaction in exchange and contract.[5] The commutation involved (the "=" between price and commodity or price and performance of service) in market interaction is the focus of justice in a commercial society, as Smith styled it, and is what counts as "real justice."[6] This view of justice as an outcome of bargaining works to confirm and validate other moral judgments at the level of ordinary social interactions and imbue them with the characteristics of the market – in other words, to create a decorum of social relations as bargaining.

To relegate broader questions of just treatment to private preferences in social decorum, as I indicated in my reading of Friedman's argument, is to pretend that the only abuse of power is by government. Ordinary social decorum, as we commonly understand it, is not sufficient to successfully bear the burden of distributive justice because of its partiality to a dominant group. Keeping in mind that any decorum is connected to a discourse community, primary communities will occur where people live and work in proximity to each other (while others will be symbolically mediated communities). I say "primary" to indicate the relevance and even significance of daily life. In a society of bodily encounters, a social decorum will necessarily have its own symbolic codes that have a history. In a pluralist society, differences and residues of former hierarchies, at the least, cannot help but hold themselves as the correct order of things. (To glance ahead to Chapter 7, one of the functions of identity politics is to push back against this sort of thing.) The limitation of ordinary social decorum is its tendency to tend to its traditions; in this respect, social decorum is attached to a form of life that desires its own continuance. This is not necessarily bad, but its own history may prevent it from giving free voice to those who feel excluded or injured by it, which would raise questions of justice.

Market decorum in and of itself is likewise not bad. The problem is that none of the three – material distribution, social decorum, and market decorum – are adequate to the task of distributive justice in an age of freedom because none of them support public argument on relational issues; relational matters, except in contract relations, are considered to be private – in colloquial terms, "none of your business."

Distributive justice's role of relational social coordination has been neglected in these developments. Relational social coordination depends on each person understanding their position relative to others; this is partly status, as in what one's standing is, but it is also position, as in what one's place is. Social understanding, in this view, is necessary to self-understanding as well; recognition is the process by which the understandings of self and other are activated. The web of social connection through which people locate themselves and others is the background condition against which judgments of distributive justice can be made; equals cannot be treated equally without that background knowledge because that background knowledge is the basis for identifying equals as such.

This description of distributive justice is functional rather than normative. It can describe different societies organized around different sets of norms. The normative condition Adam Smith faced in the late eighteenth century was a society whose relational norms were still heavily based on birth and social rank; his task, in harmony with a developing political liberalism, was to make the argument that liberalizing economic relations would be more productive than the traditional relations, making everyone better off. As successful as Smith's argument eventually was in turning attention to a broader division of labor, he underestimated the relational problems. Nevertheless, his description of how moral judgment happens, through sympathies with resentments at mistreatment, continues to be a valuable insight.

Distribution as justice

The first consequence of the elevation of commutative justice as "real justice" was to identify the operations of the market as the source for distributive equity. As I noted in the epigraph opening this chapter and in several footnotes so far, material distribution is commonly taken as the modern definition of distributive justice. For the study of economics as a science of market operation, this has provided both a moral purpose, as in a contribution of good to the social order, and a moral outcome in the increase of wealth in general and its wider distribution and availability. The "invisible hand" metaphor made popular by Smith rendered the moral purpose automatic, which is to say a naturally occurring feature of a properly operating market. So the achievement of the moral good of increased wealth and higher standards of living would result, in the way of unintended consequences, from a self-regulating market that did not need management aside from a commutative framework of law.

The key theoretical element through which self-regulation maintains stability, as I identified in both Adam Smith and Milton Friedman, is competition, and competition's condition is liberty to compete. This is the basic premise underlying what I have described as the logic of liberal political economy: freedom to compete forestalls any party from having another party at his mercy; competition requires participants in the market to take others' interests into account while pursuing their own. In this view, transactional agreements are mutually free – that is, freely made on both sides. This is the foundation of commutative justice, that both parties to an agreement implicitly assent to its justice, and by assenting, confirm the justness of the bargain.

In plain language the dominance of commutative justice can be explained as the primacy of the freedom of property and contract. The Lockean principle – that property, as a natural right, both precedes and is the *rationale for* government – is the lodestar of classical liberalism, and one that Adam Smith incorporated forthrightly into his explanation of the development of government.[7]

What is at stake for the market in the elevation of commutative justice is that the distortion of commutative and distributive justice threatens the stability promised by the theory of the self-regulating market. The advent of modern economic theory, marked by Adam Smith's work, promised a productive, self-regulating market that would operate as an independent social system; the self-regulating nature of the market would provide a solution to the perennial historical problem that the uncontrolled pursuit of self-interest had posed to social stability. Independence here refers to a separation of market operations from the political domain, and the theory of self-regulation grounds the argument for systemic independence on an analysis of the market's own dynamics, or natural laws of operation (the unintended beneficial consequences of pursuing self-interest), within a framework of commutative justice (laws of property, exchange, and contract), famously underwritten by the concept of laissez-faire.

Smith's theory of economic growth through an expanded division of labor set the tone for the group of early theorists referred to as the classical political economists; their central concern was with economic growth and development. Economic growth offered a promise of employment for the poor and a rising standard of living, in which lay the promise of justice, and the self-regulating nature of the market promised a new stability. This helped establish the thesis that productivity promotes justice by putting the poor on more stable ground, a theme that has infused market economics ever since, with the corresponding corollary that poverty indicates a problem either of virtue (e.g., laziness of the poor) or of justice (collusion of producers).

A materialized distributive justice came to be seen in commutative terms of market transactions and behaviors. The shape this took in the nineteenth century following Smith was the extent to which the distribution achieved by the market was thought to be just. Within liberal political economy this developed into two broad views: (1) Market distribution by its very nature was just; fair bargains yielded fair outcomes. This was the view we saw articulated by Milton Friedman. (2) Practically speaking, market distribution was *for the most part* just because of its productive expansion of wealth (Smith's own view), so any problem of material distributive justice could be a relatively small matter of material redistribution, or (again, Smith's view) could be adjusted through infrastructure investments by government that would correct ill consequences of failures of the market to operate.[8] I will refer to these positions generally as the classical liberal and modern liberal perspectives.[9] The classical liberal tended to view poverty as a problem of virtue,[10] and modern liberals, eventually, as a problem of justice.[11]

Within a classical liberal framework, the market does distributive justice *ipso facto* through its normal economic interactions; within a modern liberal perspective the market *mostly* does so. In the classical liberal framework, the only political requirements for justice are the standards of commutative justice enforced by a Lockean minimum-government framework. In the modern liberal framework, market failures generate warrants for government regulation. Market failures may take a variety of forms, ranging from negative externalities that impose costs on outside parties, to problems of monopoly or "combination" (Smith's term) choking growth, to problems of collusion or oligopoly in various markets, including such markets as the longstanding color and gender barriers in labor markets. Both the classical and modern liberal perspectives, however, are dominated by the elevation of commutative justice.

Both classical and modern liberal perspectives also share the productivity thesis about economic activity promoting justice in distribution by reducing poverty, with the main difference between them being the market's cultivation of virtue. The maximizing of material production, itself a good, would also have a salutary effect on the laborers' cultivation of sobriety, thrift, and similar virtues of commercial value, much like Smith's industrious and thrifty peasant.[12]

Moral philosophy also continued to follow economic thought. While classical liberalism has tended to remain strongly focused on a Lockean conception of natural rights, translated into a positive rights (i.e., legal) framework, modern liberalism has been influenced by two significant ethical philosophies: utilitarianism in the nineteenth century and John Rawls's theory of justice as fairness in the late twentieth century. These have long histories and extensive literatures of their own, of course. In my admittedly brief account of them, what I want to focus on is the extent to which they accept fundamental ideas about contract and material distribution.

Jeremy Bentham's articulation of utilitarianism rejected the idea of natural rights (and of the social contract) in favor of defining rights through positive law (i.e., legislated law). In this respect, he shared a developmental view of government with Smith. The principle of utility had been part of the vocabulary of both moral philosophy and economic thinking for David Hume and Adam Smith. For

Smith, utility meant usefulness; the capacity for reason made assessing useful-ness possible. Bentham (1988) defined utility more directly with the Epicurean (hedonist) psychology that humans avoid pain and seek pleasure; from this Bentham articulated the general principle of utilitarianism as seeking the greatest good for the greatest number.

Bentham's purpose was primarily political in the sense of providing guidance for policymaking decisions, but utilitarianism did also develop as an ethic of self-interest that was later incorporated into neoclassical economics under the rubric of individual preference. Though his effort to create a scale for calculating pleasures and pains failed (the felicific calculus of measuring them in utiles), Bentham's work was instrumental in reinforcing the idea of rational behavior as the calculation of utility in the preference-ordering of individuals. In this trans-formation, the ghost of Bentham's pleasure/pain scheme appears in the form of whatever utility an individual assigns to her preferences – a conceptual place-holder for preference. Closely related is the rejection of the possibility of any interpersonal comparisons of utility in economics. For all its philosophic differ-ences with Lockean natural rights, utilitarianism reinforced the centrality of indi-vidual choice in economic thought and the significance of legal contract, though through the greatest happiness principle, it did provide an avenue in economic policy argument for distributional support as a potential social good.[13] Even in its contemporary shape of keeping aggregate (average) utility in mind, utilitari-anism tends strongly to define utility in terms of material goods and opportunities.

Utilitarianism was originally controversial because its consequentialist orien-tation seemed to vitiate issues of moral duty. Some things were thought to be right in and of themselves, and not a matter of consequences. John Rawls's (1971, 1993) theory of justice in the late twentieth century was an attempt to challenge utilitarianism's dominance as a theory of justice by revisioning the idea of a social contract within a Kantian-inspired conception of duty to reason. While Rawls includes respect for persons within his considerations, two aspects of his theory of Justice as Fairness reinforce the commutative–distributional trend. The first is Rawls's Difference Principle, which allows for inequalities to be considered just if the social arrangements that create them are to the advant-age the least well off, presuming the first principle, maximum liberty consistent with the liberty of all, and the second principle, genuine fair opportunity, are also observed.

The second and perhaps more significant aspect of Rawls's Justice as Fair-ness concept is the structure he uses to arrive at it. In reconstructing the idea of a social contract as a thought experiment, Rawls (1971) implicitly uses a structure of bargaining. His efforts to construct his "original position" from behind a "veil of ignorance" amount to an attempt to construct a bargaining situation that rec-ognizes the existence of self-interest but is drained of any substance of self-interest.[14] The moral value in Rawls's approach is the autonomy of reasoned choice that would eventuate from this type of situation, reflecting Rawls's adap-tation of Kant's principles of autonomous reasoned choice that ground the idea of obligation in morality in the self-consistency of not violating one's own reason.[15]

Putting these two aspects of Justice as Fairness together, we have a decision-context of a bargaining process that takes self-interest into account, without itself being tainted by self-interest (veil of ignorance in the original position), that rationally settles on a condition in which the least advantaged would be materially favored by inequalities. While this approach is skeptical about the ability of the market to satisfy all claims, its foremost terms still operate within a commutative–distributional horizon.

A further problem, to be considered more in the next chapter, is how the background knowledge Rawls supplies to his original position is supposed to be available. How is it not a form of selective amnesia, a kind of philosophical counterpart to Plato's theory of *anamnesis* ("un-forgetting") in the *Phaedrus*? I propose that Rawls is appealing to our intuitions about what constitutes basic knowledge for human beings – that society will likely consist of haves and have-nots, for instance – when such intuitions are nothing more than the distilled background knowledge we have of our own experience of the world, not some feature of human nature. But if that is the case, then is relying on such an intuition very different from our understanding of the decorum of a situation we find ourselves in? The point I aim at here is that drawing on an awareness of background conditions cannot be separated from any reflective process, and Rawls's background conditions are in line with the commutative–distributional trend.

The naturalization of relational justice into social decorum

The second consequence of the materialization of distributive justice is the displacement of relational coordination into social decorum, which practically speaking means into the dominant social decorum. For Smith, this was not so much a displacement as a natural order of precedence showing itself. The problem that made itself felt was the enforcement of a social decorum that insisted on traditional privileges. The main social movements of the modern era – antislavery, women's suffrage, civil rights of a variety of forms – took place in the face of resistance anchored in tradition as well as self-interest. One of Friedman's key arguments, for example, was that people should be free to live as they please, even if that means being exclusionary. This was the basis for his argument against Federal civil rights legislation, under his principle of local governance being less oppressive than more centralized government.

Friedman's example that people should be free to live as they wish – say, as their ancestors did – points up the dilemma that the social decorum of a given way of life, while workable for those who are members of its community, may also continue traditions that were objectionable to others who shared the same spaces, as was the case with the second-class citizen status of African-Americans in the southern U.S. when Friedman was writing. The tendency of any social decorum to preserve itself can mean a resistance to change (or perhaps more precisely, a tendency to manage change in harmony with its standards of appropriateness); in the American south, this translated into a refusal of equal membership in the community. To make a claim about injustice in that case required moving outside the dominant traditional social decorum.

A second problem that can arise from reliance on traditional social decorums is the exploitation of ambiguity over whether, for a given situation, a market decorum (emphasizing individual choice and contract) is the appropriate one, or the traditional social decorum is. The "old money" "new money" antagonism, often cloaked in the guise of culture or even latter-day aristocracy, is an example of using one as a cover for the other – e.g., in the novels of Henry James, protecting family wealth through claims about social proprieties; practices of excluding "others" (race, gender) from markets on grounds of social inappropriateness.

The effects of a commercial decorum

Commutative justice itself becomes distorted in taking on the burden of social coordination that is the broader function of distributive justice – that is, social coordination in the sense of being placed in society, of knowing where one stands.[16] This becomes a distortion of commutative justice because of the pressure it puts on the market as an institution to form identity as well as provide material sustenance, a pressure that cuts exactly counter to the need to preserve fair competition. While the formation of identity does have material dimensions and symbolic manifestations, it is not reducible to a set of commodities, but the insufficiency of "buying" an identity is not the only problem to be faced. Identity *is* closely bound up with interaction, so market behavior, not simply the commodities in the market, can become a significant distorting factor. When the motive to bargain is reinforced by the motive to do everything possible to be in a position of advantage, to have the upper hand, to bring a power advantage to an exchange, then the desire for advantage can distort commutative justice by rendering problematic the free agreement by which a transaction is constituted as just. The moral principle of freedom of choice is threatened by the structuring of market contexts, including guidelines for market interaction, through power and advantage.[17]

From this perspective, classical liberalism and modern liberalism each views the market vis-à-vis the justice of its distributions, and they each foreground the primary virtues that mark their respective principles of decorum. By virtue, I mean here the qualities of character that are admired and valued, that find a corresponding resonance in different decorums of expectations of appropriateness. Classical liberalism is organized around the ideas of *achievement* and *earning*. Modern liberalism is organized around the ideas of *opportunity* and *achievement*.[18] Both share an orientation to success in the market through achievement, particularly when taken as the consequence of prudent judgment, hard work, thriftiness, and similar virtues.[19] Classical liberalism, taking mutual agreements in contract as just in and of themselves, counts success has having been *earned*.

Modern liberalism, acknowledging the potential for market failures that could close off competition, admires success as the product of virtues but emphasizes *opportunity* as the key to keeping markets open.

Objection to the case: decorum is insufficient to bear the weight of justice

In saying that considerations of appropriateness cross a number of levels of social interaction, the natural question is which parts of that range are matters of justice. If we fail in our manners – say, failing to reply to a greeting – have we committed an injustice? Adam Smith, in his argument for what counts as "real justice" in *TMS*, would say no. It is important to remember that, for Smith, the crucial factor is the extent to which we sympathize with the appropriateness of the resentment provoked by a slight; according to him, only the strongest resentments – those identified with harms to life, liberty (which encompasses property), and reputation[20] – are sufficient to move us to approve the power of the state to redress the situation. This is the psychology of moral judgment on which his construction of commutative justice rests.

The claim that decorum is insufficient to bear the weight of claims about justice tends to cast decorum only in the light of conventional preferences for everyday behaviors like manners and etiquette. In this light, decorum is a social-intercourse version of prudence, a tactical ability to judge situations aptly in terms of how others will perceive one's words and deeds. This view of decorum lends itself to an instrumental view of rhetoric, which I am at pains to argue against.[21] This view of decorum can be found in the commentary on Adam Smith. For Gloria Vivenza (2001), decorum is a primarily linguistic idea that only relates to a "low" sense of conventional morality and is not equivalent to Smith's concept of propriety.[22] She interprets Smith's moral accounts as consisting of higher and lower virtues. In this framework, prudence (as developed in *WN*) stands as a lower-order virtue in relation to the higher-order virtue of benevolence (as developed in *TMS*).[23]

Pace Vivenza, though, while decorum does have a linguistic sense, it does not merely mean conventionality. To say that decorum simply means observing conventions begs the question of how one knows what the appropriate conventions are for a given type of situation, much less an actual one. The limit to conventionality *simpliciter* ("everybody knows that…") is that convention is only a record, as it were, of what has already happened. It is at best a guide to present situations, which need to be judged afresh for their differences from the past. It is just this attitude that I take to be Aristotle's (1987) point in discussing virtue in *Nicomachean Ethics* that actual situations in life are too variable to be calculated in advance by formula, a principle I find in his rhetorical theory as well.

The focus on higher and lower-order virtues in Adam Smith's work distracts commentators like Vivenza from the architectonic principle propriety plays in his work. Steven McKenna (2006) ably sets out the other-directed sensibilities that inform Smith's work.[24] McKenna sees Smith's ethics (in *TMS*) evolving from his rhetoric rather than vice versa. Rhetorical propriety, in this view, serves as an "infrastructure" for Smith's moral psychology (McKenna 2006: 85). Propriety offers a framework for judgment in both aesthetics (rhetorical style) and ethics because of the role emotion plays in each. In both cases, emotion matters if and only if it matters to an audience of onlookers. What counts is the pressing need to keep the other in mind as audience, as observer, as someone whose own approval matters, and this awareness and attention to others, we should not forget, is the connecting point of Smith's moral theory with his economic theory and the disapprobation of evading competition that balances out the pursuit of self-interest.

The problem of conceptualizing decorum from the perspective of higher and lower-order personal virtues is aggravated by the intense methodological individualism in contemporary social science that is especially strong in economics.[25] Anthony Giddens (1984) takes up the problem of methodological individualism in outlining his theory of structuration, in which he attempts to identify the possibilities for individual agency in the midst of the constraints of pre-existing and ongoing social structures. Giddens's effort to describe action in the face of institutional, cultural, and other constraints is harmonious with a rhetorical view of constrained choice, as is his acknowledgment of the possibilities for, and limits to, human reflexivity (self-awareness) in generating opportunities for action under constrained conditions.

In calling methodological individualism into question, Giddens's concern with the problem of sorting out structure–agent dynamics is part of the ongoing heritage of structuralism. Whatever their limitations (such as an overemphasis on determinism), structuralists have contributed important insights into the influence of social institutions and practices on human development. It is important to understand that Giddens does not dispense with the choosing individual entirely, as some structuralists do, but rather emphasizes that structuration theory's purpose is to examine the possibilities for an agent's choice as they exist within actually situated circumstances – historically, culturally, and so on. Choice occurs only within structured constraints, in other words. Giddens's theory is a reasonable model for the concept of rhetoric I argue for here: not an instrumental mode of persuasive communication wielded by one abstracted and detached individual upon another in order to achieve a particular outcome, but rather the crafting of persuasive communication within a shared and living context. The *dunamis* of rhetoric is the capacity to understand the state of the living context and to employ the *technai*, the modes of persuasion, in a way that communicates that understanding as the ground which makes the persuasion's goal compelling. Such an understanding articulates a view of what the proper decorum for *this* situation is. This second view is not purely instrumental because the genuine rhetor cannot be either detached or merely self-interested; the costs in ethos would be too great.[26]

In keeping with my argument that discourse communities constitute a kind of rhetorical home for the development of identity, the relationship between decorum and character is reciprocal. They shape each other. Decorum, taken as a kind of situational awareness or sensitivity, represents a dynamic by which situations are assessed with regard to fittingness of actions within them; rhetorical decorum, as part of that larger awareness, is awareness of what can be communicated, which would include refinements of tone, emphasis, etc. – the nonverbals of communication as well as the articulations. The virtue of a well-suited action would be demonstrated through its fitness as a response to the situation at hand. To refer to a particular decorum, as in pointing to a commercial decorum or to a traditional social decorum, is to refer to a set of expectations that constitute a common understanding of particular situation types. Any social group will have a repertoire of types of decorum for differing situations. While the specific content of a decorum will depend on the group of people who share it, the consistent idea is that there are conceptions of fittingness, of appropriateness. Decorum is relevant to investigating distributive justice in their similarities of purpose in identifying what people are due by virtue of their places in their community. Decorum and distributive justice both resonate with the idea of fitting responses. The difference between them is that distributive justice allows its constructs of fittingness to be questioned.

McCloskey's virtue ethics

The problem of remaining caught up in methodological individualism reaches a kind of apotheosis with Deirdre McCloskey's (2006) *The Bourgeois Virtues*, or, as she might prefer, a redemption. In many ways, McCloskey's vision of the bourgeois virtues – the virtues inculcated by the development of commercial society – is an attractive picture of the pursuit of self-interest reined in by the need to find and satisfy customers. In this respect, her project is in harmony with an optimistic interpretation of Adam Smith's trajectory from the psychology of moral judgment in *TMS* to the playing-out of economic incentives within a society self-organized by those dynamics of moral judgment in *WN*. The influence of "*doux commerce*" (sweet commerce) elevates the poor (McCloskey 2006: 31). McCloskey highlights the positive advances of higher productivity, increasing incomes, and improved public health that accompanied liberal political economy.[27]

At the same time, she shades in darkly the efforts to criticize its shortcomings and find alternatives. Her history is chiaroscuro; its greatest evils come from opposition (the clerisy, bureaucracy, socialism), while its lesser evils come from a fading traditional social order that liberalism is in the process of gradually wearing away (slavery, racism, sexism). This is not to say McCloskey's history lacks detail; her history is lavishly detailed but starkly drawn. What is missing from her account are the unintended consequences of the successes of liberal political economy themselves. While McCloskey is correct that positive outcomes happen in markets, she misses or discounts the weaknesses of the market in being susceptible to the influence of power. The problems of power are not simply matters of personal virtue – e.g., in whether or not buyers and sellers are honest – so much as they are embedded in the opportunities for gain that make achieving a position of advantage to thwart competition a rational move in the marketplace. For McCloskey, as for Adam Smith, the interpersonal interaction through which business is done will lead people to mitigate excesses of self-interest; the decorum of the market will settle the fractious and grasping.[28] My doubts about McCloskey's picture, as with Smith's, stem from the limits of face-to-face constraints on behavior (i.e., on power) characteristic of small communities.

McCloskey's advantage over other virtue ethicists is her explicit argument that virtue is cultivated by a climate of expectations – decorum – in her case, a decorum of commercial interaction, of doing business. In this respect (and again, much like Smith), McCloskey does see the commercial virtues as being cultivated by the civil enforcements of propriety. Virtues do not spring *ex nihilo* out of a pure goodwill but out of historically and culturally situated people. In this respect, her view is harmonious with my claims about decorum.

But the decorum of the market that McCloskey and Smith rely on can undermine its pacifying tendencies by the transformation of character that happens where success in the market transactions themselves becomes the arbiter of virtue. When the concept of "earning" shifts from a mutually agreed upon exchange to pressing an advantage over an adversary, then what is at stake is not merely the market transaction, but also the claim to rightness and good character for the participants. To use an everyday example, the cliché of business is that success is achieved by buying low and selling high. Yet, if we take that seriously, each success may well be matched by a failure, by someone who is selling low and buying high on the other side of the transaction.[29]

So the decorum of the market can form character in negative as well as positive ways. The claim I make is that the rise of commutative justice, in its displacement of distributive justice, necessarily takes on part of distributive justice's functions of providing a sense of place and an understanding of where people stand in relation to each other. The distortion arises when the distributive criteria – what people are due by virtue of their membership (their place) in the community – become merit defined as "earning" in the marketplace. When that happens, people's economic achievements become the criteria not simply for the material resources they have at their disposal, but also for their sense of self and of place, the *honor* (or dishonor) that they enjoy, and the kind of relationship they can have to their fellows.

Arguably, these deleterious effects would be most likely in circumstances where alternate modes of decorum with their accompanying standards of virtue and character were absent. So in circumstances where a traditional community held sway, its standards of appropriate behavior in the market (and elsewhere socially) could presumably temper a purely market mentality.[30] But, in what is now a commonplace of analysis in modernity, traditional communities endure a constant pressure from the market that threatens to dissolve or fracture them. The freedom of movement that liberalism brought was a great good, but not an unmitigated one. Children move from small towns to cities and don't come back. Poor neighborhoods lose vital businesses and institutions, and become islands of poverty. When their residents are ethnically and racially coded, mobility becomes a serious challenge, and itself can be seen as a danger to the sense of community vital to people in such circumstances. Alternate modes of decorum are hard to come by, and while a commercial decorum can do much in the way of promoting important virtues, it has serious weaknesses, especially as it moves out of the sphere of interpersonal interactions that ground McCloskey's bourgeois virtues.

Conclusion

The elevation of commutative justice has several effects on distributive justice; it partly becomes understood in commutative (i.e., market) terms as material distribution. This aspect of distributive justice remains in the domain of public concern but is subordinated to commutative justice. Classical liberal and modern liberal characterizations of justice in distribution agree on the material dimension but disagree over the primacy of *earning* or *opportunity*. Classical liberals emphasize freedom of contract, admire risk-taking, and valorize self-reliance. Modern liberals emphasize regulated markets (working conditions, financial reporting, and so on), admire coordinated productivity, and valorize open opportunity. For classical liberals, material distribution conceived as *re*distribution outside the market is an injustice. For modern liberals, gross inequities in material distribution indicate the possibility of a market failure with respect to opportunity that creates a warrant for government action for regulation or redistribution.

Both views of liberalism, however, develop a distorted view of what people are due by virtue of their membership in the community because the reliance on commutative justice to provide an ordering principle to social relations winds up defining those social relations as market relations. It is not news, of course, to identify a hyperdeveloped individualism as the root of liberalism's troubles, but I hope to provide a clearer focus on how it is not simply, or not a *simple* individualism, but one that is strongly influenced by the effect of economic thinking on our understanding of justice. The elevation of commutative justice ultimately has the effect of overlooking the ways in which our individual development is formed within social relations that cannot be captured in the market. The problem that arises from that is a lack – or refusal – of recognition, and I turn to the matter of distributive justice and recognition in the next chapter. What I argue *for*, is not to do away with commutative justice, which would perpetrate its own ills, but to acknowledge that its concern with justice in exchange cannot be all there is to justice.

6 Recognition and the relational demands of distributive justice

Respect and recognition offer starting points for thinking about justice in relational terms, insofar as those terms invoke attention to people as they are actually situated and are not reduced to admiration for achievement as in the commutative–distributional paradigm. These qualifiers suggest that respect and recognition must occupy ground somewhere between a general respect for people on the basis of their humanity and esteem for a specific achievement, if respect and recognition are to successfully manifest the relational imperatives of distributive justice. This is in keeping with the need for a relational background of place and position that I have argued we should understand as a function of discourse communities, a background condition that makes self-understanding possible along with an understanding of relation to others. Some degree of fellow-connection, in other words, is implied with respect and recognition aside from, and in addition to, sheer human existence and excellence of accomplishment, some feeling of belonging that contributes to a sense of identity. In the model of discourse community I have been setting out, "belonging" is about one's membership, one's being among fellows.

As the preceding chapter argued, however, the commutative–distributional paradigm has become a habit of thought deeply ingrained in liberal thought. Escaping the influence of the commutative–distributional paradigm is not easy. The pull of the commutative–distributional paradigm in economics, what I earlier referred to as a "gravitational force," is felt in moral philosophy as well, as I indicated in the preceding chapter's discussion of utilitarianism and John Rawls's effort at fusing Kantian deontology with the concept of a social contract. My point in the prior chapter's discussion was to note how commutative themes were supported by developments in moral philosophy that served as justifications for the elevation of commutative justice and its role in confirming the market's standing as a social-ordering institution. It is not a surprise, in other words, that philosophical justifications would develop in harmony with the commutative–distributional paradigm to confirm the preeminent status of the market. On the other hand, what may be surprising is that even efforts to critique the market's status show signs of the pervasiveness of the commutative–distributional paradigm, undermining efforts to generate a solidarity capable of resisting the market's dominance.

An initial approximation of this problem is that even market-critical perspectives carry over too many commutative presumptions and are not adequately cognizant of relational matters. To illustrate the problem, I examine two critiques of market dominance, in this chapter Jürgen Habermas's ongoing critical analysis of the development of modernity, and in the next chapter a critique stemming from an interchange between Nancy Fraser and Axel Honneth (2003) in *Redistribution or Recognition? A Political–Philosophical Exchange*. I begin with Habermas to assess his account of language as the basis for his theory of reason as communicative in nature. His account of speech-act theory as developed in universal pragmatics turns out to be insufficiently relational, belying the interaction dynamics of his theory of communicative action; ultimately, the discourse of normativity underwriting the challenge of claims to normative validity are too susceptible to be judged in commutative terms. This problem can be ameliorated by amending his theory of language with a rhetorical sensibility more attuned to the relational connections among ethos, decorum, and discourse communities.

From Habermas's language theory, I move to his adaptation of Lawrence Kohlberg's (1981, 1984) theory of moral development, which is steeped in the presumptions of the commutative paradigm. A theory of moral–psychological development is necessary to Habermas's project because, together with language, a moral psychology creates the possibility for ethical communicative interaction, which is Habermas's key to fully formed human reason. Taken together, they comprise Habermas's philosophical anthropology: language, psychological development, and moral development.

Kohlberg's theory, though, takes as basic presumptions commutative–distributional concepts of justice. Its limits are clarified in Carol Gilligan's (1982a) early critique of Kohlberg, a critique that illustrates the differences between a propositional moral theory revolving around questions of ownership (Kohlberg's) and a form of moral questioning that focuses on looking for relational networks to help resolve moral conflicts (Gilligan's). The narrative invention of Gilligan's female subject, Amy, demonstrates the deployment of narrative as a tool of the moral imagination, in line with the rhetorical dimensions of narrative used in reading Smith's and Friedman's works to examine ethos as an issue of character. The justice vs. care debate that evolved out of the Kohlberg–Gilligan interchanges (notice the terminology) is an instance of the commutative–distributional paradigm being challenged over its relational shortcomings. Grace Clement's (1998) suggestion of using autonomy as a test in the justice–care debate offers a way to examine problems in moral decision-making in concrete terms that are compatible with the concept of discourse communities as resources for practical reasoning about relational matters.

I conclude the chapter by reviewing the relational sensibilities made available by a rhetorical perspective on discourse communities: the interplay between ethos and audience/discourse community in the development of both communicative and moral capacities; the role of narrative as a form of developmental play through the exercise of the moral imagination; and the need for concrete expression of self-identity – *and* its recognition – in order to achieve belonging in a discourse community.

The hope of achieving solidarity through belonging in a discourse community, while necessary for human flourishing, is not yet sufficient, however. The condition of modernity is such that discourse communities are multiple and may be conflicting. If relational recognition and respect are the way to re-establish a fully operative distributive justice, they need to work across discourse communities, or perhaps more accurately, constitute an overarching discourse community. I take up that issue in the subsequent and final chapter.

Distributive justice outside commutative terms

To bring into better focus the relational issue at stake in reinvigorating distributive justice in non-commutative terms, let me review the framework I develop in this argument. Distributive justice's operational principle of treating equals equally relies on a background condition through which it is possible to understand how members of a society are positioned in relation to each other. Understanding this background as a network of social relations is indispensable to identifying what it means to occupy a certain position, and hence the very possibility of determining "equals." In my view, this springs from a social constructionist view of reality[1]; it implies that the formation of a sense of self, a sense of subjective identity, a sense of one's *character*, relies on understanding oneself in relation to others, a relation that encompasses their reciprocal awareness.[2] Self-awareness is achieved in significant degree by incorporating an awareness of *others'* awareness of oneself. This view of the individual shifts the abstract view of methodological individualism to that of a situated and historically entangled individual.[3]

In claiming a regulative function for distributive justice in sustaining a social ordering, a relational social network establishes the ground of such an ordering – by identifying the background condition of the ground where each person stands. The problem I addressed in the previous chapter was that elevating commutative justice had the ill if unintended consequence of making market relations the basis for understanding one's own place and one's relation to others, as well as undermining the core commutative principle of free agreement itself by foregrounding the seeking of advantage, which in turn renders doubtful the market's claims to self-regulation.

If, as I claim, distributive justice has been naturalized and been made difficult to talk about *as* justice, the challenge now is to imagine how else we might see those relations and the network they form. I take up that challenge as a problem of recognition – a problem of being able to see the positions and understand the network of relations, especially in considering anew what it may mean to ground political relations on a principle of equality. The problem of recognition is the problem wrought by the elevation of commutative justice and the diminishment of distributive justice (now provisionally linked to recognition) that distorts liberalism's promise of freedom. And let me repeat here, again, my theme that a rhetorical dynamic is at the heart of things: not simply that the elevation of commutative justice happens through a moral persuasion, but that the diminishment of distributive justice amounts to a silencing. If this is the case, then the solution – finding recognition – must needs be finding a voice, or giving voice. This invokes a conception of a public sphere that is primarily a place for persuasion in a sense that exceeds the bargaining processes of negotiating among differing interests. The counterpart to finding a voice or giving voice is being heard or being given a hearing. The problem with a naturalized distributive justice I have been emphasizing is its being ruled out of bounds as a fitting topic of such persuasion.

Silencing complaints about justice will create resistance, and symptoms of resistance are clues to locating problems of recognition. Consider the issue of how to interpret the history of social movements – the abolition of slavery and the women's suffrage movement in the nineteenth century and continuing campaigns for racial and gender rights in the twentieth century.[4] It is possible to frame an interpretation that emphasizes the aspirational nature of liberal political philosophy as a way of acknowledging failures to live up to its principles while still claiming a steady progress of eroding traditional forms of social domination. This interpretation lends itself to identifying the core social problem as one of excluding individuals from the groups to whom rights belonged.[5] As those exclusions are remedied, the argument goes, the justice of the commutative regime can be extended to those formerly shut out. This is the happy interpretation of how social movements gradually overcome exclusions.[6]

Skepticism about this happy interpretation springs from seeing how exclusions were created and justified in the first place through the ways people were identified and positioned. A primary form of identification was by appeal to an already-existing decorum embodied in accepted (or enforced) conventions organized around a traditional social hierarchy, a hierarchy that also functioned to identify features such as rights and capacities, and especially moral capacities. The defenders of slavery justified their positions not merely on commutative grounds (ownership rights) but on grounds of the moral deficiencies of slaves;[7] similar arguments were advanced by those opposed to women's suffrage, with the added claim that women's natures were too delicate to engage in public life. The claims about moral deficiency continued to persist in the resistance faced by social movements as they developed in the nineteenth and twentieth centuries, reappearing not just in stories of welfare queens (and irresponsible borrowers in the more recent subprime mortgage defaults) but also in recent theories of moral development in the justice–care debates.

The dilemma involved in the naturalization of distributive justice and the problems of recognition that arise from it, is that the principles underlying social organization seem to be limited to only one of two forms, making for two types of decorum – a market decorum and a dominant social decorum. Market decorum, as I argued in the previous chapter, taken as a foundational principle of social organization, turns the question of distributive justice into one of material distribution and turns the issue of recognition to market success. The nature of a social decorum would depend on which tradition it claims or is claimed by, as well as the power of those who claim it, and the restrictions on membership they enforce. Here, the recognition problem has manifested as guarding privileges through a refusal to recognize others as members.

I call this a dilemma partly because it suggests that at the level of navigating our personal lives we may be torn between two worlds that may not necessarily be compatible with each other. A commonplace of modern life has become the disjunction between our enjoyment of freedoms to be as we wish and the concern that our lives are fragmented and out of sync. The cognitive dissonance of navigating life across disjunctive sets of decorums can be a burden, particularly when the disharmonies become stark.[8]

A second, more subtle aspect of the dilemma is that the disjunction has led our thinking about the relation between the market and our social identities into pathways dominated by the shift toward commutative justice. In a parallel development to the public–private distinction that is a hallmark of liberalism, the distinction between morality and ethics has become important. The version of this distinction that interests me is the Kantian-influenced view of morality as the domain of moral obligation based on a universalizable conception of human reason; the counterpart of such a morality is an ethical domain that articulates a view of what constitutes the good life. (This moral–ethical distinction also appears as a distinction between the right vs. the good.)

I say "*the* moral domain" and "*an* ethical domain" to underscore the point that in this view, matters of moral obligation are duties that are abstracted (universalized) out of actual circumstances according to foundational capacities (human reason) that are themselves universal, while the question of what constitutes a good life can only be fully answered from within a particular way of life. The pertinent consequence of this distinction is that there is only one morality but many ethical frameworks. While the Kantian moral framework is not identical to the Lockean liberal framework, it is harmonious in holding this distinction.[9] The practical outcome of this distinction in the political–social order is the condition of pluralism: multiple and competing ways of life that are held together by a neutral set of rules. My contention is that the rules, being strongly organized around commutative justice, are not neutral, as I will argue for Habermas's effort to recuperate Kantian thought in constructing his vision of the public sphere.

Habermas: reason; language; and moral development

Jürgen Habermas (1984a, b) takes up the Kantian model in a distinctive way with his model of communicative action. Habermas claims Kant's error lay in his conception of human reason as a process of solitary, individual mental reflection, which Habermas sees as still caught up in a Cartesian dualism of subject and object. Instead, Habermas proposes that human reason is actually a process of communicative interaction – a reason-giving, communicatively interactive process of producing better arguments that is necessarily social rather than just solitary mental reflection. This process of communicative interaction introduces a third area – the intersubjective – which partakes partly of the subjectivity of the communicators and partly of the objective product of their communication. The intersubjective domain is what is created through communicative inter- action; it consists of those things that people create together or come to agree- ment about, and thus is the actual domain of human reason.[10]

Intersubjectivity therefore becomes an important dimension of Habermas's extension of Kantian morality into the political domain: because human reason relies on the ability to engage in sustained interactive discussion, the problem of political freedom in democracy is the problem of open public discussion as a condition for the full flourishing of human reason.[11] This is the foundation of Habermas's concern that a healthy public sphere may be poorly served by a mass media driven by the pressures of corporatized business performance to turn its contents relentlessly in the direction of sensation and spectacle in the competi- tion to attract audiences.[12] His account of the conglomeration of media busi- nesses into corporate industries forms a substantial portion of his critiques of the late twentieth century.

For Habermas, this domination of the public sphere by money casts political pluralism into doubt, producing what he has long called a legitimation crisis.[13] But even solving the media problem (how money and power direct media content), were it possible, is not in itself sufficient. The rest of the solution, for Habermas, is for public discussion to be conducted according to rules of rational debate; to achieve that goal, Habermas attempts to create a procedural normativ- ity for public discourse, which is to say norms of public discussion that fall under a rubric of morality (right) rather than of ethics (the good life). In that attempt, he relies heavily on two sources: a theory of language (Habermas 1979c) and a theory of moral development (Habermas 1979d). Between them, the two influence the conception of normativity underlying his proceduralist approach to rational argument in the public sphere. But both of these influences, I argue, continue to be heavily implicated not only in the Cartesian dualism Hab- ermas seeks to escape, but also in the liberal view dominated by commutative justice.[14] With respect to both language and moral development, I argue that the key intersubjective aspect that is neglected is relational in nature, that recogni- tion is at the heart of the issue, and that the intersubjective dynamic is better explained by reference to rhetorical concepts of ethos and decorum. This is less obvious in Habermas's theory of language, so I turn to that first.

Habermas's revision of Kantian reason into a model of intersubjective com- munication makes his theory of language, universal pragmatics,[15] a keystone in his theoretical structure. He organizes his theory of language around the linguis- tic concept of speech acts. Robert Holub summarizes the principles of universal pragmatics, noting that Habermas, influenced by Karl Bühler (1934) and Karl Popper (1979),

> assumes that we exist simultaneously in (1) an external world of states of affairs and objects; (2) an internal world of ideas, thoughts, emotions; and

(3) a normative world of intersubjectively determined norms and values. Every statement, according to Habermas, relates to these three worlds because implicit in all utterances is a relationship to (1) an external state of affairs; (2) an internal motivation or intention; and (3) a normative reality … [when we test those claims for validity, we do three types of tests:] With regard to the first world: to study acts of reference and predication [constatives]; with regard to the second world, to study linguistic expression of intention [avowals]; and with regard to the third world, to study via illocutionary speech acts the way in which interpersonal relations are established [regulatives].

(Holub 1991: 13)[16]

The tests of validity become tests of truth about the external world, of truthfulness about the expression of the internal-subjective world, and of appropriateness about the shared, intersubjective normative world. I contend that the expression of subjective intention (in avowals) and the establishment of interpersonal relations (in regulatives) are the parts of universal pragmatics that fail to measure up to the relational demands I claim as essential to a genuinely intersubjective domain; I take them up in reverse order, assessing claims to normativity through regulatives first.

Habermas claims the establishment of an interpersonal relationship for normative speech acts through the concept of *illocutionary force*. This is an adaptation from J. L. Austin's (1976) distinction between locution (the propositional meaning of a statement) and illocution (a coinage meaning the communicative function the statement is meant to perform: requesting, commanding, promising, etc.). The illocutionary force of a regulative speech act – that is, an appeal or invocation of a norm – implicitly places speaker and hearer into a relationship; a simple example would be that saying "Stop!" not only imputes an intention to say it but also implicitly puts the speaker into a position of authority to command it and the hearer into a position of compliance/defiance.[17]

The rightness of the interpersonal relationship invoked by illocutionary force is a key part of the test of a regulative's appropriateness as a validity claim. The point of understanding a statement as a validity claim is to have a standard of judgment to which communicators can appeal in order to adjudicate disputes of understanding. Because this is key to keeping communication ongoing, and because communication's continuance is essential to the full development of human reasoning for Habermas, adjudicating differences about the nature of a relationship is a pivotal matter. For Habermas, such a standard of judgment will take shape in discourses on appropriateness. Just as we consult, say, the discourse of Newtonian mechanics when the validity claim at issue is a question of mass and energy (for a constative speech act), so too do we similarly consult discourses on normative rightness in the case of disputes about appropriateness.

When we turn to those adjudicating discourses for help, we encounter the morality–ethics distinction. If the context of appropriateness is how to live a good life as a member of a form of life (say, as a young Amish woman), we look to that form of life's ethical discourses – its oral traditions, stories, philosophical and theological reflections, rituals, and so on. The opportunities for irresolvable disagreement and rupture of communication in the face of conflicting forms of life no doubt flock readily to mind. But what if the context needs to be a moral framework, in order to transcend such potential conflicts? This is, of course, just the sort of consideration that has motivated Kant and Habermas and any number of others. To take a transcendent position, one must abstract the moral elements from the situated forms of life and universalize the moral principles – i.e., so that they apply to everyone.

Two connected questions and an unforeseen complication arise at this point. The first question concerns the kind of interpersonal relationship posited by a transcendental universalized set of norms of appropriateness. The second question, which has been hovering alongside the entire discussion of interpersonal relationship, concerns the implications of such universalized norms for subjectivity and self-identity. To sharpen the more general point, to make a claim about interpersonal relationship is to impute some*ones* some*where*; interpersonal relationships can only occur between persons. This cannot but help influence how we think about expressing the experience of subjectivity (the domain of a different type of speech act, the avowal), suggesting that the lines between the subjective and intersubjective in universal pragmatics may not be possible to draw as cleanly as Habermas would like, and suggesting as well that the connection between the experience of subjectivity and the interaction in relationships must involve recognition in some way – of self (in subjectivity) and of other (in relationship).

Before I turn to those considerations, however, the unforeseen complication needs to be addressed. It concerns the first question, about the kind of interpersonal relationship posited by a transcendental universalized set of norms of appropriateness. Habermas's view is that such norms are viable because they cast persons into the position of autonomous rational agents who observe the norms of rational discussion as a set of procedures for arriving at consensus. This is Habermas's (1995, 2007) view of rational public deliberation. The complication, however, is that another set of norms casts itself as a universally transcendent context in which rational agents are free to act: the liberal framework of commutative justice. So, because redemption claims of normative rightness are referred to discourses of normative rightness, if the validity challenge is to a normative claim about distributive justice, the discourse to which one would appeal is organized around ideas of commutative justice, which is to say the commutative–distributional paradigm. A kind of catch-22 ensues[18] wherein recognitional claims to distributive justice are ruled out of bounds by the norms of commutative justice – in economic theory and moral philosophy, as well as in social and market decorums. This is a major complication that universal pragmatics does not appear to notice, and it suggests that Habermas's moral abstraction and universalization solves the problem of conflicting ethical perspectives at the price of unintentionally edging onto the ground of commutative justice. The redemption test for regulatives is seriously compromised by the pervasiveness of the norms of the commutative–distributional paradigm.

Morality and commutative justice converge in a shared focus on equivalence. The principle of abstract reciprocity (the "=") introduces a kind of fungibility into moral reflection. In commutative justice, the equivalence is between commodity or service and payment that together comprise a transaction, and, as I noted in the last chapter, the justice of transactions in the modern era has come increasingly to bear directly on the fact of agreement between the transacting parties. In morality, the equivalence is an equivalence of persons, such that any principle applying to one must apply to all.[19] Yet the actual principles themselves tend to be commutative principles – negative prohibitions against doing harm rather than positive responsibilities to act in certain ways.

The problems with the treatment of subjectivity in universal pragmatics are as significant as the problems just rehearsed about norms of intersubjectivity. The treatment of subjectivity in universal pragmatics is the simplest and weakest of all the speech acts. The mode of communication is expressive (i.e., of the speaker's own condition) and the test for validity is veracity, or truthfulness.[20] There is no discursive court of appeal; the only test offered for truthfulness is consistency across time (Habermas 1976: 159). Habermas's rationale for this is that it replicates the model of a solitary consciousness contemplating the world – i.e., the experience of subjectivity. Even if only an analytic convenience, this view does not acknowledge the degree to which consciousness is never solitary in the sense of having an unformed encounter with anything. Habermas has not escaped the limitations of the Cartesian subject–object dualism with this model of subjectivity, and it substantially weakens not only his treatment of communicative subjectivity but also by implication his attempt to define norms of relationship between subjects. Certainly, individuals do experience themselves subjectively; it is a commonplace that they do. Understanding, however, is always pre-structured in some way; this is the function and point of discourse communities, to provide a ground of meaning. I fully grant that some experiences of subjectivity, being ineffable, fall outside the domain of speech acts (though the recreation of ineffability through art opens another avenue of communication). What is at stake here, however, is how subjectivity-in-the-world (or more precisely, subject-in-discursive-community) is structured into a self-understanding that takes shape as an understanding of identity.[21]

Habermas must deal with the question of subjectivity in universal pragmatics because of the communicative problem of trustworthiness. A lack of trust halts the communicative process and therefore hinders the operation of reason. Here is where a rhetorical conception of communication may help reconfigure universal pragmatics. Trustworthiness, in rhetoric, is talked about in terms of ethos. In my readings of Smith and Friedman, I employed ethos as a way of interpreting the portrayal of character, particularly in the invocation of virtues or vices. The narrow interpretation of ethos, to which I do not subscribe, is that it merely projects a semblance of credibility, exemplified by the old joke that the most important factor in politics is sincerity – once you can fake that, you have it made. This limited view of ethos lends itself readily to a manipulative view of rhetoric. Self-image becomes, in effect, an object to be manipulated, a projection of a persona that is measured purely according to its instrumental effect on others. To put it in Kantian terms, it treats others solely as objects for achieving one's own end.

Ethos, however, is a richer and more complex phenomenon than that. At its root, ethos describes a subjectivity already engaged with others; that is, ethos is the name given to a self-expression that is crafted with an audience in mind. It is this audience-mindedness, as McKenna (2006) argued about Adam Smith, that links Smith's theory of communication with his moral theory. It is likewise this audience-mindedness that I emphasize in my interpretation of Aristotle's principles of persuasion. Aristotle's point that the judgment of a communicator's ethos rests with the audience is tempered by the implicit anticipation of such a judgment by the communicator who takes account of her audience. This (subjective) imaginative process of taking-into-account is able to happen because the communicator has a sense of the situation's decorum, which is to say a sense of how the audience views the situation's constraints of appropriateness. The subjective and intersubjective are already imaginatively at play with each other.

Ethos, understood this way, is an expression of character, and as such is a type of self-creation. The issue of trustworthiness, in this light, can be understood as a matter of commitment, of the speaker meaning what she says, standing by what she says, staking herself to her claims.[22] At the same time, the communicative act is an expression of identity. So trustworthiness is not merely strategic, it is constitutive as well. The ethical implication of this is not simply that it avoids a detached instrumentalism with respect to others, but that it is a significant, even necessary aspect of self-creation. In this sense, identity is not "discovered" as if it had a prior independent existence, but rather is generated by being performed.

This way of thinking of ethos as the self-creating aspect of developing character suggests that authenticity is an important factor in its communicative power. Authenticity here refers not so much to what one *is*, as to what one commits to. So being authentic does not mean "discovering" a real self (as if already-existing) so much as meaning what one says. In that respect, Habermas is not far off in noting consistency as one of the features of self-expression, but consistency is a by-product, as it were, of ethos's communicative pledge that creates the need for recognition as an integral part of the communicative process. The point is not whether a given self-expression will never change (which is a simple but straitened way to interpret consistency); the point is to stay in communication with the other, to speak up when the situation changes.

So far, this account of ethos still does not yet address Habermas's argument for the need for recourse to a discursive standard to which communicators can appeal in cases of misunderstanding or dispute, as Newtonian mechanics serves as a standard for constative claims about the physics of motion. To be sure, the avowal, for Habermas, cannot have such a standard because its only test is veracity as measured by consistency. But this conclusion on his part appears to be the case because of his picture of subjectivity as an isolated state. I have suggested that avowals and regulatives – that is, the subjective and intersubjective domains

– are not so clearly separable from each other. If we amend the concept of avowal with the rhetorical concept of ethos, we have a claim about self advanced to an audience (even if that audience is imagined). Ethos *does* have a potential gauge: the appropriateness to occasion called decorum. So I suggest that the concept of decorum is a way to describe the discursive field against which a particular performance – call it a self-statement – of ethos would be judged. Yet decorum, as a register of appropriateness, would seem to point to criteria of normativity, and hence belong to the domain of regulatives; if so, how could it also function as a reference for avowals? The answer to this question lies in understanding the relations between pathos and ethos as they fall under the aegis of decorum.

First, let me review again Farrell's (1993) identification of the two distinct operative features in Aristotle's theory of rhetoric, the *dunamis* of the capacity to size up situations for their persuasive possibilities, and the *technai* (arts) of the three modes of persuasion (logos, pathos, and ethos). The term decorum, understood as what is fitting in a given time and place, is a key feature of the *dunamis* of rhetoric; it is a capacity of understanding that can take general rules (say, of convention) and judge their actual applicability through modes of persuasion in a given case according to criteria of fittingness. But the "given case" is not just a situation in which audiences have conventions of expectations, such as with genres, it is also a situation which is uniquely *live* in its actual audience, its historical time and place, and so on.[23] Decorum, in other words, acts as a governor in the inventional process across variable situations and for all the modes of persuasion in a living moment.[24] Because of this, decorum covers not only what can be said, or what must not be said, but also who may speak, and how they ought to speak; decorum is both substantive and relational.

As deployed under the aegis of decorum, pathos and ethos have a reciprocal relation to each other. Pathos is described as a "frame of mind,"[25] which I interpret as attitude or emotional context; pathos is the emotional framing of how we should perceive what is important about the situation we face. Any claim to frame an emotional context through an appeal to pathos is also implicitly an appeal to ethos – namely, such a frame is how people of good character would react to the situation (with anger, with compassion, etc.). In reciprocal fashion, an appeal to character (ethos) is an invitation to identify with the speaker's perception. Pathos is emotion connected to the subject of the communication, while ethos is emotion connected to the communicator.[26] Artful persuasion depends on the synergy of the two. This has been the core of my argument about the operation of moral persuasion in my interpretations of Smith's and Friedman's writing in the earlier chapters. Smith and Friedman invoke particular decorums by appeals to character (praising good and condemning bad) while also inviting emotional identification with (or repulsion from) their authorial ethos; this is the ethos–pathos synergy at work.

So my criticism of universal pragmatics leads to the conclusion that the pathos–ethos interaction offers a more coherent explanation than Habermas's regulative–avowal structure of the subjective–intersubjective communication dynamic, with the proviso that a single, universal discursive standard for assessing normative and subjective criticizability cannot be certified (and with the corollary claim that attempting to define a universal standard would be necessarily Procrustean). While a rhetorical conception of language enriches the understanding of performative communication, it does not yet answer the question of whether a rhetorical conception of language as communicative reasoning can bridge differences arising from differing ethical forms of life.[27]

I have taken the time to examine Habermas's universal pragmatics so closely in order to show how his concern with redeeming speech acts by recourse to a discursive standard does not, by itself, avoid the problems of the commutative–distributional paradigm. The possibility of a complaint of recognition being heard in a court of commutative normativity is all too real, and the close interconnection of the subjective with the intersubjective can turn the relational problem into a problem of subjectivity – i.e., a problem of self-understanding that results from a refusal to be heard.

This is not to say that Habermas's interest in discursive touchstones and guidance is misdirected; indeed, my own argument about the function of discourse communities as backgrounds for subjective–intersubjective understanding shares the basic idea that our perceptions and feelings arise out of our symbolic–linguistic interactions with each other. The difference between us lies in Habermas's desire to find, for normative matters, the kind of surety for normative and subjective communication that science provides for claims about the material world. Normative and subjective claims, however, being attached to a multiplicity of discourse communities, offer no such ready redemption.[28]

This problem of validity redemption in Habermas's language theory increases the burden on his theory of moral development, because the psychology of moral development underwrites the substance of what becomes the discursive standard for normative appeals. When we turn from language to moral development in Habermas's theory, we run across a more explicit emplacement of the commutative–distributional paradigm in Lawrence Kohlberg's (1981, 1984) theory of moral development.

Kohlberg's theory of moral development is a model of maturation across phases of pre-conventional, conventional, and post-conventional moral thinking, each of which contains two stages. These six stages comprise the model of coming to full moral development: obedience/punishment and self-interest stages in the pre-conventional phase; social norms (good boy/girl) and authoritative social order in the conventional phase; and social contract and universal ethics in the post-conventional phase. The pre-conventional stages are hedonic: avoiding pain and seeking pleasure. The conventional stages are socio-normative: social relationships and social systems. The post-conventional stages are abstract: contractual–legal (freedom of choice) and universal ethical principle.[29] The stages are roughly experiential in one through three, and increasingly abstract thereafter (four through six). According to the model, individuals proceed through the stages of moral development as they mature, though there is no guarantee that people will achieve stage six, which is characterized by freedom of conscience and moral reasoning based on universal principles of equality, reciprocity, and human dignity. Stage six is harmonious with the Kantian model of universalized morality that Habermas adapts, shifting the basis of reason from solitary reflection to social interaction but keeping the principle of establishing impartiality by abstraction.

Kohlberg's theory holds several attractions. It connects moral reasoning to natural human development, helping create a philosophical anthropology (i.e., theory of human nature) that is not just metaphysical. It also connects moral reasoning with self-development; that is, moral reasoning reflects processes of identity-formation necessary for self-formation as well as of socialization for interaction with others. It helps account for variation in the range of moral systems by implicitly laying out a spectrum of development, explaining relativistic moral approaches as insufficiently developed (notice the hedonic dynamics of the pre-conventional stages and think of Bentham's efforts to find a lowest-common-denominator for human motivation in utilitarianism). At the same time, Kohlberg's model holds to a view of the highest moral development as being a process of rational and impartial reflection on moral conflicts guided by principles of equality and reciprocity, similar to Kantian moral duty. Habermas (1979d) adds a seventh to Kohlberg's six stages in order to include the communicative discourse about moral principles that serves as the discursive touchstone for validity claims in public discussion.

Kohlberg refers to his model as a model of justice, but one that he develops social-scientifically (rather than philosophically[30]) from observing processes of moral reasoning in children, teens, and young adults. His method is to present his subjects with a moral dilemma and analyze the justifications for their decisions; Kohlberg's stages were developed from these analyses. The dilemma is framed as a story: Heinz's wife contracts a rare and deadly disease. A pharmacist in town has created a drug that will cure the disease, but it is rare and expensive. Heinz cannot afford it. The moral dilemma: should Heinz steal the drug? For Kohlberg's purposes, what matters most are the reasons given for why Heinz should or should not steal the drug; the reasoning shows the stage of moral development, according to Kohlberg. There is no "correct" answer per se, but the question is framed in terms of rightness – that is, it asks for justification, not merely expediency.

Carol Gilligan's (1982a) critique of Kohlberg's theory famously started what became known as the justice–care debate. Gilligan posed a methodological and substantive critique of Kohlberg's theory. The methodological critique was that Kohlberg only included boys in his samples while developing his theory; her substantive critique was that he missed the moral reasoning that develops among girls out of a primary orientation to care rather than to justice. As a result, Gilligan argued, Kohlberg's scale, when applied to girls, would systematically show them to be less morally developed than boys.

Gilligan illustrated her argument by contrasting the responses of "Jake" and "Amy," eleven year olds. Jake looks at the dilemma as a logic of conflicting values (as Gilligan claims Kohlberg frames the dilemma) and decides that, life being more important than money, Heinz should steal the drug. His answers locate him in the conventional stages, but with flashes of the abstract thinking that mark the post-conventional stages. Amy, however, resists the framing and keeps trying to find other alternatives (could Heinz find a loan? could others talk to the druggist for him?). Gilligan describes Amy's responses this way:

> Seeing in the dilemma not a math problem with humans [Jake's approach] but a narrative of relationships that extends over time, she [Amy] envisions the wife's continuing need for her husband and the husband's continuing concern for his wife and seeks to respond to the druggist's need in a way that would sustain rather than sever connection. As she ties the wife's survival to the preservation of relationships, so she considers the value of her life in a context of relationships, saying that it would be wrong to let her die because, "if she died, it hurts a lot of people and it hurts her." Since her moral judgment is grounded in the belief that "if somebody has something that would keep somebody alive, then it's not right not to give it to them," she considers the problem in the dilemma to arise not from the druggist's assertion of rights but from his failure of response.
>
> (Gilligan 1982a: 204)

The standard outcome for responses like Amy's is that they lead to evaluations of lower levels of moral development on Kohlberg's scale. To the extent that Jake's and Amy's responses are representative of their peers, girls appear to be less capable of the abstract moral reasoning of the post-conventional phase – and, as Gilligan indicates, the direction of questioning in the interview to renew the framing of the dilemma as one of justice lessens Amy's confidence in her judgment.

Gilligan's account of Amy's resistance to framing the moral problem of the Heinz dilemma as one of theft points up the fairly explicit framing of Kohlberg's scale in commutative–distributional terms. Justice is defined in a strongly commutative light, and responsiveness does not register as a moral matter. As taken up by Habermas, Kohlberg's stages of moral development fit Habermas's requirements for a universal moral position, or at least possibility, but relational responsiveness and the ethic of care only appear to qualify as a good, not as a matter of right, and in that respect fall into the domain of private life. Habermas's moral–ethical distinction reflects the public–private distinction and the commutative–distributional paradigm that underlies it. Between his theory of language in universal pragmatics and his adaptation of Kohlberg's theory of moral development, Habermas's effort to locate a universalized moral touchstone upon which communicative reason can ground itself does not escape the relational limitations of the commutative–distributional paradigm.

As Amy's moral intuitions help clarify, understanding *how* moral questions are framed and whose voices matter are relational issues that have their own moral import. As Gilligan noted in her account of Amy, dealing with a moral dilemma as a relational problem takes a fundamentally narrative turn – that is, it must work itself out as a story, as an imagined course of action and interaction, so consequences can be thought through, including the consequences of self-creation. Narratives of this sort are inherently rhetorical, not simply because they are about characters (i.e., they help us imagine actions) but because they help us form our own character, in the sense of becoming the persons we want to be. To reconstitute distributive justice in a serious way would be to frame such a formation of character as a way of making public narratives.

But it is not just what we say, but *how* we talk about our relations that matters, which means how we listen, what we are willing to hear, and who we are willing to listen to, to be an audience for.[31] My argument about the diminution of distributive justice is that its worst effect has been in subordinating our talk to either the decorum of the marketplace or the decorum of a traditional social order (or at least to the defenders of its remains), if not ruling it out of bounds altogether. In both decorums, the exercise of power remains beyond criticism by being ruled out of bounds as properly public talk. Even in a modern liberal perspective such as Rawls's, there is the limit of being "above reproach,"[32] of having done all one could, which means no longer being obliged to listen. Habermas's procedural public reason suffers from similar problems. But if a moral framework such as Habermas tries for does not work, perhaps adapting an ethical framework can. That is one of the promises of solidarity, to which I turn in the next chapter.

7 Recognition and the problem of solidarity

A defining feature of the modern era is the intractable fact of pluralism, of differences of viewpoints on what constitutes a good life, what some have called "value pluralism."[1] The variety and incommensurability of beliefs and values contribute to the feeling of fragmentation of modern life. These differences pose an insurmountable obstacle to achieving solidarity without some form of transcendence or loss of liberty. Liberalism offers itself as a moderate degree of transcendence in offering common ground based on maintaining as much freedom as possible.[2] I have argued that liberalism's success in delivering on its offer has been mixed, largely due to the strains that developed from the commutative–distributional paradigm.

This chapter takes up the question of solidarity, of possibilities for "standing together," in terms of discourse communities and the problem of belonging. My argument has been that the neglect of relational issues as matters of distributive justice has aggravated the feelings of fragmentation and alienation so commonly identified with modern life. As a result of this neglect, we miss out on a form of public relationship that could provide a basis for connection across our different value orientations. We are left with respect for humanity at one extreme and esteem for excellences and intimates at the other. Both of these are worthy, but inadequate to the task of recognition as a public relation. What they miss, that falls between them, is the recognition that can be afforded within a society of strangers, people of diverse backgrounds and forms of life.[3]

Rhetoric as attitudinal reasoning within a discourse community is how any solidarity is/can be achieved. Recognition is needed for being (rather than esteem for achievement), but in a concrete rather than generalized way (so "respect for humanity" is not sufficient). Recognition starts with people-as-they-are.

In claiming that recognition is an inherently rhetorical dynamic, I have insisted on contextualizing rhetoric as an emotional–attitudinal framing of reasoned communication that occurs within the relational (and hence ethical) borders of a discourse community. As there are many kinds of discourse communities, there are many levels of rhetorical interaction. Some of these discourse communities take the form of institutions, where codification and habitual practice coordinate the activity of large numbers of people; others may be small and personal and take the form of play. The point of identifying the rhetorical dynamics they all share is to explicitly acknowledge the interplay of emotional attitudes, modes of reasoning, and ethical commitment; this interplay, embodied in an ever-shifting rhetor–audience relation, is the means by which identity is formed by being performed in its social–discursive environment. As I indicated in my analysis of Habermas's treatment of intersubjectivity and subjectivity in universal pragmatics, the interaction between the two makes separating them of limited usefulness, particularly if the analytic distinction distracts attention from their interpenetration.

To put this in plainer language, having a recognized place in society is something people need in order to develop their own identities, as is being able to recognize others. Recognition as a human being is too abstract. Recognition through esteem is too particular. The point of recognition is simply to invoke belonging, to be "one of us." This level of recognition implies that people *as-they-are* are recognized as belonging, as being members. For some people, this happens easily and even unconsciously if they are part of a dominant social order, whatever it may be. For those who are not, however, their differences may mark them as not-belonging. In an era underwritten by a concept of liberty based on an equality of persons, those who are left out face denying themselves, living a double life, or accepting second-class status. Any of these create a burden of alienation that affects both the person and their social connections. So for recognition to revive a relational distributive justice, it needs to be of a kind that lets persons be who they are.

Solidarity is not enough if it only stems from a shared social decorum (this is the problem of so-called organic solidarity – shared ethnicity, religion, etc.). The step beyond organic solidarity is not into abstraction, as with Kant, or into a universalized humanitarianism like Sen's (2006).[4] Benhabib (1990), in a critique of Habermas's communicative ethics, argues for communication that searches for common ground in practical concerns: the need for resources to live healthily, to raise children, to have productive work, to have access to social resources.

I have proposed the concept of discourse community as a way of understanding the communicative work through which membership in a group is established and maintained, and therefore an integral part of how identity is formed and social connection established. The sociological categories that Saalmann (2002) reviews – Tönnies's *Gemeinschaft* (community) and *Gesellschaft* (society), Durkheim's organic solidarity through the social division of labor, Parsons's functional solidarity of social roles – lead Saalmann to describe a new way of thinking about solidarity, with strangers being a reflexive solidarity that comes from common social interests, what might more properly be called public interests, as in social movements where people share values but are and remain strangers to each other. I find Saalmann's concept of reflexivity compatible with my concept of the rhetorical workings of discourse communities that combine reflection in the sense of thoughtfulness, and thoughtful interchange, and also in the sense of mirroring, of seeing something about oneself. But even here, Saalmann's interest is in what people consciously and deliberately take on as a project, like a social movement, and I want to insist that affective and aesthetic factors of ways of being cannot be entirely captured by conscious deliberation. Wanting to be a certain kind of person carries more than rational purposiveness with it.

The concept of a rhetorical discourse community also provides a way of thinking about how habits of thought develop and persist; hence, my interest in the rhetoric of moral judgment in economic thought, as it worked to construct a picture of justice in a social order in which market relations would function freely and productively. The unintended malfunctioning of that social order, in what I have called the commutative–distributional paradigm, indicates that the discourse community of liberalism needs to extend its awareness to the need to be open to complaints of injustice. That is not easy, however, because our habits of thought are so strongly influenced by the commutative–distributional para-digm. This is the case even for critics of the commutative–distributional social order.

Redistribution vs. recognition: Nancy Fraser and Axel Honneth

The exchange between Nancy Fraser and Axel Honneth in *Redistribution or Recognition? A Political–Philosophical Exchange* (2003) illustrates just such an influence of the commutative–distributional paradigm. Fraser's and Honneth's exchange is prompted by the development of multiculturalism and identity pol-itics in the late twentieth century. Fraser worries that identity politics undermines a political solidarity of class necessary to solve economic inequities, while Honneth argues that identity politics reveals the central importance of misrecog-nition as the rationale for inequities. Fraser acknowledges the importance of rec-ognition as status but discounts self-identity by holding too strongly to a Kantian morality–ethics distinction, much like Habermas. Honneth acknowledges the significance of self-identity as well as status, but he holds too strongly to social achievement as the basis for recognition. Both of them remain somewhat fuzzy in what they mean by a social institution, insofar as they mainly appear to mean something with a juridical form (i.e., formally codified); this provides an opening to expand and refine the connections among attitude formation, social practices, and institutions with the rhetorical concepts of discourse community and decorum.

As a first approximation, the positions Fraser and Honneth take can be seen as articulating an updated version of the difference between Kant's and Hegel's conceptions, respectively, of the relationship between morality and ethics. Fraser insists on a Kantian morality–ethics distinction in large part because of the desire to preserve a universal justificatory method (morality) in the face of a diverse political pluralism of different ethical systems. Ethics, in other words, must necessarily be relative in a pluralist society – relative to the beliefs about a good life of the groups holding them (the groups as discourse communities, in my argument). In an important way, Fraser's devotion to the morality–ethics frame-work is for the sake of its *persuasive* power – that is, in terms of its intellectual

gravitas as a mode of justification. As a consequence of her position, Fraser constructs recognition as a question of status-rights to social participation, with misrecognition constituting an injustice. Fraser defines recognition-as-status as a
moral issue (i.e., of justice), while recognition as self-actualization is only an
ethical issue.

Honneth, in contrast, takes up Hegel's argument about moral judgment's
anchorage in concrete forms of life. This does not quite mean taking the ethical
side of the moral–ethical framework because Hegel's understanding of the relation between morality and ethics differs from Kant's. Hegel's conception is
developmental, with morality constituting a kind of minimum condition that can
further develop into ethical life.[5] Instead of Fraser's status-vs.-self-actualization
framing, Honneth argues for the primacy of recognition; he wants to foreground
recognition, with "distributional issues ... understood as the institutional expression of social disrespect – or, better said, of unjustified relations of recognition"
(2003: 114). "Maldistribution," to use Fraser's term, is a *consequence* of misrecognition in Honneth's argument rather than a parallel harm as Fraser has it. The
key issue here, for both of them, is what "institutional expression" means, which
is not at all clear for either of them. Whether "institutional" means formally codified or means traditional or customary practice, it will have an attendant discourse, and that discourse will have guidelines for "what is fitting in this
situation." This is the domain of decorum, and understanding the operation of
decorum is of utmost importance. Neither Fraser nor Honneth appear to take this
into account.

Honneth goes on to say, "[as] counter-thesis to Fraser's: I would like to demonstrate that without anticipating a conception of the good life, it is impossible
to adequately criticize any of the contemporary injustices she tries to conceive..." (ibid. 114). This explicitly foregrounds ethical reflection (the good
life). Honneth denies the charge of metaphysical reflection by arguing that he is
concerned with the conditions of recognition, not its ends or substance; rather,
his argument outlines a phenomenology of misrecognition.

For Fraser, like Habermas, morality in the Kantian moral–ethical framework
depends on an abstracted universalized model that evaluates equal reciprocity;
the rule of morality is that it applies equally to all, and the initial test of a moral
conflict is whether two persons in conflict could switch places without changing
the moral judgment. The equivalence inherent in the universalization model
reproduces the "=" of commutative justice and its limitations. The problem is
more a sin of omission, as it were, than commission; as in the commutative–
distributional paradigm, the moral–ethical framework shortchanges the ethical
(as the commutative does the distributive) by diminishing its role.[6]

Kant's universal principle was the appeal to reason via the categorical
imperative – the articulation of a moral maxim all rational persons would
necessarily agree that all should follow. Habermas, correcting what he saw as
the limiting influence of Cartesian dualism on Kant, reconceived the locus of
rationality as happening in the interchange of ideas through argument rather
than in a process of solitary mental reflection.[7] Reason, for Habermas, happens

through communication, and thus has an intersubjective dimension.[8] So Habermas's primary concern is to foster public reason through communicative interaction, and transforms morality from Kant's categorical imperative to universal procedures for open communication.

Fraser's primary value is parity of participation in social life, with political participation as a core value, not so much in a civic–republican sense of participation being self-development through self-governance, but as in a quasi-Rawlsian sense that everyone should be free to engage in the deliberations of public decision-making.[9] In short, participatory democracy is Fraser's highest good, so if people are not able to participate, there is an injustice. If they are unable because of material inequities, then there is a problem of material distributive justice – what Fraser calls "maldistribution" (2003: 74). If they are unable because institutionalized patterns of misrecognition block them, then there is a moral claim (i.e., a problem of justice). So participatory democracy is leavened with moral theory, which serves as a court of appeals for questions of justice.

In cultivating the opportunity for practical politics, Fraser's moral goal is "participatory parity," which has parallel economic and cultural dimensions: (a) material distribution adequate to provide "independence and 'voice'"; and (b) the requirement "that institutionalized patterns of cultural value express equal respect for all participants and ensure equal opportunity for achieving social esteem" (Fraser 2003: 36). The economic dimension is Fraser's objective condition for participatory parity, and equal respect (i.e., recognition for Fraser) is the intersubjective condition (i.e., the cultural dimension); taking the two together Fraser calls "perspectival dualism" (63), which is Fraser's strategy to keep economic interests from being eclipsed by identity interests.

Similarly, Fraser's emphasis on the immanence–transcendence issue is connected to practical politics. What she means by immanence–transcendence is that the purpose of critical theory has become to identify exactly what, in the current condition (the immanent), holds the possibility of future transformation (the transcendent), in order to then be able to encourage development in that direction through practical politics. Because for Fraser the motive for political action comes out of the practical political conditions of a given moment, the point of critical theory is to examine social movements for the sign of resentments that have risen to the level of public expression, creating a possibility for practical politics.

When active expression emerges in a social movement, Fraser claims, critical theory can provide a coordinated analytic framework that puts together moral theory (2003: 26 ff.), social theory (ibid. 48 ff.), and political theory (ibid. 70 ff.). The framework is coordinated in the sense that each theory has a focus on the issue of participatory parity. In moral theory, recognition should be based on a moral claim of status with regard to participatory rights. Harm to participation is the criterion for identifying an injustice. Social theory supplies the analysis that class and status are the correct categories for assessing maldistribution and misrecognition. Political theory, in turn, provides grounds for assessing democratic debate and deconstructive criticism.[10]

The problems Fraser's argument encounters can be usefully reflected as responses to what she claims as the four advantages of her approach to recognition as status for social participation:

> (1) The approach "permits one to justify claims for recognition as morally binding under modern conditions of value pluralism".
>
> (Fraser 2003: 30)

This claim functions to solidify the Kantian morality–ethics framework in moral philosophy as compatible with political value pluralism: value pluralism is about ethics. At the same time, the political domain is provided with an escape from the relativism inherent in pluralism through the appeal to morality as a final arbiter.

> (2) "[recognition-as-status] locates the wrong [of status subordination] in social relations, not in individual or interpersonal psychology".
>
> (ibid. 31)

This articulates Fraser's separation of recognition into either status or self-actualization, corresponding with the moral–ethical structure. Honneth's objection, by way of his phenomenology of suffering, is that experiences of depreciation, which Fraser frames as a problem of self-actualization, provoke suffering in persons that pervades their lives. Degraded status can be internalized; it does not necessarily have to be written in law or come out of the mouth of authorities. It could, for example, be part of a dominant social decorum. Fraser's second point also presumes and reinforces a public–private distinction; status subordination matters when it is public in a systematic way, not when it is a "quirk" of individual personality. This suggests that personal taste and public attitudes can be separate, which I have been working to problematize with the close interpenetration of identities, discourse communities, and decorum. While private and public expression may be governed by rules of decorum (i.e., of what may or may not be said in each setting), the attitudes and their connections to particular identities that underlie expression find their articulation in the discourse community – for instance, about race, about gender, and so on.[11] To put this more plainly, Fraser's separation of institutional status from self-actualization is as problematic as Habermas's separation of subjectivity from intersubjectivity in his theory of language.

> (3) "…the status model avoids the view that everyone has an equal right to social esteem. That view is patently untenable, of course, because it renders meaningless the notion of esteem".
>
> (ibid. 32)

Fraser aims this as an argument against Honneth's adoption of an achievement principle as the basis for recognition (more on this shortly). The contrast between respect and esteem, which Fraser takes as a commonplace,[12] is that respect is for basic humanity, while esteem is for accomplishment. As I argued at the beginning of this chapter, the gap between respect for humanity and esteem for achievement is conceptually too wide; it leaves out consideration of people as-they-are. Humanity is too abstract a category, and achievement too narrow. There is an intermediate place where we have a sense of belonging in a discourse community, apart from and prior to any achievement of excellence within it. Honneth is subject to this criticism as well.

> (4) "By construing misrecognition as a violation of justice, it facilitates the integration of claims for recognition with claims for the redistribution of resources and wealth. Here, in other words, recognition is assigned to the universally binding domain of deontological morality, as is distributive justice ... the self-realization view, in contrast ... treats recognition as an ethical question, which makes it incommensurable with distributive justice".
>
> (ibid. 33)

Two parts of this claim stand out: first, the identification of material distribution as distributive justice, which I claim is part of the heritage of the commutative–distributional paradigm, and second, the reliance on deontological morality as discursive power – a neatly accurate account of the commutative–distributional paradigm as filtered through a radical critical lens. The radical aspect is Fraser's primary value of participatory parity. It's not at all clear how its primary status is arrived at, a point Honneth makes, too (ibid. 170–189). While it is consistent with Fraser's desire for the transformations of socialism and deconstructed heteronormative sexuality, it is not clear how either of these are supposed to come about.

Fraser's problem with Honneth is that she sees him engaged in a metaphysical project of articulating desiderata for a good life.[13] Fraser insists, like Habermas, that we are in a post-metaphysical era, by which she means that philosophical reflection alone cannot discover or articulate a set of principles that identify the good for us.[14]

Honneth's response is that identity is so fundamental a need it cannot be subsumed under class. He proposes to reconfigure Hegel's account of recognition as a phenomenology of suffering (Honneth 2003: 114). This is a positive movement toward relational distributive justice in that the mutuality of recognition takes better account of the overlapping subjective–intersubjective dynamic, but it is undermined by Honneth's apparent acceptance of the achievement principle that pervades the commutative–distributional paradigm.

Hegel's categories of family, civil society, and state are Honneth's point of departure. For Hegel, recognition was a feature of the highest development of the person as a citizen, a culmination of a dialectical process from rights-bearing individual through moral social actor to ethical citizen. The lack of recognition of the earlier stages drove the dialectic forward (Honneth 2000).

Honneth transposes Hegel's stages of development to distinct domains of recognition – family, state, and civil society – each of which has its own forms of recognition: in the family, love and intimacy; in the state, equality in law; and in civil society, achievement and social norms. In the end, however, his focus is primarily on the question of equality in law, relying on it to address shortcomings in the other two domains: "it seems above all to be processes of legalization – expanding the principle of legal equal treatment – that have the inherent potential to correctively intervene into other recognition spheres, ensuring the protection of the minimum preconditions of identity" (Honneth 2003: 187), though in his conclusion he cautions that an expanding legalism would be resisted on grounds of morality or social norms (i.e., the domains represent distinct and separate areas of life). In this respect, Honneth is not that far removed from Fraser in seeking a solution of a trump against attitudes of exclusion: for Honneth, legal; for Fraser, deontological (and presumably subsequently legal).

But Honneth's structure of the three domains of recognition derive from the same broad historical changes that I examined as the development of the commutative–distributive split. It becomes explicit in this extended passage:

> The normative structural transformation that went along with the idea of legal equality should not be underestimated, since it led to the establishment of two completely different spheres of recognition, revolutionizing the moral order of society: the individual could now – certainly not in actual practice, but at least according to the normative idea – know that he or she was respected as a legal person with the same rights as all other members of society, while still owing his or her social esteem to a hierarchical scale of values – which had, however, also been set on a new foundation.... With the institutionalization of the normative idea of legal equality, "individual achievement" emerged as a leading cultural idea under the influence of the religious valorization of paid work ... the estate-based principle of honor conversely lost its validity, so that the individual's social standing now became independent of origin and possessions. The esteem the individual legitimately deserved within society was no longer decided by membership in an estate with corresponding codes of honor, but rather by individual achievement within the structure of the industrially organized division of labor... [141] ... [which split] the premodern concept of honor into two opposed ideas: one part of the honor assured by hierarchy was in a sense democratized by according all members of society equal respect for their dignity and autonomy as legal persons, while the other part in a sense "meritocracized": each was to enjoy social esteem according to his or her achievement as a "productive citizen."
>
> (Honneth 2003: 140–141)

Honneth's disclaimer, "certainly not in actual practice, but at least according to the normative idea," is a weak prop. He is cognizant of the split of "honor," but leaves untouched the historical commencement of that split in the elevation of commutative justice. Both the democraticization and the meritocratization of which he speaks were of use initially only to some, not to all. While it is true that the language of the ideal of equality provoked and gave hope to those excluded, the history of social movements (in the U.S. at least) shows the intensity of *opposition* to more-inclusive definitions of equality by classical liberals who claimed the principles of commutative justice and social and market norms as their own principled argument. In the end, Honneth does not have a problem with the social norms of achievement. His acceptance of them is, I believe, meant to indicate his realism.

So Honneth's position on identity politics appears to accept the individualism of modernity.[15] His objection to Fraser's argument winds up implying that her strategy of economic grounds for redistribution and cultural grounds for recognition could ironically strengthen identity–political movements by giving them more purchase than his theory of recognition domains (in which their primary recourse is in legal equality). Self-actualization is a necessary part of recognition for Honneth, in all of the domains, so he avoids the public–private split that Fraser creates, but his structure of the domains reintroduces it in almost the exact shape of the commutative–distributional paradigm.

A rhetorical view of autonomy

It may be objected that I am disregarding the most fundamental aspects of freedom in the development of liberalism and Kantian moral theory, subordinating free individual choice to the imperatives of a discourse community either as a structural matter (i.e., our "choice" is illusory because our choices are determined) or as a moral matter (i.e., our values derive from our discourse memberships, therefore dominate our thinking). Neither of these is the case, though we are indeed hemmed in by structures and motivated by values. What I protest is an individualism that pretends detachment from lived conditions. Intellectual detachment in the processes of abstraction can be a useful tool, but abstraction pays a price of stripping away the particulars of life.

So I do argue against a concept of autonomy that is "pure" in the sense of having no constraints, just as I argue against a concept of identity that is detached from any form of life and its accompanying discourse.[16] Instead, I argue for an understanding of constrained autonomy – that is, autonomy under limits.[17] This is a rhetorical view of autonomy: self-willing, but only contingently so, looking for opportunities for change while wrestling with the structures of the current state of affairs, dependent on understandings of meaning that are only available in discourse communities, and consumed by the inventional processes of shaping opportunities in terms of the audiences constituted by the discourse communities. To paraphrase Nancy Fraser in another context (1990), actually existing autonomy is always constrained.

The imbrication of identity with its sources of discourse communities is why the separation that Nancy Fraser makes between social status and self-actualization is impossible; the condition of its impossibility is the distortion of whichever dimension is disowned. The discourse community is an active constituent in identity, not simply a genealogical or sociological datum. The issue is not simply whether a flesh and blood community of like-minded fellows can be located; the discourse community is as symbolic and discursive as it is of the flesh. To put it another way, being symbolic and discursive, it is of the imagination, and therefore able to escape a fully embodied determination, while at the same time unable to fully escape embodiment into abstraction. This (and only this) is why individuals with many disparate personal experiences lived in diverse circumstances can nevertheless identify with a common unifying thread such as race, gender, ethnicity, etc., in ways that cannot be ascribed either wholly to harms from personal depreciation or wholly to an ongoing engaged communitarian experience.

Nor must this imply a deterministic view of discourse communities. The metaphoricity of rhetorical invention is a longstanding antidote to the idea that we are prisoners of past ways of seeing the world. The very inadequacy of our conceptions in the face of our lived experience is a continual goad to make new sense of the world, but we always do it by readjusting our interpretive filters to gain new insights.[18]

Stanley Cavell's moral perfectionism

An improved alternative to Fraser and Honneth's treatment of recognition is Stanley Cavell's concept of acknowledgement in what he calls "moral perfectionism." Moral perfectionism he defines as "a condition in which you can at once want the world and want it to change – even change it" (Cavell 2004: 18). Wanting the world and wanting it to change captures the interplay of acceptance and creative reinvention I have attributed to the relationship between identity and discourse community. Cavell transposes the relational demand for acknowledgement in intimate relations that he set out in *Pursuits of Happiness* (1981) into the relational demand for acknowledgment in civic friendship in *Cities of Words* (2004).

Civic friendship, in Cavell's usage, is a way of thinking through the ethical demands of the communicative relationship of citizens. It is not the solidarity of the like-minded, except insofar as the ground that may be shared concerns citizens' communication with each other. Nor is it exactly an Hegelian or civic–republican idea of civic participation as the full flowering of human potential. Civic friendship is something that can be shared in a society of strangers, perhaps even something that can *only* be shared in a society of strangers, since not being strangers would supply some other basis for affiliation. Yet it is also not exactly Saalman's (2002) reflexive "society of strangers" solidarity which helps account for a common cause on particular public issues. Cavell's moral perfectionism is characterized by a attitude of attention to the ethical demands of friendship.

Chief among these ethical demands is the demand to be heard, to be recognized (acknowledged, in Cavell's language). It is a specific demand, not to approve an identity on the grounds of excellence, but rather on the grounds of the rightness of my desire for my identity. In an odd way, this is an appeal to the most fundamental kind of "property" right, in the sense of *propre* (L.) as being what is nearest to me: I have the right to be myself in the concrete way I embrace. This is not a possession, though, so much as an enactment of desires to be a certain way. But what of possible objections to someone desiring to be a certain way?

One of the objections from a moral perspective is that ethical forms of life – ways of being a certain way – may include conduct that violates moral precepts about, say, individual freedom (cultural practices of forcing female circumcision represent a current example of this kind of controversy). This is the potential problem of relativism that ethical forms of life face. Such controversies typically arrange themselves into at least two sides: the liberal defense of individual liberty against the cultural proponents of what is claimed as a religious practice and cultural tradition. The resulting controversy falls neatly into a familiar individualism vs. communitarianism standoff.

Cavell's "wanting the world and wanting it to change" aims at acknowledgment that still leaves room for moral discussion: are there better and worse ways of acting within a way of being? Wanting the world as it is and finding it still lacking means wanting people as they are and finding them (and me, and you) still not yet what we could be. The mark of Cavell's moral perfectionism, as he develops it, is an acknowledgment that whatever *has* been accomplished nevertheless has still not measured up, that there are no laurels to rest upon, and that more still needs doing: wanting the world and wanting it to change can be "a step of political encouragement, one that assures us that we are not alone in our sense of compromise with justice" (Cavell 2004: 18).

Cavell distinguishes moral perfectionism from utilitarian and deontological ethical frameworks not so much by posing it as an alternative, as by noting the intensive relational orientation it demands – actual engagement with another:

> Utilitarianism proposes a means of calculation to determine the good of an action. Kantianism proposes a principle of judgment to determine the rightness of an action. Perfectionism proposes confrontation and conversation as the means of determining whether we can live together, accept one another into the aspirations of our lives.
>
> (Cavell 2004: 25)

The first two can be done as thought experiments; the last requires an other with whom to interact. Cavell's "confrontation" focuses on "the moral demand for intelligibility" (ibid. 25) that raises the question not just of audience, but an audience who matters – "the other to whom I can use the words I discover in which to express myself is the Friend" (ibid. 27).

The intelligibility that Cavell foregrounds is as much intelligibility to self as it is to others. The need to express intelligibly what is morally unsatisfactory with my life or with our relationship is as much my own need for understanding as it is for our communication. This view of intelligibility encompasses more than the intelligibility condition in Habermas's universal pragmatics. For

Habermas, intelligibility concerns basic comprehension of words, syntax, and so on; Cavell's sense of the word raises the stakes to the problem of articulating meaning, the problem of finding the right words, finding the right way to put the problem.

At this point, a limit of solidarity may begin to become perceptible: that "standing together," especially as an achievement of "we have managed to overcome obstacles and now stand together," may be threatened by the confrontation of which Cavell speaks approvingly. The standing-together of solidarity runs the risk of hardening, the risk of choking off the expression of the feeling that, despite wanting the world as it is, I (or you, or they) might yet want it to change, might realize something is yet lacking.

The lack that Cavell focuses on most directly is the lack of willing engagement, primarily as expressed through conversation. This is a central theme of his earlier (1981) work, *Pursuits of Happiness: The Hollywood Comedy of Remarriage*. In examining a range of the so-called "screwball comedies"[19] in films from the 1930s and 1940s onward, Cavell notes their common theme as a crisis of communication, of intelligibility within a marriage, necessitating the hard choice of either dissolving or reconstituting the marriage relationship. The crisis is specifically a crisis of intimacy, of an inability to speak freely and be heard; the comic resolution in the films is the recovery of expression that is only made possible by a self-discovery, or perhaps *re*discovery, of the sources of one's desire for the other.

Cavell theorizes that the genre of remarriage occurs at a unique historical moment when the equality of women put traditional marriage practices into doubt. The practical manifestation of this equality was an equality of divorce, which meant among other things that the pursuit of personal happiness became more clearly identified with personal desire, rather than, say, with duty – such as the duty to stay in an unhappy marriage.[20]

But desire for Cavell is not merely of the body, though neither is it *not* of the body; it is also the desire for friendship, which is identified with talk, with being heard. The centrality of conversation, including the conditions of its possibility – chief among them the prospect of being heard – are at the heart of Cavell's (2004) project in *Cities of Words*, in which he transposes intimate friendship into civic friendship. The stakes are remarkably similar: in the civic friendship, the possibility for speaking and being heard is key.

And what of desire? How do the desires of an intimate relationship transpose to desires of civic relationship? Cavell's aim in both levels of analysis is to focus on something other than what would be good or right (ethical or moral); instead, the point of his moral perfectionism is about discovering what one's desires are, of owning them as one's own, of admitting, or confessing, or even shouting them from rooftops. Saying what one *really* thinks, what one really wants, is a form of self-creation, and the interaction of conversation made possible by friendship is what enables the cultivation of self-creation.

Habermas does not hope for so much from the public sphere. He holds to the promise of rationality in a quasi-Kantian universalized procedural rationality, in the face of irresolvable differences in the pluralism of different ethical conceptions of the good life. Those irresolvable (because incommensurable) differences mean no possibility of a rational choice among them. For a similar reason, in Nancy Fraser's (2003) view, identity politics threatens the solidarity of working class-oriented politics with fragmentation and political impotence – a pluralism of interests as well as identities, with a correspondingly diluted and fragmentary ability to advance political initiatives of (material) redistribution. Axel Honneth (2003) acknowledges the connection between the personal experience of suffering and public recognition, but accepts the standards of achievement in what must be social norms dominated by market principles.

How is Cavell able to avoid this problem of incommensurable desires? As I understand his logic of conversation, what matters is not the substance of a desire per se (in terms of its goodness or rightness) but rather the acknowledgment of its genuineness as something to be desired, something worth desiring because of its being one's own desire. In transposing the desire of the body from the intimate to the civic domain, I suggest Cavell provides a different way to think about identity politics. The political desire of the body is to *be* the body one is, to let those desires be voiced and be heard, and not have to pretend *not* to be that body, to keep quiet about it. The problem this creates is the need for those outside the standard norms to live a double life, to cultivate a public persona for the sake of recognition and to hide the private person. This is a relational problem of injustice, in the sense that it voids the very possibility of civic friendship, like living a lie inside a marriage. The expression of identity is the voicing of the insistence that my desire is right for me to have. This does not mean my desire is immune from tests of goodness or rightness, but rather that it is a primary part of my self.

Cavell's "wanting the world and wanting it to change" casts the tension between past and future[21] in a different light from the pattern we saw in the Kantian–Hegelian opposition, replicated in another form in the Habermas–Gadamer debates, and in still yet other forms in the Fraser–Honneth exchange and the Kohlberg–Gilligan debate. In all four of these positional disputes, the rational–universalist deontological position (Kant, Habermas, Fraser, Kohlberg) aim is to escape from the partialities and distortions of self-interest through the process of universalizing abstraction.[22] The critics (Hegel, Gadamer, Honneth, Gilligan) protest that moral life is drained of meaning without its historical and cultural contexts, the network of relationships in which moral choices must be made.

While Cavell's "wanting the world and wanting it to change" is generally in harmony with the historical–cultural position, he makes even clearer the way in which the historical and the cultural – all the circumstances of life – form a context and setting out of which we must necessarily act if we are to do so at all. So, like Gadamer, Cavell acknowledges that wherever we start from, we are trying to make sense of our lives as we look back on them. But the issue for Cavell is not so much being able to escape a past as to create a genuine future, which for Cavell means to fully become oneself.

Becoming fully oneself through friendship and conversation means communication is at the core of the process, and as I have been arguing throughout this book, communication is at heart rhetorical – which is to say expressive as well as didactic or suasory and relational as well as goal-oriented. Rhetoric is not just the manipulative I-will-talk-you-into-this, it is communicating the emotional attitudes of appropriateness (pathos) and communicating authenticity of commitment (ethos) that make a line of reasoned argument (logos) cogent and compelling.

The pressure of Cavell's moral perfectionism is a demand to be attentive to others even, or *especially* even, when they make uncomfortable complaints. Call this a willingness to listen – even further, call it a willingness to be an audience. This suggests that to take seriously the idea that rhetoric occurs within a discourse community, is to acknowledge the need to be audience as well as to be rhetor (the speaker). Listening is a corresponding part, call it a responsibility whose root is responsiveness, of the rhetorical relationship among members of a discourse community. Such a relationship does not mean automatic approval or immunity from questioning; on the contrary, it might mean a vigorous contestation.

This resembles what Honneth calls a potential fourth domain of recognition coming into being, one that would require us to recognize one another across cultural difference to the extent that we would offer "well-meaning attention" to the possible value of norms other than our own (2003: 169). The risk to be guarded against is the risk of a solidarity calcifying into a crust of convention and closing its ears to complaint. This is the problem Cavell finds with Rawls's "above reproach" conclusion (2004: 171); that the moral reflection Rawls advises could become a rationale for ceasing to listen.

Conclusion

What began as a long historical process to shed the social divisions of feudalism has borne fruit in the development of liberalism, but in a gradual and intermittent way. The problem we face now is how our habits of thought influence our perception of what freedom means, as members of the multiple discourse communities of liberalism – political economy, moral philosophy, political theory, communication in the public sphere, to name a few.

By paying close attention to the use of language of moral judgment in important texts on political economy, I have pointed out a process of legitimizing a particular view of justice – the elevation of commutative justice and diminishment of distributive justice – that is a necessary background condition for the claim that economic activity in market interaction can be a naturally self-regulating and just social system. The process of legitimization functioned to valorize competition – or more specifically, to cultivate resentment at the evasion of competition – as the condition which would provide a regulative pressure and prevent economic activity from being an exercise of power in the pursuit of self-interest dominated by the wealthy.

This process of legitimation included a diminished distributive justice as an essential part of conceptually reducing the moral obligation of community-to-member to the standards of social or market decorum. This was a "naturalization" of distributive justice that relegated it to private life, and that gave an imprimatur of natural authority to dominant social and market conventions as the proper registers of decorum. In addition, the combination of an elevated commutative justice and a diminished distributive justice led to a modern conception of distributive justice meaning primarily material distribution (or opportunity for it). In classical liberalism, the market itself within a commutative framework is the model of just distribution; in modern liberalism, a degree of worry about market failure led to warrants for government distribution and access to opportunity. Both, however, remain within the broader view of a commutative–distributional paradigm.

This historical process generated a distortion in our understanding of justice by elevating the role of individualism and individual moral choice at the expense of acknowledging the relational significance of being social beings embedded in particular networks of social relationships. This has compromised liberalism's promise of freedom by leaving social and market conventions largely unchallengeable as matters of justice because of their assignment to private life as matters of taste and opinion; to challenge them would violate the (reduced) decorum associated with them. As a result, a substantial form of social power is left in place, albeit formally changed from the residual feudal relations of rank that preceded liberalism. Evidence for the difficulty in challenging social conventions is the persistent resistance to admitting categorically-excluded persons as full-fledged members into the community – and not just ad hoc resistance, but resistance grounded in principled appeals to liberty.

A parallel development in moral philosophy, in the development of a Kantian moral–ethical distinction, has worked to reinforce the commutative–distributional paradigm. What they share in common is a reification of the analytic distinction between the individual and the individual's embedment in social context. This foregrounds the act of individual choice – in the act of contract and sovereignty of possession in commutative justice, and in the exercise of moral choice in deontological morality – while at the same time diminishing, respectively, distributive justice as what individuals are due by virtue of their membership in the community and the ethical framework that constitutes a community's vision of what is good. As a consequence, I argued, the relational aspects of distributive justice are shortchanged, and the distortion of the commutative–distributional paradigm pervades not only the defenders of both classical and modern liberalism, but also modern critics as well.

The parallels between the commutative paradigm and the moral–ethical framework can be seen in Jürgen Habermas's theory of communicative action.[23] While Habermas's model of human reason as a collaborative, interactive process is an improvement over the model of solitary reflection, he relies too much on a theory of language and on a theory of moral development that reproduce the separation of the individual from her networks of relationships. Nancy Fraser's effort to resolve material inequities leads her to frame recognition in terms of deontological morality, inadvertently confirming the commutative–distributional paradigm. Axel Honneth avoids entangling recognition with morality, but accepts the achievement-oriented standard of recognition in civil society, one dominated by the commutative–distributional paradigm.

Stanley Cavell's moral perfectionism offers a way out of the habits of thought of the commutative–distributional paradigm by a decided attention specifically to the relational dynamics of civic communication. Cavell's argument about civic friendship brings us around again to the fullness of communication understood as rhetorical persuasion: not only reasoned argument about public purposes, but also reasons why we should care that contextualize the reasoning, and passionate commitment to being the kind of person who does care. Just as rhetorical understanding helps us to recognize the epideictic moment of valuation that precedes and frames the deliberative decision and gives it meaning, Cavell's concept of civic friendship helps us to recognize that our identities are comprised of our commitments, and that acknowledgment of those identities must frame our decisions if we are not to be in a Hobbesian war with each other.

The critique I have offered here is an attempt to intervene in the discourse of liberalism to demonstrate the shortcomings of its understanding of justice. Our efforts to define individual freedom have hewed so closely to an individualist framework that we have difficulty connecting our understanding of our social identities and communities to it. Those of us fortunate enough to feel at home in the dominant social structures may enjoy the benefits of belonging, but with little awareness of our privilege and little sympathy for those who do not feel at home, even as we contribute to their discomfort. This is not a recipe for nourishing freedom.

I believe the effort of intervention is worth it. Ideas do matter in discourse communities, and the more so when the discourse communities of political economy, moral philosophy, political theory, and public communication all attempt to come to bear on how to understand our problems. Francis Fukuyama's (1992) reflection on the end of the cold war was a worthy provocation, for example, even though his interpretation of Hegel that liberalism was the "end" of history was, to be kind, vastly premature. Fukuyama's project was thoughtful in the sense of making the case that ideas matter, but even Fukuyama was well aware that there is no necessary connection between capitalism as an economic system and democracy as a political system.[24] Liberalism put the two together, but recall that even in Milton Friedman's (2002) reflections in the preface to *Capitalism and Freedom*, the one thing he thought better of after forty years was the emphasis on political freedom; civil and economic freedoms would be enough for his purposes – and recall that Friedman named himself a classical liberal. While state socialism in the Soviet model has largely collapsed, the efforts of the People's Republic of China and other Asian states to foster markets under the umbrella of overarching state controls offer a state-centric version of crony capitalism (i.e., economic oligarchy). The definitive characteristic of capitalism in any political system still appears to be the ability to concentrate capital, and the rewards for achieving large concentrations of capital are great wealth and influence.

The problem of crony capitalism is that it violates the principles of competition that we saw as necessary conditions in Adam Smith and Milton Friedman. Today, the principle of competition in liberal societies has turned into opportunities for profitability.[25] The recent housing bubble and financial crisis exemplify the race to find increasingly profitable opportunities, to the point that the economy becomes hostage to a series of bets (i.e., zero-sum contracts where one party wins what the other party loses) of enormous size.[26] The commutative–distributional paradigm is incapable of identifying this kind of economic activity as a problem because the parties consented to the agreements, and market actions themselves do not constitute externalities, however destructive they may turn out to be. Yet the promise of Smith's and Friedman's arguments about the self-regulating nature of the market was that, unlike the Mercantilists and others, economic activity would be ongoingly productive, not zero-sum. Modern liberals recognize the financial crisis as a problem of market failure and are attempting to find a regulatory solution, but the resistance to regulation is very strong, not least because of the influence of money: keeping the opportunities for profit as unrestricted as possible is a primary goal of classical liberals, and it fuels the subsequent influence of money on the political process.

But even modern liberal efforts to find regulatory solutions for market failures does not fully encompass the problems we face. The problem is not simply financial; the pursuit of financial success also pervades our recognitional perspectives today, with the consequence that the race for achievement is motivated not just by the desire for gain but by the fear of being left behind, of being left out. This motivated not only sub-prime borrowers who feared being forever frozen out of the housing markets by skyrocketing prices, but also investors, even rich ones, who viewed those ahead of them as pulling out of reach. Overreach, especially through borrowing against the future, was as much a distorted recognitional matter as it was a rational investment decision, especially under conditions of financial musical chairs. The ensuing recession has affected millions more with blighted prospects. The blight is partly financial, but also partly the frightening prospect of not-belonging, of being abandoned; we should not forget that. "Liberty and justice for some" cannot work as a rallying cry. Distributive justice in its full sense is our unfinished business.

Notes

Introduction: economic thought, moral persuasion, and justice

1 A note on terminology: a number of rhetorical terms that originated in Greek or Latin
   are used commonly in English (e.g., decorum, pathos, ethos) and I leave these unitali-
   cized. Other terms are rarer in English, so I italicize them (*dunamis, anamnesis, tekne*).

1 Moral rhetoric and political economy

1 For discussion of different types of political economy, see Caporaso and Levine
   (1992), especially Chapters 1 and 2, and Clark (1998). For an excellent overview of
   the historical development of political economy from Adam Smith's time forward,
   see Clark's second chapter.
      There is yet another tradition of usage that casts political economy in Marxist
   terms. Marx used the term to signify the work of the classical political economists,
   whose theories he criticized as misunderstanding the nature of value such that the
   bourgeoisie were enabled by the state to exploit the working class. Thus political
   economy in the Marxist sense refers to the use of political power to manage the state
   in the interest of the bourgeoisie (capitalists). This tradition of usage informs Marxist-
   inspired criticism from the nineteenth century into the twentieth, including critical
   theory understood broadly as the writings of the Frankfurt School, the Marxist sociology of Raymond Williams, and other Marxist-inspired social critics.
      I use the term liberal political economy both to indicate that political economy, as
   a term, encompasses a broad range of meanings – broader than the Marxist usage –
   and, as I noted at the outset, to draw attention to the close affinity between the political economy of classical liberalism and the political theory of liberal individualism,
   both of which mark the beginnings of capitalism. While my analysis is a critique of
   liberal political economy, it does not rest on Marxist precepts, but rather addresses the
   fit among the internal logics of moral, economic, and social systems that liberal political economy claims for itself.
2 See Clark (1998), Ch. 2, for a good account of the distinction between classical liberalism and modern liberalism. Classical liberalism was the strongly market-oriented
   political philosophy of individualism of the late 1700s into the 1800s; modern liberalism developed late in the 1800s out of a variety of progressive movements that sought
   more government regulation of business practices, control of monopoly, and so on.
3 Distributive justice defined as what people are due as members of a society is part of
   Aristotle's definition of justice in *Nicomachean Ethics* (1987), bk. V. See especially
   where Aristotle discusses "those who have a share in the constitution" in Chapter 5.
4 Aristotle (1987), Bk. V, ch. 5. See also Berns (1994) for discussion of the parallels
   between Aristotle's and Smith's discussions of justice. As Berns sums up Aristotle's perspective, "distributive justice ... carries into practice the notions of what

is appropriate and fitting that dominate society and are reflected in its laws" (80). Berns, however, does not draw his assessment of distributive justice through in his analysis of Smith, apparently accepting Smith's taking for granted the distributive order of the status quo and concentrating instead on commutative justice.

A vital methodological question at the very heart of this book's argument is whether it is possible to adapt ideas from Aristotle's work (or anyone's, for that matter) without thereby invoking the author's entire metaphysical frame, including a teleology of human nature. This is partly a hermeneutic problem (one of interpretation) and partly a question about how another's ideas may be fairly and legitimately appropriated – that is, without distortion and with relevant application. This question is as important for rhetoric as it is for discussions of justice, and in both cases my approach is similar: I look to the dynamic principle that I see operating in Aristotle's analysis. In understanding rhetoric, this means taking up the dynamics of his social-psychology without necessarily also taking up his specific understanding of Athenian psychology or his specific values. I do so by adapting his principles – for example, that people reason about probabilities (logos) within emotional (pathos) and relational (ethos) frameworks in order to adequately set contexts for judgment. Similarly, in taking up Aristotle's discussion of justice, I focus on the distinction he makes that distributive justice's core principle is proportionality according to merit – that equals be treated equally – but without taking up his specific definitions of merit.

These principles of proportionality and merit are a point of departure for me to interpret distributive justice as being concerned with what people are due by virtue of their place in the community. The constitution of the community matters: in a society organized around social rank, that rank is what determines what one is due, and distributive justice consists in treating people of the same rank equally, that is, in a consistent manner. I am interested here in exploring what treating equals equally might mean in the development of liberalism, wherein equality is a first principle. The interpretation I make in transposing Aristotle's principles to our era is that distributive justice relies on an understanding of the place of persons within a community – that is, how they are placed in relation to each other. That placement gives persons their standing, their status, their position, from which it is possible to identify who equals actually are. The concept of "standing" lends itself directly to considerations of decorum – which is to say, to considerations of appropriateness in action, in treatment, and so on. Such considerations cross a number of levels of social interaction, from the minutiae of everyday life, in which simple matters of manners and etiquette are ever present, to significant life-affecting demands on one's own liberty, such as paying taxes or serving in the military.

Each set of appropriate actions and behaviors carries with it accompanying frames of thought and guides to communication – which is to say, rhetorical decorum – that encompass not only the capacity to understand what would be fitting to do in a given situation but also what is say-able – and by extension, what should not be said, or cannot be said because of a refusal to hear it, to give it a hearing, to countenance it, which is to say, to face it or be faced by it. So the principle of proportionality in distributive justice, of treating equals equally, invariably calls up the problem of how to do so appropriately. In this respect, distributive justice and decorum are alike concerned with fitness, with appropriateness of treatment. In that respect, it should not be a surprise that a naturalized distributive justice would find a place in decorum.

5 For a related argument, see Brewer (1989). Brewer describes the late eighteenth-century British state as "Janus-faced" in the difference between its domestic and colonial orientations toward questions of rights, being careful of preserving rights in the face of domestic criticisms of excessive consolidation of power, but insisting on the legitimacy of its total authority in the colonies.
6 Giddens (1984), xxxv.
7 In claiming to study moral judgment, I am not engaged in the social–psychological

investigations like Jonathan Haidt (2008), who attempts to translate philosophical dilemmas like the trolley problem (see Michael Sandel 2009) into matters of taste (literally, of disgust). While Haidt's appreciation of moral judgment as anchored in emotional response is good, his methodological individualism pushes him too far into taste as an individual (or at best, conventional) phenomenon, without adequate consideration of how tastes are formed within the horizon of a discourse community. See also Chapter 5's discussion of Lawrence Kohlberg's (1981, 1984) developmental theory of moral judgment.

8 For an overview of early rhetoric, including Plato's attitudes, see Bizzell and Herzberg (1990: 1–35).

9 Bizzell and Herzberg (1990: 637–669).

10 Bizzell and Herzberg (1990: 711–727).

11 Aristotle (1987).

12 A point of controversy within the study of rhetoric is its scope – whether "everything is rhetorical" or not, the criticism being that the "everything" position makes rhetoric trivial. My own view is that the issue is not that everything is rhetorical; it is that untangling the rhetorical aspects from a communicative situation can only be accomplished by killing and stuffing it. It can be done, but at the cost of losing the living creature. See Gross and Keith (1997), and Schiappa (2001) for more on rhetoric's scope.

13 This is why the Athenian mass juries were a problem for Aristotle in a way the Assembly was not. Aristotle's condemnation of rhetoric in the courts is not a condemnation of rhetoric per se, but of the structure of the court system. His oft-quoted line about not warping the carpenter's rule is not a blanket condemnation of rhetoric, but rather a complaint about how the audience for persuasion in courts should be structured. The system of mass juries led to rhetorical situations that could favor a distraction from judging rules of law by setting the possibilities for persuasion too broadly.

14 See, e.g., Charland (1994) and Gaonkar (1994).

15 By way of example, Farrell's reading of Franklin Roosevelt's inaugural address is far too hagiographic to be a comprehensive account of the public culture of his day. There were many people who completely and bitterly opposed Roosevelt, people for whom his speech would have represented the worst kind of sophistic manipulation. Farrell may admire Roosevelt's sentiments and think them worthy of emulation; that would be reasonable as rhetorical criticism. He cannot offer them as evidence of what the public culture as a whole was at the time, however, only that it was good enough to get Roosevelt elected.

16 See Sahlins (2009: 2) for a discussion of this point:

> As against the idea prevalent since Aristotle that the family of parents and children is a natural self-generated entity and the germ of the larger society, Levi-Strauss argued that no human family could exist if there were not first a society.

17 See Hariman (1995).

18 My conception of constitutive rhetoric shares a similarity with Maurice Charland's (1987), but the major difference is Charland's reliance on Louis Althusser's concept of interpellation, which Althusser developed out of his effort to combine Marxist social analysis with a Freudian psychoanalytic theory of identity development. Although interpellation has come to be used more loosely in recent years (sometimes so loosely as to simply mean social influence), I still find Althusser's concept too structural–determinist. Therefore, I attempt to develop my concept of constitutive rhetoric out of the elements of rhetoric itself.

19 Booth (1983: 9).

20 Booth's project is a contribution to the larger area of study referred to as reader-response theory, or more broadly, reception theory. While there are a range of differences among those working in this area, what they share in common is attention

to the audience's role in meaning-making, in contrast to the older view that meaning resided in authorial intention (see, e.g., Barthes (1977) "The Death of the Author"). For an overview, see Tompkins (1980); the main conflict Tompkins points out is between formalists and reader-response; what is at issue is the location of meaning, whether in the object of the text or in the reader's interpretation. Rosenblatt (1978) is strongly on the uniqueness, even idiosyncrasy, of the reader's interpretation, though her specific topic is the process of reading poetry. Jauss (1982) focuses more on audience capacities for interpretation, as does Fish (1980), and his concept of interpretive communities and for a fascinating account of audience reception in film, see Hansen (1999).

I selected Booth's framework as a conceptual centerpiece because of his interest in distinguishing the imaginative personae authors and readers occupy in their inter-action through a text. Booth's early work perhaps over-emphasized the text as a struc-ture controlled by the author (which was Rosenblatt's main criticism of him), but Booth's work was usefully expanded into audience considerations by Rabinowitz (1977, 1980) and into examination of inferential structures in the text that may escape intentional design by Phelan (1996), and Phelan and Rabinowitz (1994).

All of these writers make important contributions that do not necessarily contradict the others'. Rosenblatt is correct to say that individuals may interpret poetic readings in meaningfully different ways at different times in their own experience. Barthes and other poststructuralists are correct to point to the massive momentum of symbols and meaning-making in cultures. Booth's contribution is to acknowledge that we cannot deny the intentionality present in writing, while also acknowledging that its reception cannot be fully controlled, and to place the act of writing and reading in a rhetorical context.

21 Chaim Perelman (1994) also recognizes this connection in his recuperation of Aristo-telian rhetoric in "The New Rhetoric: A Theory of Practical Reasoning"; Perelman refers to the treatment of epideictic as a version of literary artistry in oral form as a "misleading analysis," going on to say,

> The orator's aim in the epideictic genre is not just to gain a passive adherence from his audience but to provoke the action wished for or, at least, to awaken a disposition so to act. This is achieved by forming a community of minds, which Kenneth Burke, who is well aware of the importance of this genre, calls identifica-tion.... In fact, any persuasive discourse seeks to have an effect on an audience, although the audience may consist of only one person and the discourse be an inward deliberation.
>
> (150f.)

22 Aristotle (1954), 1366a, 24–29. The translator's footnote at this passage refers the reader back to 1356a, lines 2 and 5 under the "modes of persuasion." Line 5 reads, "Persuasion is achieved by the speaker's personal character when the speech is so spoken as to make us think him credible."
23 See also Sullivan (1993: 117).
24 Fisher (1970: 137–138).
25 Stigler quoting Smith from *WN* Glasgow Ed. (Oxford: Clarendon Press, 1976) I, 43–44.
26 Stigler (1982: 4).
27 See, e.g., Cannan (1904), Raphael and Macfie (1984).
28 Smith (1776: 1-16).
29 Metanoia: A "change of mind or heart; a correction." Lanham (1991: 100).
30 Thomas Leitch (1986) uses the term "narrativity" to describe the audience's ability to fill in the blanks of what is unsaid in order to make a coherent story.

2 Sympathy and justice in *Theory of Moral Sentiments*

1 Winch (1983a: 254).
2 For concise reviews of Das Adam Smith Problem, see Teichgraeber (1981), Peters-Fransen (2001), Otteson (2001), and Montes (2003). Montes is especially thorough in his exposition of the German Historical School critiques of Smith.
3 See Heilbroner (1982) for an example of the prudential argument.
4 See Haakonssen (1996), ch. 1, and Grotius ([1625], 1990).
5 See Hont and Ignatieff (1983: 2): "Our argument is that the *Wealth of Nations* was centrally concerned with the issue of justice, with finding a market mechanism capable of reconciling inequality of property with adequate provision for the excluded."
6 See, for instance, Aristotle's (1987) discussion of exchange in Book V, section 5.
7 Wood (2002).
8   the origin of quarrels and complaints [is] when either equals have and are awarded unequal shares, or unequals equal shares. Further, this is plain from the fact that awards should be 'according to merit'; for all men agree that what is just in distribution must be according to merit in some sense, though they do not all specify the same sort of merit, but democrats identify it with the status of freeman, supporters of oligarchy with wealth (or with noble birth), and supporters of aristocracy with excellence.

   The just, then, is a species of the proportionate.
                                                      Aristotle (1987: Bk. V, ch. 5)
9 Tawney (1926), Wood (2002).
10 Tawney (1926), Rothschild (2001).
11 An interesting present-day version of this principle can be found in Habitat for Humanity. Well known for building housing for poor people, the organization's religious and charitable impetus finds one expression in its no-interest loans to its clients. See Fuller (1990).
12 See Wood (2002), ch. 7 and 8.
13 See Tawney (1926) and Robbins (1998) for Christian influences on economic thought.
14 Tawney (1926), Hardin (1999), Robbins (1998), Rothschild (2001).
15 Rothschild (2001), especially in her discussion of Montesquieu.
16 Haakonssen (1996).
17 While the reason/emotion divide was not the only problem in philosophy at the time, it was an important one that is still continuing; see MacIntyre (1988).
18 Hobbes ([1651], 1962), Grotius ([1625], 1990).
19 The references to Smith's *Theory of Moral Sentiments* (*TMS*) will follow the convention of the Glasgow edition of Smith's works, using, in this case, an abbreviation of the book's title (*TMS*) followed by Part (VII), Section (ii), Chapter (4), and Paragraph (6). Thus, *TMS* VII.ii.4.6 refers to Part VII, section ii, chapter 4, and paragraph 6. In some cases, as in Part III, there may be no section headings, and hence no section notation.
20 See also Wood (2002), ch. 1.
21 See Haakonssen (1996) and Cremaschi (1989) for Smith's empiricist/emotivist stance as solving the problem of unacceptably rationalist foundations for the natural law separation of commutative and distributive justice. Cremaschi in particular makes the argument that Smith's fundamental critique of a rationalist foundation was that it was a type of dogmatism.
22 Smith's theory of moral development strongly prefigures Lawrence Kohlberg's stages of moral development, though Kohlberg misreads Smith as solely an emotivist (Kohlberg 1984: 288–293). See Macfie (1959) for the argument that Smith used emotion as the impetus for rational reflection.

23 See Haakonssen (1981: 64) for a discussion of direct and indirect sympathy.
24 See Cremaschi (1989).
25 See Haakonssen (1981: 99–100). The commutative–distributive distinction and separation is consistent with the distinction between perfect and imperfect rights and the
corresponding perfect and imperfect duties that appear as a central argument in
Smith's Lectures on Laws and Justice (LJA and LJB). As Haakonssen notes, perfect
rights (to liberty of person and property) incur a perfect duty (obligation) to observe
those rights under the rules of justice. Imperfect rights only establish imperfect duties
– recommended rather than obliged behavior – and are not properly part of justice.
26 As Haakonssen put it, Smith's conception of justice ultimately becomes an appeal to
the self-understanding of the impartial spectator – and as I argue, hence the implied
reader:

> "right," like "justice," is dependent upon the concept of "injury" ... The object of
> natural jurisprudence is justice; and the rules of justice define our rights by laying
> down what actions constitute injuries against us. The concept of "injury" is under-
> stood in pure spectator-terms: what the relevant, actual spectators – such as judges
> and juries – in a given society recognize as injury is in legal terms injury in that
> society at that time and is definitive of it rights and laws.
>
> (Haakonssen 1981: 99–100)

27 Smith contrasts reactions to impropriety and demerit in terms of hate vs. resentment:
"hatred, a passion which is naturally excited by impropriety of sentiment and behavi-
our; not of resentment, a passion which is never properly called forth but by actions
which tend to do real and positive hurt to some particular persons" (TMS II.ii.1.3).
28 It is also a straightforwardly Lockean sentiment. See Locke (1952), ch. 2 "Of the
State of Nature."
29 "offices" here has the sense of "duties," as in Cicero's (1913) *De Officiis* (*On Duty*).
30   the Moral Sentiments are attempts to apply [Smith's] understanding of Newtonian
scientific methods to the study of society. Much that seems obscure or irrelevant
in the Moral Sentiments falls into place when this book is regarded as an explanation of the social origin and function of moral rules.

> (Campbell 1971: 21)

3 Sympathy and moral horizons in *Wealth of Nations*

1 The full title is *An Inquiry into the Nature and Causes of the Wealth of Nations*. For
citations to *Wealth of Nations* (*WN*), I follow the format used in the reproduction of
the Cannan (1904) combined edition of both volumes, which is: volume and page
number: thus (*WN* i 493) is *Wealth of Nations* Vol. 1, p. 493.
2 This is part of Smith's difference from the civic humanists, insofar as the tendency in
Smith is to remove the necessity of practicing virtue from civic/public life (and con-
sequently to privatize virtue). See, e.g., Teichgraeber (1986: 27, 42–49).
3 For arguments specifically about economic distributive justice, see Boulding (1969,
1985), and Young (1997). Young makes the specific case that Adam Smith's contribution was to point out the good distributive effects of free markets. Both Boulding
and Young differ from my argument in that they define distributive justice *only* in
economic terms, rather than in terms of a larger social order.
4 Das Adam Smith Problem (DAS Problem) has generated nearly two centuries of
scholarly comment. The two most comprehensive and current reviews of DAS
Problem are Peters-Fransen (2001) and Montes (2003). Montes includes an excellent
section on the nineteenth-century German Historical School criticisms of Smith.
5 Cited in Peters-Fransen (2001: 190).
6 "Selfishness" critiques like Kames and Reid's, cited in Peters-Fransen (2001: 190).
7 Brown (1994), Heilbroner (1982).

8 West (1976), Fitzgibbons (1995), Otteson (2002).
9 Bitterman (1940a, 1940b) sees justice as the connection between *TMS* and *WN*, but holds that Smith's view of it is utilitarian – that is, rational rather than based on the sentiments. Bitterman's reading of sympathy and propriety is extremely thin.
10 See Cropsey ([1957] 2001: vii; Evensky (1993a: 395–397), (1992: 68).
11 See Elliott (2000).
12 See Alvey (2003) for an extensive investigation into optimistic and pessimistic passages in *WN*. Alvey's title is informative: *Adam Smith: Optimist or Pessimist? A New Problem Concerning the Teleological Basis of Commercial Society*. Teleology is Alvey's term for the natural dynamic that produces and sustains society, what I have been referring to as its self-regulating dynamic. For Alvey, the optimistic side of Smith is both immanent and historical, but Alvey apparently considers pessimism only in historical terms. I say "apparently" because Alvey does not directly address the difference. My argument differs from Alvey's in my claim that Smith's pessimism can also be said to be immanent (that is, in the nature of things) insofar as self-interest needs to be controlled.
13 One of Smith's criticisms of the Mercantilists was that they represented their own interests as being coincident with the interests of the country as a whole; his analysis aimed to prove that claim wrong.
14 Several commentators have remarked on the stylistic differences between *TMS* and *WN* as evidence of Smith's own rhetorical sensibilities. See Pack's (1997: 136) argument that writing style differences between *TMS* and *WN* can be laid to Smith's Aristotelian approach in *TMS* vs. Socratic approach in *WN*, each suited to friendly and hostile audiences, respectively. See also Matthews and Ortmann (2002: 390):

> Smith, whose earlier lectures demonstrate a remarkable command over rhetorical principles, chooses to emphasize first the desirable properties of economic freedom in Books I, II, and III – he writes in obvious but not explicit opposition to mercantilism – and to postpone his direct criticism of mercantilist principles until Book IV, when the reader's confidence has been won.

15 See Ortmann and Meardon's (1995) argument that game theory can illustrate the operation of sympathy in long-run considerations.
16 Choi (1990) is one of the few references I found that framed DAS Problem in terms of sympathy in *WN*. See also Peters-Fransen (2001), who cites Choi, and Ortmann and Meardon (1995) who implicitly address the question. Contrast also Macfie (1967: 104): "The impartial spectator in fact makes no appearance in *The Wealth of Nations*. He there becomes the impersonal market."
17 See Campbell (1971: 34–41), for an extensive treatment of Smith's connection of familiarity as the starting point of learning.
18 See Campbell (1971) for an extended discussion of Smith's admiration and emulation of a Newtonian scientific method. For a critique, see Cremaschi (1989).
19 Sorites: a figure of speech to indicate an argument "of the heap" – piling up examples.
20 Locke (1952, ch. 5, sec. 41), quoted in Muller (1993: 65).
21 Similar themes of power-seeking and dependency-creating have informed debates about welfare over the last several decades, with conservatives portraying liberals as being like Mercantilists in favoring misguided benevolent schemes of government.
22 Theoretically, that is; see Mannheim's (1936) argument that there was an inherent contradiction between a religion of charity and equality and a feudal social order of hierarchy and domination.
23 Not just startling, but prophetic as well, given *WN*'s 1776 date of publication. While the eruption of the American revolution (from the English perspective, a rebellion) was not entirely unforeseen, neither was there widespread expectation of it. The only other example of timely analysis on a similar scale that comes to mind is Francis Fukuyama's (1989) essay "The End of History?" which in effect predicted the dissolution of the Soviet Union.

24 See, for example, *WN* ii 462, where Smith describes how much shorter wars that were directly paid for would likely be:

> The people feeling, during the continuance of the war, the complete burden of it, would soon grow weary of it, and government, in order to humour [sic] them, would not be under the necessity of carrying it on any longer than it was necessary to do so.

25 See Teichgraeber (1981, 1986).

4 The subordination of distributive justice in Milton Friedman's *Capitalism and Freedom*

1 Citations in the text to *Capitalism and Freedom* will follow the model of *Wealth of Nations*; thus, (*CF* 20) means *Capitalism and Freedom*, page 20. The original publication was 1962, and it was reprinted in 1982 and 2002. The later reprints included new prefaces, but the original text and pagination were maintained. Each subsequent printing included all prior material, so the 2002 text is comprised of the original text and pagination, and the prefaces from all three printings.
2 A brief example of how even small elements work to construct character: In chapter one, in criticizing the Social Security program, Friedman writes, "True, the number of citizens who regard compulsory old age insurance as a deprivation of freedom may be few, but the believer in freedom has never counted noses" (*CF* 9). The last clause of the sentence is as compact a portrait of character as could be, not only a description of Friedman himself but also an invitation to the reader to join him as a believer in freedom. It simultaneously frames the political process in pejorative terms ("counting noses") and makes a clear contrast between adherence to first principles ("believer in freedom") and mere expediency.
3 See Friedman's discussion of types of monopoly (*CF* 26–32). Ordinary collusion is short-lived, according to Friedman.
4 "I am led to the view that it [the capitalist ethic] cannot in and of itself be regarded as an ethical principle; that it must be regarded an instrumental or a corollary of some other principle such as freedom" (*CF* 165).
5 Schumpeter (1954: 394) quoted in Friedman (1962: 5).
6 This is Friedman's interpretation of Marx's theory of surplus value and its expropriation.
7 See note 2, above.
8 Contrast, for example, with "The central defect of these measures [of government reform] is that they seek through government to force people to act against their own immediate interests in order to promote a supposedly general interest" (CF 200). Friedman takes for granted that people acting in their own interests would not thwart competition, claiming that only government or collusive monopoly thwarts competition in any meaningful way.

5 The materialization of distributive justice

1 Lamont and Favor (2008).
2 Samuel Fleischacker voices a substantial objection to the idea of viewing older, Aristotelian ideas of distributive justice as the progenitors of the modern idea, especially if such lineage is used to claim a distortion in the modern era. Fleischacker's (2004b) response to arguments about distorted understandings of distributive justice is to claim, in *A Short History of Distributive Justice*, that the different theories of distributive justice are, actually, distinctly different theories of justice, not perverse changes in a single, holistic view. In particular, he singles out reference to Aristotelian principles as being inappropriate because of Aristotle's definitions of merit, the

incomprehensibility (to Aristotle) of giving money to the poor as a matter of justice, and similar issues relating to Aristotle's argument in *Nicomachean Ethics* (1987: Bk. V, ch. 6). Instead, Fleischacker argues that an entirely new view of distributive justice as specifically about material distribution only arises in the modern era when economic understanding finally enabled markets to generate theretofore unheard-of wealth. It is only this wealth, he claims, that made it possible to conceive of distributive justice materially.

Fleischacker's argument, however, reinforces rather than undermines my case about materialization. The difference between my interpretation of Aristotle and his lies in what we each appropriate from Aristotle's discussions of justice. Fleischacker concentrates on how Aristotle's teleological conception of human nature is the basis for the excellences he (Aristotle) foregrounds as the basis for determining merit and therefore the proper object of distributive justice. I take up the principle that equals be treated equally.

3 See Samuels (1966: 22–23) for his articulation of the "market-plus" framework of classical political economy, and especially the nonlegal forces of social control.

4 See Berns (1994: 81–82) for his account of distributive justice as the contextual background for commutative justice.

5 Cropsey (2001) on Smith's view of commutative justice:

> ...an aspect of freedom as we now commonly understand it, which aspect is called freedom of contract. Freedom of contract is a defensible principle only in virtue of two of Smith's fundamental tenets: (1) that all men are sufficiently prudent in their own affairs; and (2) that justice is created by contract, or in other words that any exchange to which sane men commit themselves cannot be unjust since each is acquiring something which he values at least as highly as that which he gives up.
>
> (64)

> Justice as he [Smith] defines it is compatible with, indeed requires, the freest republican government; and this very justice, the substitute for and ouster of benevolence, is at the same time the soul of commerce. *In order to elevate strictly commutative justice* to be the ruling principle of polity, and thus to guarantee freedom, it was necessary for Smith to obviate duty and virtue. His reprobation of the moral and intellectual defects of commercial society may be regarded as the tokens of his regret over the price that must be paid for humane, civilized life as he understood it.... Civilization and commerce he thought were inseparably joined.
>
> (94, emphasis added)

6 *TMS* II.ii.1.1–7.

7 With the caveat that Smith's view was of property as a developed right, not an absolute right. See Paul (1997).

8 Smith's third duty of government, after defense and the administration of justice, was

> the duty of erecting and maintaining certain public works and certain public institutions, which it can never be for the interest of any individual or small number of individuals, though it may frequently do much more than repay it to a great society
>
> (*WN* ii 209)

This is a line famously open to interpretation, and is cited by Ellen Frankel Paul's (1997) libertarian critique of Smith as a utilitarian departure from property as a Lockean natural right. Paul's critique, while correct that Smith is not a libertarian, misses his point that a natural right is a starting point, and the articulation of actual property rights is a developmental process that happens historically through government. This "public works" rationale is the basis for Smith's argument for public funding of basic education, though he was caustically skeptical of the state of higher education at the time (see *WN* ii 301–307 for the discussion of education).

9 See Barry Clark's (1998) account of the development of political-economic ideologies. His approach is functional in defining ideological positions according to their value-commitments. He highlights two sets of value tensions characteristic of the development of economic thought: the tension between the individual and community, and the tension between equality and hierarchy. Mapping these tensions against each other provides a two-by-two model. The classical liberal is individual-hierarchy; the modern liberal is individual-equality. The other two positions are conservative (community-hierarchy) and radical (community-equality). Both classical and modern liberals are strong market proponents, but modern liberals are more prone to skepticism about the market's ability to self-regulate.

10 See Schwartz (2000) *Fighting Poverty with Virtue: Moral Reform and America's Urban Poor, 1825–2000* for a classical liberal account of the place of virtue in poverty.

11 I say "eventually" because, as Clark's (1998) account makes clear, modern liberalism gradually developed over the course of the nineteenth century because of increasing doubts about the self-correcting nature of the market. While virtue continued to be emphasized as a way out of poverty even for modern liberals, structural problems, such as unemployment rates, became seen as pervasive enough to warrant welfare provision by the state. The Great Depression of the 1930s provided the warrant for Franklin D. Roosevelt to create the Social Security program that accelerated the twentieth-century American welfare state.

12 For contemporary accounts of the market as a cultivator of virtue, see West (1976), Boulding (1969, 1985), Fitzgibbons (1995), Young (1997), Young and Gordon (1996), Otteson (2002), and McCloskey (2006). Of these, McCloskey makes the most ambitious argument about the cultivation of the bourgeois virtues; I address her work later in this chapter.

13 John Stuart Mill's (1993) effort to rescue utilitarianism from Carlyle's "pig philosophy" charge was to introduce a distinction between higher and lower pleasures ("better to be Socrates dissatisfied than a fool satisfied"). Mill's distinction relied on a concept of judgment that, interestingly, invokes the sense of a social place by referring to Socrates, but leaves it implicit.

14 i.e., the original position is the imaginary place of entering into a social contract, where its terms are as yet undecided. The veil of ignorance is the condition that, while knowing people may have differing interests and endowments, no one in the original position knows what those will actually be. Rawls poses this situation to inquire what rational persons would agree to under these conditions; his answer is Justice as Fairness.

15 It is also worth noting that Kant, too, relies on an appeal to the market (in fact, a consequentialist appeal) in his defense of the categorical imperative. In "On a supposed right to lie from philanthropy," Kant argues that being able to excuse oneself from the moral maxim "never lie" would lead to a situation where contracts could not be trusted, and the operation of markets would grind to a halt (Kant 1996c).

16 This implicitly frames distributive justice as identifying everyone's place, not in a substantive sense but in the sense of the proper network of relationships according to which proportionality can be assessed. This does not presume equality of identity, only that equals be treated equally.

17 It is worth noting that only in liberalism does commutative justice take on its pure commutative form. In earlier articulations, there is an attempt to identify price, e.g., with an objective referent – an idea repeated in theories of natural price, or just price, or a labor theory of value.

See John Médaille's (2007: 63–71) discussion of the marginal revolution in economics as the justice of a transaction comes increasingly to bear directly on the fact of agreement (i.e., not on a sense of a natural or just price); the labor theory of value offered a brief replacement for the older ideas (and gave Marx the opportunity to make an expropriation argument about surplus value), but the marginal revolution entirely swept away all but agreement on market exchange as the basis for transactional justice.

18 The separation of modern liberalism from classical liberalism came about in part because of practical doubts about the fairness of the market, but also because of the development of utilitarianism. Jeremy Bentham's (1988) utilitarianism was opposed to the Lockean natural rights view and was originally a guide to policymaking that claimed a foundation in a theory of human nature (Epicurean psychology, that people seek pleasure and avoid pain). Its "greatest happiness" principle stemmed from an emancipatory impetus intended to guide policymaking away from entrenched interests (though Bentham stopped short at dispossession of the rich) and promote policies that would curb excesses and share out resources more evenly. Yet even though Bentham attacked any notion of natural rights (the Lockean view), his own adaptation of Epicurean psychology continued to develop the core principle of methodological individualism.

19 For the dark side of the self-made mythos of, especially, U.S. business, see Sandage (2005).

20 See Haakonssen's (1981, 99–100) assessment that standards of legitimate resentment are subject to historical change.

21 E.g., Cropsey's (2001: 26) interpretation of Aristotle's rhetoric as a "managerial" art (i.e., instrumental).

22 Vivenza (2001: 198–202). It is also worth noting Vivenza's complaint about distributive justice in these pages. She is skeptical of the argument that Smith "demoted" distributive justice because the entire idea of distributive justice to her is that it represents a sham, an ideological false justice that is used to keep the privileged in power and the disadvantaged down. This is not an uncommon reaction to Aristotle's own focus on virtue as merit and Aquinas's interpretation that persons of higher standing would be due more worldly goods (see Aquinas (1947), *Summa Theologica* (ST IIa IIae 61.2)).

23 The idea of higher and lower virtues is also central to Vivienne Brown's (1994) and Robert Heilbroner's (1982) arguments about de-moralization – that is, a devolution of morality traceable to the differences between *TMS* and *WN*, respectively, such that *WN* was a moral step backward from *TMS*. Compare also Raphael's (2007) treatment of prudence as an unproblematic connecting link between *TMS* and *WN*. Note also Eric Schliesser's (2008: 572) account of the higher and lower orders of prudence ("superior and inferior") added by Smith to the 6th ed. of *TMS*. Schliesser makes the case that Smith was uncomfortable by this late date (1790) with how his economic advice was being put into practice.

24 As a contrast, look at James Otteson (2002) for an effort to model Smith's architectonic theme as exchange. Otteson's argument is a good example of commutative justice taken to its fullest development as a principle idea.

25 See Giddens's (1984) discussion of methodological individualism in "Critical Notes: 'Structural Sociology' and Methodological Individualism," pp. 207–226, especially 214–220. Briefly, Giddens sets out four articulations of methodological individualism (214) which share the general idea that social phenomena are fundamentally actions undertaken by individual persons, so understanding social phenomena must (at the very least) begin with an analysis of the person, including motivations, expectations, etc. A strong version of this was British Prime Minister Margaret Thatcher's (1987) statement, "there is no such thing as society," a remark that shows the influence of Friedrich von Hayek's (1988) version of methodological individualism. Jon Elster (1989: 105) similarly undertakes to derive norms through methodological individualism; his primary example is the anticipation of the sanction of shame at doing something forbidden.

26 Rhetors *can* be deceptive, but to do so carries great risks of its own. See also Richard Weaver's (1970a) account of the risks of propaganda and scientific detachment.

27 McCloskey uses the term capitalism freely, but I prefer to emphasize liberal political economy in order to more accurately capture the political–philosophical framework of individual rights, rule of law, and so on that McCloskey herself favors. Capitalism, as a term, usually takes a liberal framework as an assumption, but it is technically possible for capitalism to mean crony capitalism, an oligarchy of monopoly capital, or other forms of concentrating investment capital.

28 For a contrasting view on the cultivation of character by the market, see Rosenberg (1990): Commercial society leads to the decline of extended family, replacing its functions with social institutions for protection, education, etc. Rosenberg accepts Smith's definition of justice unproblematically (pp. 6–8); he is very like Fitzgibbons (1995) in seeing commerce as stimulating the development of virtues:

> The growth of commerce is instrumental in shaping character, in altering tastes, and in providing new and more powerful incentives. The growth of commerce, by increasing the importance of the capitalist class as compared to large landowners, increases the proportion of those in society devoted to parsimony and frugality.
>
> (10)

Rosenberg, however, is aware of the market's potential shortcomings:

> Finally, a commercial society can be an effective builder of moral capital, but only under competitive conditions. Although Smith's argument about the importance of competitive conditions in achieving efficient resource allocation are familiar enough, it is not commonly realized that such competition was also essential to assure that ... the moral capital of a commercial society does not quickly dissipate itself. This is a real possibility, because easily attained wealth is inherently corrupting.
>
> (16)

Rosenberg goes on to describe Smith's view that only when profits are hard to come by do capitalists maintain their prudence and parsimony.

29 In the presumption of an always-rising market, this would not be the case because "low" at one point would later become "high," which would then in turn become a new low for a subsequent high. Similarly, arbitrage works to buy low in one market in order to sell high in a different one. In a fluctuating market, real success comes in selling at the top of the market, which necessarily produces a group of buyers who bought high. The recent financial crisis has illustrated this painfully.

30 The tendency toward in-group and out-group dynamics in traditional societies, however, is a constant problem of modern civil society and political liberalism. For only a few examples, see Seligman (1992), Cheney (1999), and Putnam (1993). Even Rawls's (1993) idea of a "social union of social unions" is an attempt to transcend the problem.

6 Recognition and the relational demands of distributive justice

1 It is also possible to have other conceptions of social placement of individuals – essentialist nature (metaphysical, biological, etc.), divine ordination, and so on. Plato's (1956) catalog of different types of souls in *Phaedrus*, for instance, functions as both a description of social placement and as categories for determining the nature of one's audience. With respect to audience, his point is that rhetoric addressed to a "crowd" (a diverse public audience) cannot but appeal to base motives because the collection of souls is too diverse; his alternative is the persuasive use of language to only a few select students, as modeled in the dialogue itself between Socrates and Phaedrus (and re-enacted in the writing/reading of the dialogue between Plato and his many readers *seriatim*).

2 George Herbert Mead, a key figure in the development of the social constructionist view, himself acknowledged the influence of Adam Smith. See T. V. Smith's (1931)

account of Mead's uptake of Adam Smith's impartial spectator in formulating Mead's "generalized other." T. V. Smith's reading of the impartial spectator is too neatly framed as "an altruistic guest housed in an egoistic household for purposes of respectability" (378), reflecting the devolution-of-morality interpretation of Adam Smith's trajectory from *TMS* to *WN*.

3 Timur Kuran's (1995) claims that the kind of historical–social entanglement falls away under conditions where "true" preferences can be expressed, like the secret ballot. His concept of preference-falsification is a reasonable and even common-sense acknowledgment that the prospect of being criticized will lead people to falsify their preferences, but his scenarios are entirely about conscious decisions which might be called characteristic rational choices. His perspective does not take attitude-formation fully into account.

4 T. H. Marshall (1964) formulates a history of the development of rights in the modern era, with civil rights prominent in the eighteenth century; political rights in the nineteenth; and social rights in the twentieth, with economic rights becoming a subset of social rights. See especially the first part of ch. 4, "Citizenship and Social Class."

5 The practice of exclusion by definition is illustrated by the Dred Scott case, Scott vs. Sanford (1856), which determined that Scott, as a slave, could have no standing to sue.

Axel Honneth (1996: 165–166) appears to accept the demand for inclusion to be the demand for recognition, though he does distinguish between interest- and respect-based claims. Interest-based claims have practical political import but not moral; respect-based claims have moral motivation (i.e., *dis*respect creates a moral demand).

6 Francis Fukuyama's (1992) thesis in *The End of History and the Last Man* is a version of the happy interpretation of liberalism via Kojeve's reading of Hegel: the master–slave problem of relations of domination gives way, in liberalism, to the freedom of individuals. The American revolution was only a starting point, from which the principle of individual freedom would spread and gradually displace traditional social orders by its attractions of freedom and prosperity. This is a primary basis for the neo-conservative concept of American exceptionalism – that persons become defined by their embrace of principles of freedom rather than by heritage (blood) or language or geography – and thus is an "end" to the conflicts that define history in the sense of *telos* (what history has been aiming toward) and "end" in the sense of finishing or stopping (the end of domination).

7 See, e.g., Colfax (1833), discussed in Frederickson (1987: 49–51).

8 Hayek (1988) says, for instance, that we must learn to live in two worlds. One is the world of exchange, the other the world of family. This replicates a public–private structuring of life domains.

9 When I refer to Kantian moral framework, at the root is Kant's (1996) distinction between the categorical and hypothetical imperatives. The categorical imperative, because it is both universalizable and disinterested, can articulate what Kant argues all rational persons would agree to accept. Hypothetical imperatives may point to a good (if you want to get to Carnegie Hall, then practice, practice, practice) but are conditional – that is, interested, as in self-interested, and therefore *partial* in the sense of not impartial, tainted by partiality.

10 Stephen Toulmin's (1958) theory of everyday argument is akin to Habermas's. Toulmin's critique of philosophical method was its neglect of how everyday arguments worked, noting that the ordinary argument begins with a claim (rather than ending with one); the unfolding of the argument lies in how a series of challenges to a claim may be met. In this process, the argument may ultimately go back to the first principles underlying a chain of justifications. In this way, everyday argument looks like the reverse of philosophical argument. Toulmin makes the distinction between field-invariant dimensions of argument, such as logic, and field-dependent dimensions, such as standards of evidence that may vary across different fields of argument like

law and medicine. In this respect, Toulmin and Habermas both locate discursive communities as the final arbiter of specific domains of argument; of the two, Toulmin appears more anchored to particular bodies of practitioners, and Habermas more committed to defensible abstraction at the level of method (such as his desire to bridge normative and empirical research).

11 Habermas (2006: 24): "Political liberalism (which I defend in the specific form of a Kantian republicanism) understands itself as a nonreligious and postmetaphysical justification of the normative bases of the democratic constitutional state."

12 This is akin to Neil Postman's (1982, 1985) argument that the dynamics of modern electronic media promote sensationalism and undermine rational thought. While not identical, Postman's and Habermas's arguments are harmonious with each other. Postman's emphasis is on the psychodynamics of media interaction. Postman identifies sexualized sensationalism (1982) and the increasing tendency of television to push all programming toward entertainment (1985) as prime problems in the corruption of the public sphere.

13 See, at a minimum, Habermas (1975, 1996, 2006). The theme of legitimation problems in advanced industrialized societies runs throughout Habermas's work.

14 The connection between the power of a perspective dominated by commutative justice and Cartesian dualism is the privileged view of the subjects and the effacement or invisibility of the intersubjective grounds of their interconnection, especially conceived as a socio-cultural context; a commutative regime is preeminently individualistic, and a subjectivist position supports (or perhaps explains) such individualism.

15 See Habermas (1979c) "What is universal pragmatics?" For Habermas's own early acknowledgment of influences, see also footnote 58 in Habermas (1979b: 215). Besides Austin (1976), other influential figures in speech-act theory have been Wittgenstein (1968) and Searle (1969).

16 See also Habermas (1976).

17 What "command" and "compliance" mean would depend on a number of shadings of contextual circumstances. For Louis Althusser (1971), the concept of interpellation is the policeman's "You there, stop!" of state authority that establishes the relation between oppressor and oppressed that becomes internalized by the subject, or what the subject is subjected to.

For a complicated example of relationship invoked through illocutionary force, consider Elizabeth Bennett's reply to Darcy's first proposal of marriage in Jane Austen's (1813) *Pride and Prejudice*. Her refusal of Darcy moves swiftly to the insults implicit in his proposal, insults that are not merely propositional (locutionary) but also imply a type of relationship between them (the illocutionary) that she rejects, not simply by rejecting his suit but by criticizing his proposal *as a proposal* – that is, as a proposal that disqualifies itself from being a serious proposal.

18 The phrase "catch-22" was popularized by Joseph Heller's (1961) eponymous novel. In the story of the character Yossarian's attempt to escape the idiocy of the war (WWII) his attempt to disqualify himself from flying on the grounds of his insanity was taken as evidence that he was, in fact, sane.

19 The problem with the fungibility of moral actors is that the degree of abstraction required drains the examination of moral questions of the contextual details that moral actors always face. What I call fungibility here is akin to Hegel's complaint about the abstractness of Kant's conception of morality, something I will turn to in more detail in the next chapter in my discussion of Nancy Fraser and Axel Honneth (2003).

20 To clarify the relation between speech acts and validity claims: the types of validity claims are universal in the sense that all three validity claims are dimensions of all speech acts, but each validity claim may also be the special focus of particular speech acts. In general, speech acts fall into one of three categories: constatives, claims about the world whose test is truth; regulatives, claims about norms whose test is appropriateness; and avowals, claims about the speaker's veracity whose

standard is consistency. So every speech act will have a dimension of sincerity, in that the speaker means to say it, but an avowal, as a specific type of speech act that focuses on the speaker's own state (i.e., its locutionary meaning will be a claim about the speaker's own state, as in "I'm sad") will make an additional, as it were, criticizable validity claim of veracity.

21 To speak of identity is not necessarily to invoke an essentialist, pre-given, idealized, or fully conscious and self-creating version of selfhood. I use it merely to acknowledge the sense of an "I" that is culturally and historically emplaced. Anton and Peterson (2003) provide an overview-distinctions about essentialism and anti-essentialism, fragmented identities, cognitive dissonance, etc. See also Giddens's (1984) effort to make sense of structure–agent dynamics by squaring structural influences with opportunities for choices.

22 This is not to say that claims cannot be qualified with degrees of surety. Toulmin's (1958) model of argumentation uses the term "qualifier" to cover this aspect of claim-making. General examples include both contextual information ("according to her usual habits") and degrees of certainty (probably, maybe, etc.). Given the importance of appropriateness in ethos, an unwarranted certainty could be just as damaging as a timorous uncertainty.

23 See Anstey (2006) for an intriguing perspective from architecture on how fresh beauty in decorum keeps conventions from calcifying.

24 For an interesting angle on aliveness, see Dreyfus (1999) on how to understand "playing" as an act of live engagement.

25 Aristotle (1954: 1356a).

26 The possibility for mixed messages and failed persuasion is always present, of course.

27 Habermas himself begins to turn to ethical life as a resource in his later work, e.g. (1996). For a similar critique of Habermas, see Aune's (2007) reading of Hegel's concept of *Sittlichkeit* (from "custom") as a rhetoric-friendly addition to the morality–ethics framework.

28 I should note again that Habermas has recently shifted his ground to admit to the need for a motivated incentive for action that cannot come from a neutral set of rules. For that reason, he now argues that motivations will spring from ethical ways of life, though he retains the goal of achieving a rational morality. See Habermas (1996, and 2010).

29 See Kohlberg (1981, 1984), and Habermas (1979d) has a chart on p. 77.

30 Kohlberg does indicate that there is a convergence between "natural" moral reasoning and philosophical imperatives at the highest stages.

31 This argument is in harmony with Benhabib's (1990) critique of Habermas; her amendment to Habermas's discourse ethics is to stay communicatively engaged.

32 See Cavell's (2004: 171) extended discussion of Rawls.

7 Recognition and the problem of solidarity

1 See Galston (2002: 4–7) on value pluralism.

2 Benedict's (2009) *Charity in Truth*.

3 See Saalmann (2002) for an excellent concise account of sociological approaches to solidarity from Tönnies, Durkheim, and others. Saalmann's summary of Bauman's (1993) distinctions among cognitive, aesthetic, and moral social spaces suggests these as distinct areas of life. A rhetorical twist lets us think of them as articulations of logos, pathos, and ethos in a discourse community. The multiplicity of discourse communities does gibe with Baumann's point that there can be social distance even when people are physically near each other. I do not think this necessarily means that "we live in semantically empty spaces" [(Saalmann 2002: 2), referencing (Bauman 1993: 158)]. We may be in a semantically meaningful but "virtual" (i.e., symbolic) space. A consequence of such an absence of mind during a presence of the body could be taken

in some circumstances as being overlooked (socially "cut" in the old-fashioned sense of the term), which could be an actively negative consequence.

4 See Appiah's (2008) critique of Sen's (2006) argument, that while Sen correctly connects identity and solidarity, he is too rationalist in his account of identity, taking inadequate account of the nonrational dimensions of both identity and solidarity.

5 See Honneth (2000): Hegel's theory of right is a dialectical progression from a rights-bearing individual, through a moral social actor, to an ethical citizen. Because, for Hegel, the individual can only come into full development (become "determinate") within an actual social context, the earlier stages (rights, morality) lack something important, what Honneth calls "suffering from indeterminacy." The suffering motivates the progression, and the ultimate achievement is (for Hegel) the relational connection of citizenship; hence, this interpretation of Hegel is a civic–republican model wherein civic participation is a necessary part of human flourishing.

It is also worth noting that the commutative paradigm does serve as a minimum condition for Adam Smith as well; the happiest society is one whose interaction proceeds from motives of love. The commutative regime will enable a society to persist even in the absence of love,

> among different men, as among different merchants, from a sense of its utility, without any mutual love or affection.... Society may subsist, though not in the most comfortable state, without beneficence; but the prevalence of injustice must utterly destroy it see.
>
> (*TMS* II.ii.3.1–3)

6 My discussion of the subjective–intersubjective dynamic in the prior chapter's discussion of Habermas bears on this point, in particular my argument that self-identification is enacted through membership in discourse communities, and hence is bound up with the audiences that comprise them – which necessarily also means bound up with the conceptions of a good life articulated in those discourse communities. To give a simple example, morality can fairly easily generate a moral rule that murder is wrong for everyone, no exceptions allowed ("="). The clarity of the moral rule is subject, however, to the tricky part of application – that defining what "murder" actually means in a given historical place and time cannot help but participate in the ethical discourses of the time and place, as do similar concepts of "self-defense" and related ideas.

7 That reason proceeds through communication is as true for strategic and instrumental reason as it is for coordinated social action. The difference is that instrumental reason, for instance, is cultivated by interaction (at the very least, in the process of education), but may be deployed in an instrumental fashion by an individual. Coordinated action, in contrast, can only be produced *by* communication.

8 My reservations about Habermas, as developed in the preceding chapter, could be thought of as primarily that he did not acknowledge the extent to which subjectivity is also intersubjective.

9 I say "quasi"-Rawlsian because Fraser eschews the thought-experiment approach of Rawls and goes straight to the actual practice of politics.

10 In terms of what political solutions would look like, Fraser distinguishes solutions for problems of maldistribution and of recognition as follows: two alternative courses of action exist for each: affirmative and transformational (Fraser 2003: 74). Affirmative action is ameliorative but not structural; transformational action is structural, and only transformational solutions actually resolve the problems. Welfare is the affirmative shape of economic distributive justice; socialism is the transformational shape. Recognition has similar affirmative and transformative shapes. The principle is to "redress status subordination by deconstructing the symbolic oppositions that underlie currently institutionalized patterns of cultural value. Far from simply raising the self-esteem of the misrecognized, it would destabilize existing status differentiations and change *everyone's* self-identity" (ibid. 75, original emphasis). Her example is "gay

identity politics [affirmative], which aims to revalue gay and lesbian sexuality, and 'queer politics,' [transformational] which proposes to deconstruct the binary opposition between homosexuality and heterosexuality" (ibid. 75). How either the change to socialism or the deconstruction of sexuality could actually happen remains unclear, aside from the tacit suggestion that the moral force of their claims on justice would help.

11 Consider the phenomenon of "political correctness" in its multiple variants. As a term of discourse its implicit meaning is Orwellian (invoking *1984*: 1961), meaning that it is politically dangerous to say what you really think. This implies at least two audiences: one that would approve and one that would condemn; the usual use of the term further implies that the disapproving audience has illegitimate authority and the approving audience must hide from it. See Kuran (1995) on preference-falsification. Kuran notes that people may falsify their preferences (say one thing but actually think or do another) out of fear of reproach, but he does not go so far as to wonder about the burdens of living in incommensurate discourse communities, because in his economic framework, personal preferences are "purely" personal (i.e., individual) and not connected to any community.

12 See Fraser (2003: 99, fn 32).

13 As part of her critique of Honneth as engaged in metaphysics, Fraser writes "those who embrace poststructuralist thought insist that the idea of recognition carries normalizing assumptions of centered subjectivity" (2003: 11). While this is generally true as a report on poststructuralist thought, what remains to be spelled out is the extent to which the normalizing assumptions referred to are considered to be essentialized characteristics of the subject.

   A contingent and de-centered view of the subject, which I think Honneth advances, is not subject to the same criticisms. An important critique of centered subjectivity, for instance, stems from Freudian psychoanalytic concepts that delimit the scope and control of ego functions. To refer to a centered self-willing subject, in this view, is to refer to an illusion of control within a subjectivity that encompasses the desires of the body as well as contradictions and inconsistencies. Honneth (2006), however, offers an alternative interpretation of Freud's concepts by suggesting object relations as a more comprehensive explanatory framework of infant psychological development than the theory that the drives of the body (the Freudian id) are the motor, in the sense of the problem to resolve, of psychological development. The advantage of object relations is that it places the earliest psychological development as occurring within the relational context of recognition between parent and infant. For more on object relations, see Winnicott (1980). The relational emphasis is an advantage over the model of the self-maximizing hedonic individual that is implicit in the drive model, which is perhaps another instance of the dominance of the concept of the self-maximizing individual in the nineteenth century.

   In terms of the rhetorical model of identity I have been arguing for (and which I think is close to Honneth's), a critique of "normalizing assumptions of centered subjectivity" likewise misses coming to grips with the contingent nature of subjectivity. In the rhetorical model, the very idea of a centered subjectivity only comes to exist through participating in a discourse community (say, the Western metaphysical tradition) that shares it as an assumption. Indeed, one of my central claims about the rhetorical construction of identity is that *no* discourse is free of normalizing assumptions, at least in the sense that every discourse develops its own sense of fittingness, of decorum.

14 This is in line with Habermas's argument that practical reason has been detached from public life in the modern era, where it is only useful for guiding personal decisions. This is a condition of pluralism.

15 The bias, in the most neutral possible sense of an inclination to take a beaten path, of an already-individualist disposition is Honneth's ready acceptance of Bernhard

Peters's (1999) distinction between individualist and communalist forms of identity politics (Honneth 2003: 163 fn 65). The disjunctive assumption underlying the logic of treatment already participates in an individualist framework, and hence begs the question of the nature of the relation between individual and community: in Peters's view, either a given case is about the condition of an individual or it is about the condition of a group; if about an individual, the principle of universal equality in law applies; if about a group, then claims to negative freedoms (e.g., freedom from persecution) would also come under the heading of equality under law. The demand for social recognition of a minority group, however, would by definition not meet the normative requirements for achievement of civil society, and so would have no claim of injustice. Honneth's point is that recognition beyond the domain of legal equality may not be available to identity groups; it is not to be expected that social norms would expand so far as to include others' norms, though they might conceivably stretch so far through an act similar to love, but that would exceed the act of recognition. No other possibility of identity is available outside the problem of stereotype-harm to an individual on the one hand and a thoroughgoing communitarian positioning of a group on the other.

Honneth does acknowledge the possibility of a fourth domain coming into being that would require that we recognize one another across cultural difference to the extent that we would offer "well-meaning attention" to the possible value of norms other than our own (2003: 169), but appears to consider this a largely speculative activity at present.

In a similar vein, see Fish (2008) for an argument distinguishing between "interest" and "tribal" versions of identity politics. Fish classifies "interest" groups as liberal, and therefore legitimate, and "tribal" as illiberal. In all these instances, the analytic distinction between individual and group slices too sharply, losing the possible concreteness of holding them together, that is, at the same time, and hence losing the possibility of a recognition of belonging that does not weigh achievement.

16 This serves as my understanding of Derrida's (1977: 158–159) "*il n'y a pas de hors-texte*": there is nothing outside the text. Often misinterpreted (and dismissed) as an ontological statement about the nature of reality, I interpret Derrida to be referring to the world of meanings, which do indeed only exist in "text" writ large, as all discourse.

17 See Blumenberg (1987). This is also how I understand Giddens's (1984) approach in structuration theory – to examine the possibilities for human agency within the constraints of social structures, including roles which individuals play out. In particular, see Clement (1998), who uses the concept of autonomy as a way of testing positions in the justice vs. care debate; ch. two has a particularly good discussion of how to understand the socially constituted aspects of autonomy.

18 Most of the works on rhetoric cited in this book touch on rhetorical invention. For metaphor, see Anstey (2006), Corbett (1990), Eubanks (2000), Hansen (1999), Hauser (1999), Kauffman (1990), Lakoff, and Johnson (1980), Leff (1983), McCloskey (1985), McKeon (1973), Ricoeur (1977), Rosenblatt (1978), Turpin (2003), Vico (1990).

19 Cavell (1981) has chapters examining the films *The Lady Eve*, *It Happened One Night*, *Bringing Up Baby*, *The Philadelphia Story*, *His Girl Friday*, *Adam's Rib*, and *The Awful Truth*.

20 See also Coontz (2004) and Giddens (1992) on the changes in modern understandings of marriage. Cavell's interest in the remarriage comedies is in how the cinema, as art, casts up practical efforts to understand and integrate the consequences of new equalities, slender as those equalities may have seemed at the time.

21 This tension also has the dimension of socio-cultural matrix vs. methodological individualism, or more simply community–individual (as in Clark 1998), where individualism's aim is to escape the conformity that social convention tends to press for.

22 Rawls attempts to avoid the problems of over-abstraction in his Original Position by keeping general knowledge (what society may be like) but removing specific knowledge (where you or I would stand) behind the veil of ignorance. See Richardson (2005) for an overview.

23 Habermas, in arguing for a communicative theory of reason, transforms part of Kant's two basic conditions that mark human moral capacity: (a) the capacity to reason among alternatives; and (b) the capacity to choose a good (i.e., one thing over another). Habermas's theory transforms (b) into a capacity to reason interactively, in theory to enable a collective transformation of (a) through decision making that derives from interaction in the public sphere. I have argued that Habermas's theoretical structure remains overly abstract, though there are signs that he is reconsidering the relative contribution of ethical forms of life (see, e.g., Habermas 1996: 463–490).

Grace Clement (1998), in examining the justice vs. care debate, approaches these Kantian categories in an interesting way in her first two chapters that offers a practical way to consider ethical forms of life in concrete terms. She approaches the debate by beginning with ideal types of justice and care, which she subsequently assesses with respect to autonomy as a criterion for the moral appropriateness of each. She notes that the ethic of justice, as basically a Kantian/Enlightenment notion of equal treatment of individuals, is strongly oriented to a definition of autonomy characterized by two conditions, one negative and one positive: (a) the absence of coercion, and (b) the ability to reflect critically on one's choices. This characterization of autonomy, however, is highly individualistic (and Kantian) in the sense that it emphasizes autonomy as an individual psychological and reflective process connected with the will.

If we are to find real complementarity between justice and care, Clement argues, this view of autonomy needs amendment. Her source for amendment comes from understanding the self as being socially constituted as well as individually experienced. She does not, however, *displace* the individualistic model of identity with a socially constituted one, as is often the case with continental critiques of agency; rather, she *adds* the issue of socially constituted identity to that of individually experienced identity. Then, emphasizing pragmatic observations of the world around us over rigorous definitions, she notes that we readily see that some people have more autonomy than others.

Therefore, Clement argues, the way to amend an idealized Kantian notion of autonomy with a socially constituted model of identity is as follows:

a The negative condition of freedom from coercion should be thought of as a limit-case. Our experience of differentials in social power – e.g., between the power of doctors and the power of nurses (not to mention both of them in relation to the power of patients) – should alert us to the effects of pragmatic constraints on autonomy arising from differences in social power.
b The positive condition of critical reflection on alternatives should recognize the potential for social "blinders" that might inhibit genuinely critical reflection, the remedy for which is the active encouragement of alternative critical voices in social issues.

Clement's refinement of coercion as a problem of power shifts the critical issue from a binary question (is something coercive or not?) to one of degree (how is [this] constraining?). Similarly, her refinement of critical reflection with regard to choice from an idiosyncratic-individual perspective to one that is socially informed allows for a self-questioning that actively seeks outside/other arguments.

Using constraints as a broader framework than coercion for thinking about the operation of power is highly compatible with the rhetorical ideas I have been foregrounding in my argument, particularly with respect to understanding communication as the interaction of individual-with-discourse community (I use the hyphenated form to emphasize the shifting positions of sometimes rhetor, sometimes audience). The basic dynamic of individual with discourse community is of course made complex by the many different discourse communities that actual persons participate in, so that the expression "to be of two minds about something" could represent a reflection on two competing discourse principles. In the case of doctors and nurses, say, between a discourse of technical procedure and a discourse of considering an array of patient needs.

24 An additional and ongoing problem is the tendency to use the term "democracy" as subsuming the principles of liberalism. This has become a commonplace in U.S. (especially classical liberal) discourse about Muslim countries, including George W. Bush's acceptance of the neoconservative rationale for invading Iraq to promote democracy. "Democracy," in that usage, actually means a state organized on liberal principles, not just the process of holding elections, as is confoundingly demonstrated by democratic (but not liberal) outcomes such as Hamas winning Palestinian elections. See Zakaria (2003) on this topic. Fukuyama did break with neoconservatives over the Iraq war. See Krauthammer (2004, 2005) and Fukuyama (2004, 2005) for an exchange between them in the pages of *The National Interest*, followed by Fukuyama's (2006) account of where he thought neoconservatives misinterpreted its principles in formulating Iraq and war-on-terror policy.

25 See again Becker and Posner (2009) and Drucker (1993), for example, for arguments that policies should promote profitability in order to attract investment. Generally speaking, this "supply side" orientation among classical liberals is countered by a "demand side" orientation among modern liberals, which argues for consumer-friendly policies to create market opportunities for investors.

26 See, e.g., Lewis (2010), Lowenstein (2000, 2010), and especially Roubini and Nihm (2010). For a recantation of a formerly confirmed classical liberal, see Posner (2009).

Bibliography

Althusser, L. (1971) *Lenin and Philosophy: And Other Essays*, New York, Monthly Review Press.

Alvey, J. E. (2003) *Adam Smith: Optimist or Pessimist? A New Problem Concerning the Teleological Basis of Commercial Society*, Aldershot, Eng., Ashgate.

Anstey, T. (2006) The dangers of decorum. *Architectural Research Quarterly*, 10, 131–139.

Anton, C. & Peterson, V. V. (2003) Who said what: Subject positions, rhetorical strategies and good faith. *Communication Studies*, 54, 403–419.

Appiah, K. A. (2008) Bending towards justice. *Journal of Human Development*, 9, 343–355.

Aquinas, T. (1947) *Summa Theologica/St. Thomas Aquinas;* literally translated by Fathers of the English Dominican Province, New York, Benziger Bros.

Aristotle (1954) *Rhetoric*, New York, The Modern Library.

Aristotle (1987) *The Nicomachean Ethics*, Buffalo, N.Y., Prometheus Books.

Aune, J. A. (1994) *Rhetoric and Marxism*, Boulder, Westview Press.

Aune, J. A. (2001) *Selling the Free Market: The Rhetoric of Economic Correctness*, New York, Guilford Press.

Aune, J. A. (2007) "Only connect": Between morality and ethics in Habermas' communication theory. *Communication Theory*, 17, 340–347.

Austen, J. ([1813] 1996) *Pride and Prejudice*, Norwalk CT, Easton Press.

Austen, J. ([1815] 1976) *Emma*. The Complete Novels of Jane Austen. First Vintage Books Edition; rpt. of 1950 Random House ed., New York, Random House.

Austin, J. L. (1976) *How to Do Things with Words*, London, Oxford University Press.

Azar, O. H. (2004) What sustains social norms and how do they evolve? The case of tipping. *Journal of Economic Behavior and Organization*, 54, 49–64.

Barthes, R. (1977) The death of the author. *Image, Music, Text,* New York, Hill and Wang.

Bauman, Z. (1993) *Postmodern Ethics*, Oxford, UK; Cambridge, Mass., Blackwell.

Becker, G. (2009) Government demand for drugs and drug prices–Becker. In Posner, G. B. A. R. (Ed.) *The Becker–Posner Blog.* Chicago, University of Chicago. December 27, 2009 http://uchicagolaw.typepad.com/beckerposner/2009/12/index.html February 10, 2010.

Becker, G., and R. Posner (2009) Should the government use its monopsony power to reduce the price of drugs? Chicago (http://uchicagolaw.typepad.com/beckerposner/), University of Chicago.

Bellah, R. N. (2008) *Habits of the Heart: Individualism and Commitment in American Life*, Berkeley, University of California Press.

Benedict, P. (2009) *Charity in Truth (Caritas in Veritate): Encyclical Letter*, San Francisco, Ignatius Press.

Benhabib, S. (1990) Afterword: Communicative ethics and current controversies in practical philosophy. In Dallmayr, F. and S. Benhabib (Ed.) *The Communicative Ethics Controversy*. Cambridge, Mass., MIT Press.

Bentham, J. ([1789] 1988) *The Principles of Morals and Legislation*, Buffalo, N.Y., Prometheus Books.

Berlin, I. (2002) *Liberty*, Oxford, Oxford University Press.

Berns, L. (1994) Aristotle and Adam Smith on justice: Cooperation between ancients and moderns? *The Review of Metaphysics*, 48, 71–91.

Bitterman, H. J. (1940a) Adam Smith's empiricism and the law of nature: I. *Journal of Political Economy*, 48, 487–520.

Bitterman, H. J. (1940b) Adam Smith's empiricism and the law of nature: II. *Journal of Political Economy*, 48, 703–734.

Bizzell, P., and B. Herzberg (Ed.) (1990) *The Rhetorical Tradition: Readings from Classical Times to the Present*, Boston, Bedford Books of St. Martin's Press.

Blumenberg, H. (1987) An anthropological approach to the contemporary significance of rhetoric. In Baynes, K., J. Bohman, and T. McCarthy (Ed.) *After Philosophy: End or Transformation?* Cambridge, Mass., The MIT Press.

Booth, W. C. (1974) *Modern Dogma and the Rhetoric of Assent*, Chicago, The University of Chicago Press.

Booth, W. C. (1983) *The Rhetoric of Fiction*, 2nd ed., Chicago, The University of Chicago Press.

Booth, W. C. (1988) *The Company We Keep: An Ethics of Fiction*, Berkeley, University of California Press.

Boulding, K. (1969) Economics as a moral science. *The American Economic Review*, 59, 1–12.

Boulding, K. E. (1985) *Human Betterment*, Beverly Hills, Sage.

Brewer, J. (1989) *The Sinews of Power: War, Money, and the English State, 1688–1783*, New York, Alfred A. Knopf.

Brown, V. (1991) Signifying voices: Reading the "Adam Smith Problem". *Economics and Philosophy*, 7, 187–220.

Brown, V. (1993) Decanonizing discourses: Textual analysis and the history of economic thought. In Henderson, W., T. Dudley-Evans, and R. Backhouse (Ed.) *Economics and Language*. London, Routledge.

Brown, V. (1994) *Adam Smith's Discourse: Canonicity, Commerce, and Conscience*, London, Routledge.

Brown, V. (1995) The moral self and ethical dialogism: Three genres. *Philosophy and Rhetoric*, 28, 276–299.

Brown, V. (1997) "Mere Inventions of the Imagination": A survey of recent literature on Adam Smith. *Economics and Philosophy*, 13, 281–312.

Bühler, K. (1934) *Sprachtheorie; die darstellungsfunktion der sprache*, Jena, G. Fischer.

Butterfield, H. ([1931] 1978. Reprint) *The Whig Interpretation of History*, Original publication, London, G. Bell & Sons.

Campbell, T. D. (1971) *Adam Smith's Science of Morals*, London, George Allen & Unwin Ltd.

Campbell, W. F. (1967) Adam Smith's theory of justice, prudence, and beneficence. *The American Economic Review*, 57, 571–577.

Cannan, E. ([1904], 1976) Preface, Editor's Introduction. In Cannan, E. (Ed.) *An Enquiry into the Nature and Causes of the Wealth of Nations*, by Adam Smith. Chicago, The University of Chicago Press.

Caporaso, J. A., and D. P. Levine (1992) *Theories of Political Economy*, Cambridge, Cambridge University Press.

Cavell, S. (1969) *Must We Mean What We Say? A Book of Essays*, New York, Scribner.

Cavell, S. (1979) *The Claim of Reason: Wittgenstein, Skepticism, Morality, and Tragedy*, Oxford; New York, Clarendon Press.

Cavell, S. (1981) *Pursuits of Happiness: The Hollywood Comedy of Remarriage*, Cambridge, Mass., Harvard University Press.

Cavell, S. (1994) *A Pitch of Philosophy: Autobiographical Exercises*, Cambridge, Mass., Harvard University Press.

Cavell, S. (1996) *Contesting Tears: The Hollywood Melodrama of the Unknown Woman*, Chicago, University of Chicago Press.

Cavell, S. (2004) *Cities of Words: Pedagogical Letters on a Register of the Moral Life*, Cambridge, Mass., Belknap Press of Harvard University Press.

Cavell, S. (2005) *Philosophy the Day After Tomorrow*, Cambridge, Mass., Belknap Press of Harvard University Press.

Charland, M. (1987) Constitutive rhetoric: The case of the *Peuple Quebecois*. *Quarterly Journal of Speech*, 73, 133–150.

Charland, M. (1994) Norms and laughter in rhetorical culture. *Quarterly Journal of Speech*. National Communication Association.

Cheney, G. (1999) *Values at Work : Employee Participation Meets Market Pressure at Mondragón*, Ithaca, N.Y., Cornell University Press.

Choi, Y. B. (1990) Smith's view on human nature: A problem in the interpretation of *The Wealth of Nations* and *The Theory of Moral Sentiments*. *Review of Social Economy*, 48.3, n.p.

Cicero ([1913], 1997) *De Officiis*, Cambridge, Mass., Harvard University Press.

Clark, B. (1998) *Political Economy: A Comparative Approach*, Westport, Connecticut, Praeger.

Clark, J. B. (1925) Distribution, Ethics of. In Higgs, H. (Ed.) *Palgrave's Dictionary of Political Economy*. London, Macmillan & Co., Ltd.

Clement, G. (1998) *Care, Autonomy, and Justice: Feminism and the Ethic of Care*, Boulder, CO, Westview Press.

Coase, R. H. (1960) The problem of social cost. *The Journal of Law and Economics*, 3, 1–44.

Coase, R. H. (1978) Economics and contiguous disciplines. *Journal of Legal Studies*, 7, 201–211.

Coase, R. H. (1994a) Adam Smith's view of man. *Essays on Economics and Economists*. Chicago, University of Chicago Press.

Coase, R. H. (1994b) *Essays on Economics and Economists*, Chicago, University of Chicago Press.

Coats, A. W. (1988) Economic rhetoric: The social and historical context. In Klamer, A., D. McCloskey, and R. M. Solow (Ed.) *The Consequences of Economic Rhetoric*. Cambridge, Cambridge University Press.

Colfax, R. H. ([1833], 1973) *Evidence Against the View of the Abolitionists Consisting of Physical and Moral Proofs, of the Natural Inferiority of the Negroes*, New York, J. T. M. Bleakley.

Collings, D., and A. Ortmann (1997) Reading Adam Smith's discourse: A review essay. *Research in the History of Economic Thought and Methodology*, 15, 329–336.

Cooke, M. (1997) Authenticity and autonomy: Taylor, Habermas, and the politics of recognition. *Political Theory*, 25, 258–288.

Coontz, S. (2004) The world historical transformation of marriage. *Journal of Marriage and Family*, 66, 974–979.

Corbett, E. P. J. (1990) *Classical Rhetoric for the Modern Student*, New York, Oxford University Press.

Cremaschi, S. (1989) Adam Smith: Skeptical Newtonianism, disenchanted republicanism, and the birth of social science. In Dascal, M., and O. Gruengard (Ed.) *Knowledge and Politics: Case Studies in the Relationship Between Epistemology and Political Philosophy*. Boulder, Westview Press.

Cropsey, J. (1957) *Polity and Economy; An Interpretation of the Principles of Adam Smith*, The Hague, M. Nijhoff.

Cropsey, J. (2001) *Polity and Economy: With Further Thoughts on the Principles of Adam Smith*, South Bend, Ind., St. Augustine's Press.

Crouch, C., and D. Marquand (Ed.) (1993) *Ethics and Markets: Cooperation and Competition within Capitalist Economies*, Oxford, Blackwell Publishers.

Derrida, J. (1977) *Of Grammatology*, Baltimore, Johns Hopkins University. Press.

Dreyfus, H. L. (1999) The primacy of phenomenology over logical analysis: A critique of Searle. *Philosophical Topics*, 27.

Drucker, P. F. (1993) *Post-Capitalist Society*, New York, HarperBusiness, HarperCollins.

Durkheim, É. (2008) *The Division of Labor in Society*, New York, Free Press.

Elliott, J. E. (2000) Adam Smith's conceptualization of power, markets, and politics. *Review of Social Economy*, 58, 429–454.

Elster, J. (1989) Social norms and economic theory. *The Journal of Economic Perspectives*, 3, 99–117.

Elster, J. (1989) *The Cement Of Society: A Study of Social Order*, Cambridge, Cambridge University Press.

Emerson, R. W. ([1860], 1932) Wealth. *The Works of Emerson*. New York, Black's Readers Service Co.

Etzioni, A. (1988) *The Moral Dimension: Toward a New Economics*, New York, The Free Press.

Eubanks, P. (2000) *A War of Words in the Discourse of Trade: The Rhetorical Constitution of Metaphor*, Carbondale, Southern Illinois University Press.

Evensky, J. (1987) The two voices of Adam Smith: Moral philosopher and social critic. *History of Political Economy*, 19.

Evensky, J. (1989) The evolution of Adam Smith's views on political economy. *History of Political Economy*, 21, 123–145.

Evensky, J. (1992) Ethics and the classical liberal tradition in economics. *History of Political Economy*, 24, 61–77.

Evensky, J. (1993a) Adam Smith on the human foundation of a successful liberal society. *History of Political Economy*, 25, 395–412.

Evensky, J. (1993b) Retrospectives: Ethics and the invisible hand. *Journal of Economic Perspectives*, 7, 197–205.

Evensky, J. (1998) Adam Smith's moral philosophy: The role of religion and its relationship to philosophy and ethics in the evolution of society. *History of Political Economy*, 30, 17–42.

Evensky, J. (2005) *Adam Smith's Moral Philosophy: A Historical and Contemporary Perspective on Markets, Law, Ethics, and Culture*, Cambridge, Cambridge University Press.

Faber, D. (2009) House of Cards. CNBC.com. http://classic.cnbc.com/id/28892719/ June 15, 2010.

Farrell, T. B. (1976) Knowledge, consensus, and rhetorical theory. *Quarterly Journal of Speech*, 62, 1–14.

Farrell, T. B. (1985) Narrative in natural discourse: On conversation and rhetoric. *Journal of Communication*, 35, 109–127.

Farrell, T. B. (1990) From the Parthenon to the bassinet: Death and rebirth along the epistemic trail. *Quarterly Journal of Speech*, 76, 78.

Farrell, T. B. (1993) *Norms of Rhetorical Culture*, New Haven, Yale University Press.

Farrell, T. B. (1997) An elliptical postscript. In Gross, A. G., and W. M. Keith (Ed.) *Rhetorical Hermeneutics: Invention and Interpretation in the Age of Science.* Albany, State University of New York Press.

Farrell, T. B. (2008) Rhetoric in history as theory and praxis: A blast from the past. *Philosophy and Rhetoric*, 41, 323–336.

Farrell, T. B. (2008) The weight of rhetoric: Studies in cultural delirium. *Philosophy and Rhetoric*, 41, 467–487.

Fish, S. (1980) *Is There a Text in This Class? The Authority of Interpretive Communities*, Cambridge, Mass., Harvard University Press.

Fish, S. (2008) When "identity politics" is rational. *The Opinionator Blog.* Online ed. New York, New York Times Online. February 17, http://opinionator.blogs.nytimes.com/2008/02/17/when-identity-politics-is-rational/?scp=1-b&sq=when+identity+politics+is+rational&st=nyt June 26, 2010.

Fisher, W. R. (1970) "A motive view of communication". *Quarterly Journal of Speech*, 56, 131–139.

Fisher, W. R. (1973) Reaffirmation and the subversion of the American Dream. *Quarterly Journal of Speech*, 59, 160–167.

Fisher, W. R. (1978) Toward a logic of good reasons. *Quarterly Journal of Speech*, 64, 376–384.

Fisher, W. R. (1984) Narration as human communication paradigm: The case of public moral argument. *Communication Monographs*, 51, 1–22.

Fisher, W. R. (1985a) The narrative paradigm: In the beginning. *Journal of Communication*, 35, 74–89.

Fisher, W. R. (1985b) The narrative paradigm: An elaboration. *Communication Monographs*, 52, 347–367.

Fisher, W. R. (1987) *Human Communication as Narration: Toward a Philosophy of Reason, Value, and Action*, Columbia, University of South Carolina Press.

Fisher, W. R. (1988) The narrative paradigm and the assessment of historical texts. *Argumentation and Advocacy*, 25, 49–53.

Fisher, W. R. (1989) Clarifying the narrative paradigm. *Communication Monographs*, 56, 55–58.

Fisher, W. R. (1992) Narration, reason, and community. In Brown, R. H. (Ed.) *Writing the Social Text: Poetics and Politics in Social Science Discourse.* New York, Aldine de Gruyter.

Fisher, W. R. (1994) Narrative rationality and the logic of scientific discourse. *Argumentation*, 8, 21–32.

Fisher, W. R., and S. D. O'Leary (1996) The rhetorician's quest. In Salwen, M., and D. Stacks (Ed.) *An Integrated Approach to Communication Theory and Research.* Hillsdale, NJ, Lawrence Erlbaum.

Fisk, M. (1991) Review: Elster, Marx, and method. *Nous*, 25, 215–220.

Fitzgibbons, A. (1995) *Adam Smith's System of Liberty, Wealth, and Virtue: The Moral and Political Foundations of The Wealth of Nations*, Oxford, Clarendon Press.

Fleischacker, S. (1999) *A Third Concept of Liberty: Judgment and Freedom in Kant and Adam Smith*, Princeton, NJ, Princeton University Press.

Fleischacker, S. (2002) Adam Smith's Reception among the American Founders, 1776–1790. *The William and Mary Quarterly*, 59, 897–924.

Fleischacker, S. (2004a) *On Adam Smith's* Wealth of Nations*: A Philosophical Companion*, Princeton, Princeton University Press.

Fleischacker, S. (2004b) *A Short History of Distributive Justice*, Cambridge, Mass., Harvard University Press.

Floyd, S. (2006) Thomas Aquinas: Moral philosophy. In Fieser, J., and B. Dowden (Ed.) *The Internet Encyclopedia of Philosophy.*

Frank, J. (1998) Democracy and distribution: Aristotle on just desert. *Political Theory*, 26, 784–802.

Frank, J. (2005) *A Democracy of Distinction: Aristotle and the Work of Politics*, Chicago, University of Chicago Press.

Fraser, N. (1990) Rethinking the public sphere: A contribution to the critique of actually existing democracy. *Social Text*, 25/26, 56–80.

Fraser, N. (2003) Social justice in the age of identity politics: Redistribution, recognition, and participation. *Redistribution or Recognition? A Political–Philosophical Exchange.* London, Verso.

Fraser, N., and A. Honneth (2003) *Redistribution or Recognition? A Political–Philosophical Exchange*, London, Verso.

Frederickson, G. M. (1987) *The Black Image in the White Mind: The Debate on Afro-American Character and Destiny, 1817–1914*, Middleton [Conn.], Wesleyan University Press.

Friedman, M. (1962) *Capitalism and Freedom*, Chicago, The University of Chicago Press.

Friedman, M. (1982) Preface. *Capitalism and Freedom.* Chicago, The University of Chicago Press.

Friedman, M. (2002) Preface. *Capitalism and Freedom.* Chicago, The University of Chicago Press.

Friedman, M., and P. A. Samuelson (1980) *Milton Friedman and Paul A. Samuelson Discuss the Economic Responsibility of Government*, College Station, TX, The Center for Education and Research in Free Enterprise.

Friedman, M., and R. D. Friedman (1980) *Free to Choose: A Personal Statement*, San Diego, Harcourt: Harvest Books.

Friedman, M., and R. D. Friedman (1998) *Two Lucky People: Memoirs*, Chicago, University of Chicago Press.

Fukuyama, F. (1989) The end of history? *The National Interest*, 16, 3–18.

Fukuyama, F. (1992) *The End of History and the Last Man*, New York, The Free Press: Macmillan.

Fukuyama, F. (2004) The neoconservative moment. *The National Interest*, 57–68.

Fukuyama, F. (2005) Fukuyama responds. *National Interest*, 11.

Fukuyama, F. (2006) *America at the Crossroads: Democracy, Power, and the Neoconservative Legacy*, New Haven, Yale University Press.

Fuller, M. L. (1990) *The Excitement Is Building*, Dallas, Word Publishing.

Gadamer, H. G. (1994) *Truth and Method*, New York, Continuum.

Galbraith, J. K. (1983) *The Anatomy of Power*, Boston, Houghton Mifflin Co.

Galston, W. A. (2002) *Liberal Pluralism: The Implications of Value Pluralism for Political Theory and Practice*, Cambridge, UK; New York, Cambridge University Press.

Gaonkar, D. P. (1994) The very idea of a rhetorical culture. *Quarterly Journal of Speech*, 80, 333.

Gaonkar, D. P. (1997) Close readings of the third kind: Reply to my critics. In Gross, A. G., and W. M. Keith (Ed.) *Rhetorical Hermeneutics: Invention and Interpretation in the Age of Science.* Albany, State University of New York Press.

Gaonkar, D. P. (1997) The idea of rhetoric in the rhetoric of science. In Gross, A. G., and W. M. Keith (Ed.) *Rhetorical Hermeneutics: Invention and Interpretation in the Age of Science.* Albany, State University of New York Press.

Giddens, A. (1984) *The Constitution of Society: Outline of the Theory of Structuration*, Berkeley, University of California Press.

Giddens, A. (1991) *Modernity and Self-Identity: Self and Society in the Late Modern Age*, Stanford, Stanford University Press.

Giddens, A. (1992) *The Transformation of Intimacy: Sexuality, Love and Eroticism in Modern Societies*, Stanford, CA, Stanford University Press.

Gilligan, C. (1982a) New maps of development: New visions of maturity. *American Journal of Orthopsychiatry*, 52, 199–212.

Gilligan, C. (1982b) *In a Different Voice: Psychological Theory and Women's Development*, Cambridge, Mass., Harvard University Press.

Griswold, C. L., Jr. (1991) Rhetoric and ethics: Adam Smith on theorizing about the moral sentiments. *Philosophy and Rhetoric*, 24, 213–237.

Griswold, C. L., Jr. (1995) Reassembling Smith. *Times Literary Supplement*. London.

Griswold, C. L., Jr. (1999) *Adam Smith and the Virtues of the Enlightenment*, Cambridge, Cambridge University Press.

Gross, A. G. (1990) Rhetoric of science *is* epistemic rhetoric. *Quarterly Journal of Speech*, 76, 304–306.

Gross, A. G. (1999) A theory of the rhetorical audience: Reflections on Chaim Perelman. *Quarterly Journal of Speech*, 85, 203–211.

Gross, A. G., and M. Dascal (2001) Conceptual unity of Aristotle's rhetoric. *Philosophy and Rhetoric*, 34, 275–291.

Gross, A. G., and W. M. Keith (Ed.) (1997) *Rhetorical Hermeneutics: Invention and Interpretation in the Age of Science*, Albany, State University of New York Press.

Grotius, H. ([1625], 1990. Reprint) *The Rights of War and Peace*, Original publication, London, M. Walter Dunne, 1901.

Haakonssen, K. (1981) *The Science of a Legislator: The Natural Jurisprudence of David Hume and Adam Smith*, Cambridge, Cambridge University Press.

Haakonssen, K. (1996) *Natural Law and Moral Philosophy: From Grotius to the Scottish Enlightenment*, Cambridge, Cambridge University Press.

Habermas, J. (1975) *Legitimation Crisis*, Boston, Beacon Press.

Habermas, J. (1976) Some distinctions in universal pragmatics: A working paper. *Theory and Society*, 3, 155–167.

Habermas, J. (1979a) The public sphere. In Siegelaub, A. M. A. S. (Ed.) *Communication and Class Struggle: An Anthology in 2 Volumes.* New York, International General.

Habermas, J. (1979b) *Communication and the Evolution of Society*, Boston, Beacon Press.

Habermas, J. (1979c) What is universal pragmatics? *Communication and the Evolution of Society.* Boston, Beacon Press.

Habermas, J. (1979d) Moral development and ego identity. *Communication and the evolution of society.* Boston, Beacon Press.

Habermas, J. (1984a) *The Theory of Communicative Action: Reason and the Rationalization of Society*, Boston, Beacon Press.

Habermas, J. (1984b [1981]) *The Theory of Communicative Action: Lifeworld and System: A Critique of Functionalist Reason*, Boston, Beacon Press.

Habermas, J. (1989 [1962]) *The Structural Transformation of the Public Sphere: An Inquiry into a Category of Bourgeois Society*, Cambridge, Mass., MIT Press.

Habermas, J. (1990 [1983]) *Moral Consciousness and Communicative Action*, Cambridge MA, MIT Press.

Habermas, J. (1996 [1992]) *Between Facts and Norms: Contributions to a Discourse Theory of Democracy*, Cambridge, Mass., MIT Press.

Habermas, J. (2002 [1973]) *Theory and Practice*, Boston, Beacon Press.

Habermas, J. (2006) Political communication in media society: Does democracy still enjoy an epistemic dimension? The impact of normative theory on empirical research. *Communication Theory (10503293)*, 16, 411–426.

Habermas, J. (2010) *An Awareness of What Is Missing: Faith and Reason in a Post-Secular Age*, Cambridge, Polity.

Habermas, J., and H. Constantinides (1998) What is universal pragmatics? *IEEE Transactions on Professional Communication*, 41, 143–145.

Habermas, J., J. Ratzinger (Pope Benedict), and F. Schuller (2006) *Dialectics of Secularization: On Reason and Religion*, San Francisco, Ignatius Press.

Haidt, J. (2008) What makes people vote republican? In J. Brockman (Ed.) *Edge: The Third Culture*. Edge Foundations, Inc. September 9, 2008 http://edge.org/3rd_culture/haidt08/haidt08_index.html September 15, 2008.

Hansen, M. B. (1999) The mass production of the senses: Classical cinema as vernacular modernism. *Modernism/Modernity*, 6, 59–77.

Hardin, R. (1999) From Bodo ethics to distributive justice. *Ethical Theory and Moral Practice*, 2, 399–413.

Hariman, R. (1995) *Political Style: The Artistry of Power*, Chicago, University of Chicago Press.

Hauser, G. A. (1998) Civil society and the principle of the public sphere. *Philosophy and Rhetoric*, 31, 20–41.

Hauser, G. A. (1999) Aristotle on epideictic: The formation of public morality. *Rhetoric Society Quarterly*, 29, 5–23.

Hauser, G. A. (1999) *Vernacular Voices: The Rhetoric of Publics and Public Spheres*, Columbia SC, University of South Carolina Press.

Hauser, G. A. (2008) The moral vernacular of human rights discourse. *Philosophy and Rhetoric*, 41, 440–466.

Hausman, D., and M. S. McPherson (1993) Taking ethics seriously: Economics and contemporary moral philosophy. *Journal of Economic Literature*, 31, 671–731.

Hayek, F. A. (1988) *The Fatal Conceit: The Errors of Socialism*, Chicago, The University of Chicago Press.

Hegel, G. W. F. (1995) *Reason in History: A General Introduction to the Philosophy of History*, New York, Prentice Hall.

Hegel, G. W. F. (2002) *The Philosophy of Right/Uniform Title: Grundlinien der Philosophie des Rechts*. Trans. Dyde, S. W., Newburyport, MA, Focus Pub./ R. Pullins.

Hegel, G. W. F. (2005) *Philosophy of Right*, Trans. Hartman, R. S. Mineloa, N.Y., Dover Publications.

Heilbroner, R. L. (1980) *Marxism, For and Against*, New York, Norton.

Heilbroner, R. L. (1982) The socialization of the individual in Adam Smith. *History of Political Economy*, 14, 427–439.

Heilbroner, R. L. (1985) *The Nature and Logic of Capitalism*, New York, W. W. Norton & Company.

Heilbroner, R. L. (1990) Economics as ideology. In Samuels, W. J. (Ed.) *Economics As Discourse: An Analysis of the Language of Economists.* Boston, Kluwer Academic Publishers.

Heilbroner, R. L. (1992) *The Worldly Philosophers: The Lives, Times, and Ideas of the Great Economic Thinkers*, New York, Touchstone: Simon & Schuster.

Held, V. (2006) *The Ethics of Care: Personal, Political, and Global*, Oxford, Oxford University Press.

Heller, J. (1961) *Catch-22, a novel*, New York, Simon & Schuster.

Hobbes, T. ([1651] 1962) *Leviathan: Or the Matter, Forme and Power of a Commonwealth Ecclesiasticall and Civill*, London, Collier Books.

Holub, R. C. (1991) *Jürgen Habermas: Critic in the Public Sphere*, London; New York, Routledge.

Honneth, A. (1995) *The Struggle for Recognition: The Moral Grammar of Social Conflicts*, Cambridge Mass, The MIT Press.

Honneth, A. (2000) *Suffering from Indeterminacy: An Attempt at a Reactualization of Hegel's Philosophy of Right*, Amsterdam, Van Gorcum Ltd.

Honneth, A. (2003) Redistribution as recognition: A response to Nancy Fraser. In Fraser, N. and A. Honneth *Redistribution or Recognition? A Political–Philosophical Exchange.* London, Verso.

Honneth, A. (2006) The work of negativity: A psychoanalytic revision of the theory of recognition. *Critical Horizons*, 7, 101–111.

Honneth, A. (2007) *Disrespect: The Normative Foundations of Critical Theory*, Cambridge, Polity Press.

Honneth, A. (2008) *Reification: A New Look at an Old Idea*, Oxford, Oxford University Press.

Hont, I., and M. Ignatieff (1983b) Needs and justice in the Wealth of Nations: An introductory essay. In Hont, I., and M. Ignatieff (Ed.) *Wealth and Virtue: The Shaping of Political Economy in the Scottish Enlightenment.* Cambridge, Cambridge University Press.

Hont, I., and M. Ignatieff (Ed.) (1983a) *Wealth and Virtue: The Shaping of Political Economy in the Scottish Enlightenment*, Cambridge, Cambridge University Press.

Hume, D. (1948) Enquiry Concerning the Principles of Morals. In Aiken, H. D. (Ed.) *Hume's Moral and Political Philosophy.* New York, Hafner Press.

Hume, D. (1988) *An Enquiry Concerning Human Understanding*, Buffalo, Prometheus Books.

Hume, D. (1992) *A Treatise of Human Nature*, New York, Prometheus Books.

Jamieson, K. H. and Campbell, K. K. (1982) Rhetorical hybrids: Fusions of generic elements. *Quarterly Journal of Speech*, 68, 146.

Jauss, H. R. (1982) *Toward an Aesthetic of Reception*, Minneapolis, University of Minnesota Press.

Kant, I. (1993) *Critique of Practical Reason*, Trans. Beck, L. W., Upper Saddle River, NJ, Library of Liberal Arts: Prentice-Hall.

Kant, I. (1996a) What is enlightenment? *Practical Philosophy.* Trans. Gregor, M. Cambridge, Cambridge University Press.

Kant, I. (1996b) Groundwork of the metaphysics of morals: Transition from common rational to philosophic moral cognition. *Practical Philosophy.* Trans. Gregor, M. Cambridge, Cambridge University Press.

Kant, I. (1996c) On a supposed right to lie from philanthropy. *Practical Philosophy.* Trans. Gregor, M. Cambridge, Cambridge University Press.

Kauffman, C., & Parson, D. W. (1990) Metaphor and presence in argument. In Williams, D. C., and Hazen, M.D. (Ed.) *Argumentation Theory and the Rhetoric of Assent.* Tuscaloosa, University of Alabama Press.

Kauffman, C., and D. W. Parson (1990) Metaphor and presence in argument. In Williams, D. C., and M. D. Hazen (Ed.) *Argumentation Theory and the Rhetoric of Assent.* Tuscaloosa, University of Alabama Press.

King, M. L., JR. (2000) *Why We Can't Wait*, New York, Signet Classic.

Kohlberg, L. (1981) Indoctrination versus relativity in value education. *The Philosophy of Moral Development: Moral Stages and the Idea of Justice.* San Francisco, Harper & Row.

Kohlberg, L. (1981) *The Meaning and Measurement of Moral Development*, Worcester, Mass., Clark University Press.

Kohlberg, L. (1984) *The Psychology of Moral Development: The Nature and Validity of Moral Stages*, San Francisco, Harper & Row.

Krauthammer, C. (2004) In defense of democratic realism. *National Interest*, 15–26.

Krauthammer, C. (2005) Krauthammer responds. *National Interest*, 9–10.

Kuran, T. (1995) *Private Truths, Public Lies: The Social Consequences of Preference Falsification*, Cambridge, Mass., Harvard University Press.

Kuran, T. (2004) *Islam and Mammon: The Economic Predicaments of Islamism*, Princeton, NJ, Princeton University Press.

Lakoff, G., and M. Johnson (1980) *Metaphors We Live By*, Chicago, University of Chicago Press.

Lamont, J., and Favor, C. (2008) Distributive Justice. In Zalta, E. N. (Ed.) *The Stanford Encyclopedia of Philosophy* Palo Alto, CA, The Metaphysics Research Lab, Center for the Study of Language and Information, Stanford University. September 21 2008 http://plato.stanford.edu/archives/fall2008/entries/justice-distributive/ October 13 2009.

Lanham, R. A. (1991) *A Handlist of Rhetorical Terms*, Berkeley, University of California Press.

Leff, M. (1983) Topical invention and metaphoric interaction. *The Southern Speech Communication Journal*, 48, 214–229.

Leitch, T. M. (1986) *What Stories Are: Narrative Theory and Interpretation*, University Park, PA, The Pennsylvania State University Press.

Lewis, M. (2010) *The Big Short: Inside the Doomsday Machine*, New York, W. W. Norton.

Locke, J. and Peardon, T. P. (1952) *The Second Treatise of Government*, New York, Liberal Arts Press.

Lowenstein, R. (2000) *When Genius Failed: The Rise and Fall of Long-Term Capital Management*, New York, Random House.

Lowenstein, R. (2010) *The End of Wall Street*, New York, Penguin Press.

Lukes, S. (1982) Of gods and demons: Habermas and practical reason. In Thompson, J. B. (Ed.) *Habermas: Critical Debates.* Cambridge, Mass, MIT Press.

McCloskey, D. (1981) The demoralization of economics: Can we recover from Bentham? In Hirschman, A. O. (Ed.) *Essays in Trespassing: Economics to Politics and Beyond.* Cambridge [Eng.], Cambridge University Press.

McCloskey, D. N. (1985) *The Rhetoric of Economics*, Madison, The University of Wisconsin Press.

McCloskey, D. N. (1994) Bourgeois virtue. *American Scholar*, 63, 177–191.

McCloskey, D. N. (1998) *The Rhetoric of Economics*, 2nd ed., Madison, The University of Wisconsin Press.

McCloskey, D. N. (2006) *The Bourgeois Virtues: Ethics for an Age of Commerce*, Chicago, University of Chicago Press.

McKenna, S. J. (2006) *Adam Smith: The Rhetoric of Propriety*, Albany, State University of New York Press.

McKeon, R. (1957) Communication, truth, and society. *Ethics*, 67, 89–99.

McKeon, R. (1973) Creativity and the commonplace. *Philosophy and Rhetoric*, 6, 199–210.

Macfie, A. L. (1959) Adam Smith's moral sentiments as foundation for his *Wealth of Nations. Oxford Economic Papers*, 11, 209–228.

Macfie, A. L. (1967) *The Individual in Society*, London, George Allen & Unwin.

MacIntyre, A. (1966) *A Short History of Ethics*, New York, Touchstone Books: Simon & Schuster.

MacIntyre, A. (1984) *After Virtue: A Study in Moral Theory*, Notre Dame, Indiana, University of Notre Dame Press.

MacIntyre, A. (1988) *Whose Justice? Which Rationality?* Notre Dame, Indiana, University of Notre Dame Press.

Maines, D. R. (2000) Charting futures for sociology: culture and meaning. *Contemporary Sociology.*

Mandeville, B. ([1732a], 1966) *The Fable of the Bees: Or, Private Vices, Publick Benefits*, Oxford, Clarendon Press.

Mannheim, K. (1936) *Ideology and Utopia: An Introduction to the Sociology of Knowledge*, San Diego, Harcout: Harvest Books.

Marshall, T. H. (1964) *Class, Citizenship, and Social Development*, Garden City NY, Doubleday.

Matthews, P. H., and A. Ortmann (2002) An Austrian (mis)reads Adam Smith: A critique of Rothbard as intellectual historian. *Review of Political Economy*, 14, 379–392.

Médaille, J. C. (2007) *The Vocation of Business: Social Justice in the Marketplace*, New York, Continuum.

Mill, J. S. (1993) *Utilitarianism*, London, Everyman.

Montes, L. (2003) Das Adam Smith Problem: Its origins, the stages of the current debate, and one implication for our understanding of sympathy. *Journal of the History of Economic Thought*, 25, 63–90.

Montes, L. (2004) *Adam Smith in Context: A Critical Reassessment of Some Central Components of His Thought*, New York, Palgrave Macmillan.

Montes, L. and Schliesser, E. (2006) New voices on Adam Smith. *Routledge Studies in the History of Economics*; 82. Routledge.

Mothersill, M. (1975) Review: *Must We Mean What We Say? A Book of Essays; The World Viewed: Reflections on the Ontology of Film; The Senses of Walden*, by Stanley Cavell. *Journal of Philosophy*, 72, 27–48.

Mueller-Vollmer, K. (Ed.) (1985) *The Hermeneutics Reader: Texts of the German Tradition from the Enlightenment to the Present*, New York, Continuum.

Muldrew, C. (1998) *The Economy of Obligation: The Culture of Credit and Social Relations in Early Modern England*, New York, St. Martin's Press.

Muller, J. Z. (1993) *Adam Smith in His Time and Ours: Designing the Decent Society*, Princeton, New Jersey, Princeton University Press.

Noddings, N. (1984) *Caring: A feminine approach to ethics and moral education*, Berkeley, University of California Press.

Noddings, N. (2003) *Caring: A feminine approach to ethics and moral education*, Berkeley, University of California Press.

Nussbaum, M. C. (1992) Human Functioning and Social Justice: In Defense of Aristotelian Essentialism. *Political Theory*, 20, 202–246.

nytimes.com (2010) Credit crisis – the essentials. Online ed. New York, New York Times Company. May 17, 2010 http://topics.nytimes.com/top/reference/timestopics/subjects/c/credit_crisis/index.html?ref=economy June 16, 2010.

Oakley, A. (1994) *Classical Economic Man: Human Agency and Methodology in the Political Economy of Adam Smith and J. S. Mill*, Aldershot, Cambridge University Press.

Ormiston, G. L. and Schrift, A. D. (1990) *The Hermeneutic Tradition: From Ast to Ricoeur*, Albany, NY, State University of New York Press.

Ortmann, A., and S. Meardon (1995) A game-theoretic re-evaluation of Adam Smith's Theory of Moral Sentiments and Wealth of Nations. In Rima, I. H. (Ed.) *The Classical Tradition in Economic Thought: Perspectives on the History of Economic Thought*. Aldershot, Eng., Edward Elgar.

Orwell, G. (1961) *1984: A Novel*, New York, N.Y., New American Library.

Otteson, J. R. (2000) Adam Smith: Moral philosopher. *The Freeman: Ideas on Liberty*, 50, n.p.

Otteson, J. R. (2002) *Adam Smith's Marketplace of Life*, New York, Cambridge University Press.

Pack, S. J. (1991) *Capitalism as a Moral System: Adam Smith's Critique of the Free Market Economy*, Aldershot, Eng., Edward Elgar.

Pack, S. J. (1997) Adam Smith on the virtues: A partial resolution of the Adam Smith Problem. *Journal of the History of Economic Thought*, 19, 127–140.

Paul, E. F. (1997) Adam Smith: A reappraisal. *Journal of Libertarian Studies*, 1, 289–306.

Perelman, C. (1994) The new rhetoric: A theory of practical reasoning. In Enos, T., and Brown, S.C. (Ed.) *Professing the New Rhetorics*. Englewood Cliffs, NJ, Blair Press-Prentice Hall.

Peters, B. (1999) *Understanding Multiculturalism*, Bremen, Inst. für Interkulturelle und Internat. Studien.

Peters-Fransen, I. (2001) The canon in the history of the Adam Smith Problem. In Peart, S., and E. Forget (Ed.) *Reflections on the Classical Canon in Economics: Essays in Honor of Samuel Hollander*. London, Routledge.

Phelan, J. (1996) *Narrative as Rhetoric: Technique, Audiences, Ethics, Ideology*, Columbus, Ohio State University Press.

Phelan, J., and Peter J. Rabinowitz (1994) Introduction: Understanding narrative. In Phelan, J., and P. J. Rabinowitz (Ed.) *Understanding Narrative*. Columbus, Ohio State University Press.

Plato (1956) *Phaedrus*, Upper Saddle River, NJ, Library of Liberal Arts: Prentice Hall.

Poovey, M. (1995) *Making a Social Body: British Cultural Formation, 1830–1864*, Chicago, University of Chicago Press.

Popper, K. R. (1979) Three worlds. *Michigan Quarterly Review*, 18.

Posner, R. A. (2009) *A Failure of Capitalism: The Crisis of '08 and the Descent into Depression*, Cambridge, Mass., Harvard University Press.

Posner, R. A. (2009) Should the government use its monopsony power to reduce the price of drugs? Posner. In Posner, G. B. A. R. (Ed.) *The Becker–Posner Blog*. Chicago,

University of Chicago. December 27, 2009 http://uchicagolaw.typepad.com/beckerpos-ner/2009/12/index.html February 10, 2010.

Post, F. R. (2003) The social responsibility of management: A critique of the shareholder paradigm and defense of stakeholder primacy. *American Journal of Business*, 18.

Poster, C. (2008) Whose Aristotle? Which Aristotelianism? A historical prolegomenon to Thomas Farrell's *Norms of Rhetorical Culture. Philosophy and Rhetoric*, 41, 375–401.

Postman, N. (1982) *The Disappearance of Childhood*, New York, Dell Publishing Co., Inc.

Postman, N. (1985) *Amusing Ourselves to Death: Public Discourse in the Age of Show Business*, New York, Viking.

Putnam, R., Leonardi, R., and Nanetti, R.Y. (1993) *Making Democracy Work: Civic Traditions in Modern Italy*, Princeton NJ, Princeton University Press.

Puzo, M. (1969) *The Godfather*, New York, Putnam.

Rabinowitz, P. (1977) Truth in fiction: A re-examination of audiences. *Critical Inquiry*, 4, 121–141.

Rabinowitz, P. (1980) "What's Hecuba to us?" The audience's experience of literary borrowing. In Suleiman, S., and I. Crosman (Ed.) *The Reader in the Text: Essays on Audience and Interpretation.* Princeton, Princeton University Press.

Rand, A. (1943) *The Fountainhead*, Indianapolis; New York, Bobbs-Merrill Co.

Rand, A. (2003) *Atlas Shrugged*, New York, Plume.

Raphael, D. D. (2007) *The Impartial Spectator: Adam Smith's Moral Philosophy*, Oxford; New York, Clarendon Press; Oxford University Press.

Raphael, D. D., and Macfie, A. L. (1984) Introduction. In Raphael, D. D., and Macfie, A. L. (Ed.) *The Theory of Moral Sentiments.* Indianapolis, Liberty Fund.

Rawls, J. (1971) *A Theory of Justice*, Cambridge, Mass, Harvard University Press.

Rawls, J. (1993) *Political Liberalism*, New York, Columbia University Press.

Richardson, H. (2005) John Rawls. In Fieser, J., and B. Dowden (Ed.) *The Internet Encyclopedia of Philosophy.* May 14, 2010 http://www.iep.utm.edu/rawls.

Ricoeur, P. (1977) *The Rule of Metaphor: Multi-disciplinary Studies of the Creation of Meaning in Language*, Toronto; Buffalo, University of Toronto Press.

Robbins, L. (1998) *A History of Economic Thought: The LSE Lectures*, Princeton, Princeton University Press.

Rosenberg, N. (1990) Adam Smith and the stock of moral capital. *History of Political Economy*, 22, 1–17.

Rosenblatt, L. M. (1978) *The Reader, the Text, the Poem: the Transactional Theory of the Literary Work*, Carbondale, Southern Illinois University Press.

Rothschild, E. (2001) *Economic Sentiments: Adam Smith, Condorcet, and the Enlightenment*, Cambridge, Mass., Harvard University Press.

Roubini, N., and Mihm, S. (2010) *Crisis Economics: A Crash Course in the Future of Finance*, New York, Penguin Press.

Rousseau, J.-J. (1953) *The Confessions of Jean-Jacques Rousseau*, London, Penguin Books.

Rousseau, J.-J. (1994) *Discourse on Political Economy and the Social Contract*, Oxford; New York, Oxford University Press.

Saalmann, G. (2002) *Solidarity in a Society of Strangers*. Universität Freiburg Philosophische Fakultät IV Institut für Soziologie. 2002 www.freidok.uni-freiburg.de/volltexte/567/pdf/Soli.pdf June 14, 2010.

Sahlins, M. (2009) On the anthropology of Levi-Strauss. American Anthropological Association. July 8, 2009 http://blog.aaanet.org/2009/07/07/on-the-anthropology-of-levi-strauss/ January 10, 2010.

Samuels, W. J. (1966) *The Classical Theory of Economic Policy*, Cleveland, The World Publishing Co.

Samuels, W. J. (1990) Introduction. In Samuels, W. J. (Ed.) *Economics As Discourse: An Analysis of the Language of Economists.* Boston, Kluwer Academic Publishers.

Samuels, W. J. (1990b) Introduction. In Samuels, W. J. (Ed.) *Economics As Discourse: An Analysis of the Language of Economists.* Boston, Kluwer Academic Publishers.

Samuels, W. J. (1997b) Introduction. In Samuels, W. J., S. G. Medema, and A. Schmid (Ed.) *The Economy as a Process of Valuation.* Cheltenham, UK, Edward Elgar.

Samuels, W. J. (1997d) The Concept of "Coercion" in Economics. In Samuels, W. J., S. G. Medema, and A. Schmid (Ed.) *The Economy as a Process of Valuation.* Cheltenham, UK, Edward Elgar.

Samuels, W. J. (2000) Review: Rose Friedman and Milton Friedman's *Two Lucky People. Research in the History of Economic Thought and Methodology*, 18A, 241–252.

Samuels, W. J. (Ed.) (1990a) *Economics As Discourse: An Analysis of the Language of Economists*, Boston, Kluwer Academic Publishers.

Samuels, W. J., and A. Schmid (1997c) The Concept of Cost in Economics. In Samuels, W. J., S. G. Medema, and A. Schmid (Ed.) *The Economy as a Process of Valuation.* Cheltenham, UK, Edward Elgar.

Samuels, W. J., S. G. Medema, and A. Schmid (Ed.) (1997a) *The Economy as a Process of Valuation*, Cheltenham, UK, Edward Elgar.

Sandage, S. A. (2005) *Born Losers: A History of Failure in America*, Cambridge, MA, Harvard University Press.

Sandel, M. J. (2009) *Justice: What's the Right Thing to Do?* New York, Farrar, Straus and Giroux.

Saussure, F. D. (1959) *Course in General Linguistics*, New York, McGraw-Hill.

Schiappa, E. (2001) Second thoughts on the critiques of big rhetoric. *Philosophy and Rhetoric*, 34, 260–274.

Schliesser, E. (2008) The impartial spectator: Adam Smith's moral philosophy, Review of *Adam Smith in Context: A Critical Reassessment of Some Central Components of His Thought. Ethics*, 118, 569–575.

Schopenhauer, A. (1888a) *The World As Will and Idea*, Trans. Haldane, R. B. and J. Kemp. London, Trübner & Co.

Schopenhauer, A. (1888b) On the primacy of the will in self-consciousness. *The World As Will and Idea.* Trans. Haldane, R. B. and J. Kemp. London, Trübner & Co.

Schumpeter, J. A. (1936 [1934]) *The Theory of Economic Development: An Inquiry into Profits, Capital, Credit, Interest, and the Business Cycle*, Cambridge, Mass., Harvard University Press.

Schumpeter, J. A. (1954) *History of Economic Analysis*, New York, Oxford University Press.

Schwartz, J. (2000) *Fighting Poverty with Virtue: Moral Reform and America's Urban Poor, 1825–2000.* Bloomington, Indiana University Press.

Searle, J. R. (1969) *Speech Acts: An Essay in the Philosophy of Language*, London, Cambridge University Press.

Seligman, A. B. (1992) *The Idea of Civil Society*, New York, The Free Press: Macmillan, Inc.

Sen, A. (2006) *Identity and Violence: The Illusion of Destiny*, New York, W. W. Norton & Co.

Sen, A. (2009) *The Idea of Justice*, Cambridge, Mass., Belknap Press of Harvard University Press.

Smith, A. ([1759], 1982) *The Theory of Moral Sentiments*, Indianapolis, Liberty Fund: Liberty Classics.

Smith, A. ([1776], 1976) *An Inquiry into the Nature and Causes of the Wealth of Nations*, Chicago, University of Chicago Press.

Smith, A. (1984) *The Theory of Moral Sentiments. 1976 Oxford University Press.*, Indianapolis, Liberty Fund.

Smith, A. (1985) *Lectures on Rhetoric and Belles Lettres*, Indianapolis, Liberty Fund: Liberty Classics.

Smith, T. V. (1931) The social philosophy of George Herbert Mead. *The American Journal of Sociology*, 37, 368–385.

Staveren, I. V. (2001) *The Values of Economics: An Aristotelian Perspective*, London, Routledge.

Stigler, G. J. (1982) The economist as preacher. *The Economist as Preacher and Other Essays.* Chicago, University of Chicago Press.

Sugden, R. (1989) Spontaneous order. *The Journal of Economic Perspectives*, 3, 85–97.

Sullivan, D. L. (1993) The ethos of epideictic encounter. *Philosophy and Rhetoric*, 26, 113–133.

Susan, S. F. (2007) Iris Marion Young (1949–2006): A tribute. *Antipode*, 39, 382–387.

Tabb, W. K. (1999) *Reconstructing Political Economy*, London, Routledge.

Tawney, R. H. (1926) *Religion and the Rise of Capitalism: A Historical Study*, New York, Mentor Books.

Taylor, C. (1994) The politics of recognition. In Gutmann, A. (Ed.) *Multiculturalism: Examining the Politics of Recognition.* Princeton, N.J., Princeton University Press.

Teichgraeber III, R. (1981) Rethinking das Adam Smith Problem. *The Journal of British Studies*, 20, 106–123.

Teichgraeber III, R. F. (1986) *"Free Trade" and Moral Philosophy: Rethinking the Sources of Adam Smith's Wealth of Nations*, Durham, Duke University Press.

Tompkins, J. P. (1980) An introduction to reader-response criticism. In Tompkins, J. P. (Ed.) *Reader-Response Criticism: From Formalism to Post-Structuralism.* Baltimore, The Johns Hopkins University Press.

Toulmin, S. (1958) *The Uses of Argument*, Cambridge, Cambridge University Press.

Toulmin, S. (1990) *Cosmopolis: The Hidden Agenda of Modernity*, Chicago, University of Chicago Press.

Toulmin, S. (2001) *Return to Reason*, Cambridge, Mass., Harvard University Press.

Toulmin, S., and A. R. Johnson (1988) *The Abuse of Casuistry: A History of Moral Reasoning*, Berkeley, University of California Press.

Turpin, P. (2003) Conceptual metaphor from a rhetorical perspective. *Review of Communication*, 3, 139–144.

Vico, G. (1990) On the study methods of our time. In Bizzell, P., and B. Herzberg, (Ed.) *The Rhetorical Tradition: Readings from Classical Times to the Present.* Boston, Bedford Books of St. Martin's Press. 714–727.

Vivenza, G. (2001) *Adam Smith and the Classics: The Classical Heritage in Adam Smith's Thought*, Oxford, Oxford University Press.

Waldron, J. (1995) The wisdom of the multitude: Some reflections on book 3, chapter 11 of Aristotle's *Politics. Political Theory*, 23, 563–584.

Waszek, N. (1984) Two Concepts of Morality: A distinction of Adam Smith's ethics and its stoic origin. *Journal of the History of Ideas*, 45, 591–606.

Weaver, R. M. (1970a) The *Phaedrus* and the nature of rhetoric. In Johannesen, R. L., R.

S., and R. T. Eubanks (Ed.) *Language Is Sermonic.* Baton Rouge, LA, Louisiana State University Press.

Weaver, R. M. (1970b) The cultural role of rhetoric. In Johannesen, R. L., R. Strickland, & R. T. Eubanks (Ed.) *Language Is Sermonic.* Baton Rouge, LA, Louisiana State University Press.

Weaver, R. M. (1985) *The Ethics of Rhetoric*, Davis, CA, Hermagoras Press.

Werhane, P. H. (1991) *Adam Smith and His Legacy for Modern Capitalism*, New York, Oxford University Press.

West, W. G. (1976) *Adam Smith: The Man and His Works*, Indianapolis, Liberty Fund.

Wichelns, H. A. (1925) The literary criticism of oratory. In Drummond, A. M. (Ed.) *Studies in Rhetoric and Public Speaking in Honor of James Albert Winans.* New York, The Century Co.

Winch, D. (1978) *Adam Smith's Politics: An Essay in Historiographic Revision*, Cambridge, Cambridge University Press.

Winch, D. (1983a) Adam Smith's "enduring particular result": A political and cosmopolitan perspective. In Hont, I., and M. Ignatieff (Ed.) *Wealth and Virtue: The Shaping of Political Economy in the Scottish Enlightenment.* Cambridge, Cambridge University Press.

Winch, D. (1983b) Science and the legislator: Adam Smith and after. *Economic Journal*, 93.

Winch, D. (1992) Adam Smith: Scottish philosopher as political economist. *The Historical Journal*, 35.

Winnicott, D. W. (1980) *The Maturational Processes and the Facilitating Environment: Studies in the Theory of Emotional Development*, New York, International Universities Press.

Wittgenstein, L. (1968) *Wittgenstein: The Philosophical Investigations*, London, Macmillan.

Witztum, A. (1997) Distributive considerations in Smith's conception of economic justice. *Economics and Philosophy*, 13, 241–259.

Witztum, A. (1998) A study into Smith's conception of the human character: Das Adam Smith Problem revisited. *History of Political Economy*, 30, 490–513.

Wood, D. (2002) *Medieval Economic Thought*, Cambridge, Cambridge University Press.

Woodmansee, M., and M. Osteen (Ed.) (1999) *The New Economic Criticism: Studies at the Intersection of Literature and Economics*, London, Routledge.

Yar, M. (2001) Beyond Nancy Fraser's "perspectival dualism". *Economy and Society*, 30, 288–303.

Young, I. M. (1990) *Justice and the Politics of Difference*, Princeton NJ, Princeton University Press.

Young, I. M. (2002) *Inclusion and Democracy*, Oxford, Oxford University Press.

Young, J. T. (1997) *Economics as a Moral Science: The Political Economy of Adam Smith*, Cheltenham, UK, Edward Elgar.

Young, J. T. (2001) Justice versus expediency. In Forget, E., and S. Peart (Ed.) *Reflections on the Classical Canon in Economics: Essays in Honor of Samuel Hollander.* London, Routledge.

Young, J. T. (2006) Montes's *Adam Smith in Context*. Review. *Research in the History of Economic Thought and Methodology*, 24-A, 201–208.

Young, J. T., and B. Gordon (1996) Distributive justice as a normative criterion in Adam Smith's political economy. *History of Political Economy*, 28, 1–25.

Zakaria, F. (2003) *The Future of Freedom: Illiberal Democracy at Home and Abroad*, New York, W. W. Norton.

Index

References to notes are prefixed by *n*.

For Product Safety Concerns and Information please contact our EU
representative GPSR@taylorandfrancis.com
Taylor & Francis Verlag GmbH, Kaufingerstraße 24, 80331 München, Germany

www.ingramcontent.com/pod-product-compliance
Ingram Content Group UK Ltd.
Pitfield, Milton Keynes, MK11 3LW, UK
UKHW021611240425
457818UK00018B/493